ROTH FAMILY FOUNDATION

Imprint in Music

Michael P. Roth
and Sukey Garcetti
have endowed this
imprint to honor the
memory of their parents,
Julia and Harry Roth,
whose deep love of music
they wish to share
with others.

The publisher and the University of California Press Foundation gratefully acknowledge the generous support of the Roth Family Foundation Imprint in Music, established by a major gift from Sukey and Gil Garcetti and Michael P. Roth.

Just Beyond Listening

CALIFORNIA STUDIES IN MUSIC, SOUND, AND MEDIA

James Buhler and Jean Ma, Series Editors

1. *Static in the System: Noise and the Soundscape of American Cinema Culture,* by Meredith C. Ward
2. *Hearing Luxe Pop: Glorification, Glamour, and the Middlebrow in American Popular Music,* by John Howland
3. *Thinking with an Accent: Toward a New Object, Method, and Practice,* edited by Pooja Rangan, Akshya Saxena, Ragini Tharoor Srinivasan, and Pavitra Sundar
4. *Key Constellations: Interpreting Tonality in Film,* by Táhirih Motazedian
5. *Just Beyond Listening: Essays of Sonic Encounter,* by Michael C. Heller

Just Beyond Listening

Essays of Sonic Encounter

MICHAEL C. HELLER

University of California Press

University of California Press
Oakland, California

© 2024 by Michael Heller

Cataloging-in-Publication data is on file at the Library of Congress.

ISBN 978–0-520–35077–9 (cloth)
ISBN 978–0-520–35078–6 (pbk.)
ISBN 978–0-520–97586–6 (ebook)

32 31 30 29 28 27 26 25 24 23
10 9 8 7 6 5 4 3 2 1

To Charlie and Perry

Contents

List of Illustrations — IX

Introduction — 1

PART I: LOUDNESS AND SILENCE — 9

1. Between Silence and Pain: Loudness and the Affective Encounter — 11
2. Let's Listen to Nothing: Silence and the Anechoic Chamber — 32
3. Silencing and Alternative Silences — 58

PART II: TEXTUAL INTERFERENCE — 83

4. Projecting Results: Opera Supertitles and the People Who Hated Them — 85
5. Diaries and Postcards: Archival Privilege, Empathy, and Intimacy — 106

PART III: DEATH AND DEADNESS — 139

6. Deploying Deadness in Louis Armstrong's House — 141
7. Tape Death: Mourning Sounds We Never Heard — 181

Acknowledgments — 209

Notes — 213

Bibliography — 243

Index — 257

List of Illustrations

1. Kaye's phon scale — 12
2. Acoustic locator, circa 1930s — 33
3. SONAR operator and display monitor — 34
4. Interior of the Harvard anechoic chamber — 36
5. *The Lab Echo,* issue 1 (front and back cover) — 41
6. Louis Armstrong House Museum, exterior — 142
7. Louis Armstrong on his front steps with neighborhood children — 143
8. Louis Armstrong at his front steps — 150
9 and 10. Lucille and Louis Armstrong's living room — 152
11. Louis Armstrong with reel-to-reel tape recorder — 156
12. Louis Armstrong in his first-floor mirrored bathroom — 160
13. Louis Armstrong holding a tape box covered in his collage art — 164
14. Lucille and Louis Armstrong's kitchen — 167
15. Lucille and Louis Armstrong's bedroom — 172
16. Lucille and Louis Armstrong's den — 174
17. Lucille and Louis Armstrong in the den — 175
18. Louis Armstrong composing collages on the walls of the den — 176
19. Louis Armstrong's collage wall — 177
20. Basic physical structure of magnetic tape — 188
21. Philip De Lancie's hair-dryer heating chamber — 189

Introduction

It's a sunny summer afternoon in 2007, and I am a tourist strolling alone through the streets of Paris. Perusing my map, I see that I'm not far from Notre Dame Cathedral, so I decide to wander over. The scene is pretty much as I expected. The famously imposing edifice—already familiar from so many photos—towers over a large pavilion accented by low hedges. The hedges are filled with chirping songbirds that some of the other tourists are feeding. It's crowded today, which fills the air with the chatter of multiple languages. It also makes the line to enter the church longer than I am willing to wait. So, after a few minutes of enjoying the scene, I take out my map once again to plan my next destination.

It's about now that the first bell begins to toll, marking the top of the hour. *Oh, what a nice coincidence!* I think. *I'll stay for a few minutes to listen.* The sound gradually swells as more and more of the massive bells lend their heft to the soundscape. To my surprise, though, they don't seem to evoke pleasant consonance or divine harmony so much as a cacophonous raw power. The bells seem to have very little connection in their harmonies or overtones, creating an unexpectedly chaotic and increasingly terrifying effect. It builds and builds, filling the pavilion with an ominous, seemingly unstoppable accretion of energy.[1] I didn't know it at the time, but this was a frequent criticism that had been made of the Notre Dame bells since the nineteenth century. It eventually led to most of them being replaced in 2013.[2] On the day of my visit, however, the discrepancies between their overtones create a palpable beating, which resonates not only in my ears but throughout my whole body, especially my chest and teeth. The sound envelops me, overwhelms me, fills my consciousness and takes away my breath. I have the thought that if this is supposed to invoke an image of God, this is no God of gentleness and compassion but a towering Old

Testament deity of awe-inspiring, earth-shaking power. The thunder of the skies. The crush of waves against seaside crags.

As the toll reaches its height, a totally unexpected thing happens. Seemingly out of nowhere, a bird of prey—perhaps one of the kestrels that nests in the cathedral—sweeps out of the sky and plunges into one of the hedges a few feet away. Its target is the same flock of songbirds that had, moments ago, been chirping so delightedly. The birds take flight in a panic, adding their rush of tiny flaps into the already saturated soundscape. I duck my head to dodge their escape. One of them is not so lucky. As I peek back up, I see a bird pinned under the talons of the kestrel, which savagely tears into it with beak and claws. I wonder whether the kestrel was waiting for the bells to disorient the birds, masking its approach and allowing it to attack undetected. After about thirty seconds of gore, the kestrel flies off with the songbird clenched in its claws. The bells thunder on.

Eventually—you could convince me it has been one minute or ten—the bells start to recede, fading one by one as their beating echoes decay. I stand there, trembling for quite a bit longer. My afternoon of pleasant diversions has been wrested from me, transformed into an overwhelming and entirely unexpected frenzy of sound and power, touch and death. I feel changed, moved, entirely against my will. It is quite a while before I am able to continue my journey.

· · ·

When I think back to that afternoon at Notre Dame, my encounter with the bells feels like something very different from anything that I might describe with the word "listening." To be clear, an experience of listening was certainly what I expected when the bells first began: *Oh, what a nice coincidence! I'll stay for a few minutes to listen.* But what I ended up undergoing felt like a decidedly different mode of experience. Instead of me orienting myself toward the sound—offering it my attention and seeking to understand it—the feeling was one of sound acting on me. I found myself moved before I could process what was happening. This disorientation was heightened by many factors, including a distinct cross-wiring of the senses (sound becoming touch in the bells' vibration), the gravity imbued by my own narrative interpretations (the power of an Old Testament God), and the unexpected addition of non-sonic addenda (the dramatic death of the bird). Rather than recalling these as discrete elements, all of them closely intertwine and interfere in my memory. I should note that I don't suggest that these responses were universal or "correct" interpretations in any way, but ones that were thoroughly informed by my limited subject position as the individual experiencing the encounter (as a white cisgender American male, as a tourist in Paris enjoying a pleasant sauntering afternoon, as a student of music attuned to the sonic landscape, as an ignorant novice regarding the history or sound of the Notre Dame bells, as a lapsed Catholic hazily recalling biblical tales, and so on).

I offer this vignette as an example of what I refer to in this book as a sonic encounter. I define this term as an affective interaction between an observer and a sound—often supplemented by other inputs—whose impact overflows outside of the realm of what would generally be considered "listening." The act of listening (i.e., the close attention paid to a sonic experience) can certainly be a crucial part of this process. But in various ways I argue that the mode of focused reception implied by the term "listening" comprises only a fraction of the dense network of affective relationships that we can form with sound in a particular moment. Listening processes are constantly rubbing against other inputs that contribute to the totality of an encounter. These might include other sensory data (sights, smells, touches), the residues of pre-listening preparation (texts, memories), notions of expectation (confirmation, surprise, absence), forms of cultural training (sonic syntax or musical languages, systems of meaning, privilege and bias, discourses of race, gender, class, etc.), and so on. Importantly, I argue that discursive interpretations and other non-sensory inputs do not exist in a different realm from the affective reception of sound. To the contrary, these inputs can substantively alter the affective power of a sonic encounter at the moment of impact.

My use of the term "sonic encounter" aligns in most respects with that put forward by James G. Mansell in his chapter "Hearing With: Researching the Histories of Sonic Encounter," which defines it as "a socially shaped and culturally specific affective relationship between hearer and heard."[3] Mansell uses the concept as a way to move toward a historically situated understanding of sonic affect, one that rejects the universalism of the so-called "ontological turn" or "vibrational" approaches to sound studies. Instead, he follows other scholars in treating sonic affect as a concept that is always informed by historical and cultural positionality. To this end, Mansell quotes Marie Thompson's insight that "situating rather than simply dismissing sonic ontologies enables us to ask how 'the nature of the sonic' is determined—what grounds the sonic ground—while remaining open to how it might be heard otherwise."[4]

Two additional inspirations for this project have been the writings of Nina Sun Eidsheim (her books *Sensing Sound* and *The Race of Sound*) and Anthony Braxton (his three volume *Tri-Axium Writings*).[5] In various ways both of these authors consider the impact of sonic encounters as what

Eidsheim refers to as a "thick events" that carry myriad layers of multisensory, social, and intermaterial complexities. They demonstrate that comprehending a sonic experience is impossible if one restricts their analysis to sound alone, a narrow viewpoint that Eidsheim refers to as "sonic reduction."[6] Quite to the contrary, parsing the significance of any sonic encounter (musical or otherwise) requires ongoing attention to the many factors that underlie how that encounter resonates. Braxton, for example, uses prose and schematic diagrams to interrogate the wide range of forces (individual, social, historical, vibrational, spiritual, functional, discursive) that can contribute to the impact and reception of a creative work.[7] Both authors also pay close attention to the relationships between sonic practices and histories of race, racism, and sonic control. This topic resurfaces repeatedly throughout this book, primarily informed by my background and training as a white scholar of Black American music. This focus builds upon a growing wave of sound studies scholarship that extends beyond white European and American case studies and pushes further to consider the many interrelationships between sound, sonic regulation, and cultural practices in the aftermath of the institution of slavery and colonial encounter, and/or in the contemporary global south.[8]

Just Beyond Listening draws deeply on the insight that that there is no such thing as "listening to the sound alone"—no form of sonic encounter that can exist outside the sensory and cultural networks that we live within. These points, however, manifest very differently in various chapters. I intentionally leave the title phrase "beyond listening" ambiguous and capacious, at least at this point. In some chapters I explore forces that emerge diachronically before or after listening, altering one's engagement with sonic substance through non-sonic or metasonic supplements. In others, I describe synchronic interference—sensory inputs that happen alongside and simultaneously with listening. And in still others, I refer to modes of engaging sound that don't fit neatly into any definition of listening whatsoever (remembering sound or imagining sound, for instance). Many of the case studies draw from affect theory as a framework to consider the impact of a given encounter. Indeed, a useful definition offered by Melissa Gregg and Gregory Seigworth describes affects as "forces of encounter" that can move across and/or in between disparate bodies, discourses, or realms.[9] I should be clear that although several examples include autoethnographic accounts of sound described from my own subject position, these are not intended as definitive readings of any given phenomenon. They are offered only as individual interpretations of one possible network of forces, which may or may not resonate with how others experience similar encounters.

The impact of a sonic encounter never exists in isolation. Affects are always moving and oscillating between multiple experiential frames. One of the goals of this book is to take those oscillations seriously. To borrow a phrase from Brian Massumi, the case studies attempt to consider sonic encounters via a "logic of mutual inclusion," in which multiple forces (senses, affects, memories, discourses, etc.) coexist within a single moment. Rather than attempting to explain away contradictions, I aim to consider how these forces "overlap in the unicity of the performance, without the distinction between them being lost. They are performatively fused, without becoming confused. They come together without melding together, co-occurring without coalescing."[10]

. . .

The chapters that follow offer a varied selection of case studies. They are divided into three thematic sections. Part I, "Loudness and Silence," comprises the first three chapters, which consider the two dynamic ends of the hearing spectrum: the very loud and the very soft. Chapter 1 focuses on extreme loudness, using various descriptions of loud sound to consider what kinds of impacts loudness can have on the hearing body. These observations are distilled into a selection of three "loudness effects," which I name imagined loudness, noise occupation, and listener collapse. I apply these effects to two theoretical texts about listening, asking how a consideration of loudness can enrich our affective understanding of certain sonic encounters.

Chapter 2 turns to questions of silence, beginning with an account of US military acoustics research in the 1940s that led to the creation of the world's most silent space: the so-called anechoic chamber. This same chamber would later be the site of an endlessly retold visit by the composer John Cage, who cited the story as a pivotal inspiration for the composition *4′33″*. While Cage framed his methods as being in contrast to the pragmatism of the scientists who built the chamber, I argue that much of Cage's theory of silence relies on scientific ideas, ultimately producing a somewhat limited account of silence's potential power. Chapter 3 continues this discussion, shifting from "silence" (as noun) to the verb "silencing," or creating silence. I begin by tracing how Cage sometimes used his theories about silence as a cudgel with which to silence other artists (particularly Black improvisers). I then consider two other aesthetic applications of silence that differ in crucial ways from the Cagean model: Wadada Leo Smith's composition titled *Silence* and Pauline Oliveros' *Sonic Meditations* and her ongoing practice of "Deep Listening."

Chapters 4 and 5 comprise Part II, "Textual Interference." Both deal with the potential of reading practices (either before or alongside an act of audition), to substantively alter what we experience during sonic encounters. Chapter 4 examines a flare-up in the early 1980s surrounding the adoption of supertitles (written translations of sung texts, projected in real time above the stage) in opera houses. Though the titling was enormously successful, a small but highly vocal group of detractors bemoaned the ways that supertitles changed their sensory experience of the genre by imposing a textual presence. Many of these objections were rooted in elitist forms of gatekeeping. In this chapter I consider the arguments made both for and against titling, both of which hinge on the premise that textual superimposition materially alters the way an audience must engage with live opera.

Chapter 5 turns away from textual engagement in the present and instead considers archival engagements that precede acts of listening. Specifically, I consider my own work in the personal and professional archives of a composer and an instrumentalist from the late twentieth century, both of whom I leave anonymous. Drawing from literature on archival empathy, I consider ways in which my process of listening to the pair's music was altered through my intimate engagement with their possessions. I argue that such changes resulted not from increased understanding or insight but instead through affective changes to my own listening apparatus through processes of proximity, intimacy, and empathy. I focus on the ways in which this empathy itself relies on structures of privilege and systemic inclusion/exclusion that undergird the creation of many archives in the first place.

Part III, "Death and Deadness," turns toward perceptions of death and how these perceptions can alter particular arenas of sonic encounter. Chapter 6 considers the way sound is curated at the Louis Armstrong House Museum, a national historic landmark preserved in the trumpeter's longtime home in Corona, Queens, New York. Drawing from my own experience as a tour guide at the museum in 2005–2006, I focus on the way that the museum incorporates private recordings of Armstrong's voice, which are placed strategically throughout the tour and tend to elicit powerful reactions from visitors. I argue that the recordings can be understood as evoking a process that I refer to as "antischizophonia," an acousmatic (but not schizophonic) phenomenon based around creating the impossible impression of *returning* recorded sound to its point of origin. This technique is used to stage a form of haunting that relies on interpenetrations of sound and space as well as the resurrection of dead labor that has been referred to under the rubric of "deadness." The chapter is structured as a soundwalk that guides the reader through the house tour itself.

Finally, chapter 7 considers a phenomenon I refer to as "tape death," a process of mourning the loss of recorded sounds that recurs in many journalistic accounts of audio archives. The chapter begins by considering a form of archival decay called "sticky shed syndrome," a type of degradation in archived tapes that plagues many tape stocks manufactured in the 1970s and 1980s. I then shift to consider the story of a massive fire at the vault of the Universal Music Group in 2008, an event chronicled in a widely circulated news story in 2019. In both examples I contemplate how the responses to these events can be read as a type of mourning for lost sounds, even in cases where those sounds have never actually been heard. The chapter questions how we might think about the status of commercial recordings held in record company vaults, arguing that they constitute a form of stored labor that is detached from the bodies of the artists and stockpiled for corporate profit.

. . .

As these descriptions make clear, the chapters function largely as stand-alone entities that differ in their approach as well as in the tone of the writing. Each begins with an evocative prologue that sets the stage and introduces some aspect of the discussion. It goes without saying that these are by no means the only topics that could have been chosen. Rather, they offer a collection of examples that I found illuminating in regard to particular sonic relationships.

PART I

Loudness and Silence

1 Between Silence and Pain

Loudness and the Affective Encounter

PROLOGUE

In 1937 physicist George William Clarkson Kaye delivered the presidential address for a meeting of the British Association in Nottingham, England. The speech, titled "Noise and the Nation," aimed to evaluate "the impact of [noise] on everyday life and the methods available for the abatement of the noise nuisance."[1] Kaye took exceptional pains to make the speech engaging, even producing a short film to accompany his remarks. In addition, he presented a diagram that mapped the perceived loudness of various sounds using a recently developed unit called "phons."[2] This diagram is reproduced as Figure 1.

Unlike the better-known decibel—a physical measurement of air pressure—the phon sought to measure loudness as perceived by living listeners. Kaye was not its inventor, but he designed the diagram to give his audience a general field of reference within the new perceptual system. Depicted somewhat like a thermometer, the image is designed to bolster Kaye's arguments about the growing danger of environmental noise. In the lighter sections near the bottom, one finds calming, domesticated sounds: a quiet conversation, a suburban train, a residential street. Above 70 phons, however, feverish threats appear in black: doors slam, horns blast, drills cut into rock. Through the trappings of scientific precision, the image dramatizes at the same time that it quantifies, staging modernity's mechanized assault upon the ears of the living.

Kaye's diagram is by no means unique. Similar charts pepper antinoise literature of the 1920s and 1930s, often employing a similar rhetoric of measurement and threat.[3] As more recent studies have shown, the period's rapid advances in sound measurement technology—including both the decibel and the phon—were catalyzed by strong alliances between science and the antinoise movement.[4] By emphasizing concrete statistics regarding loudness,

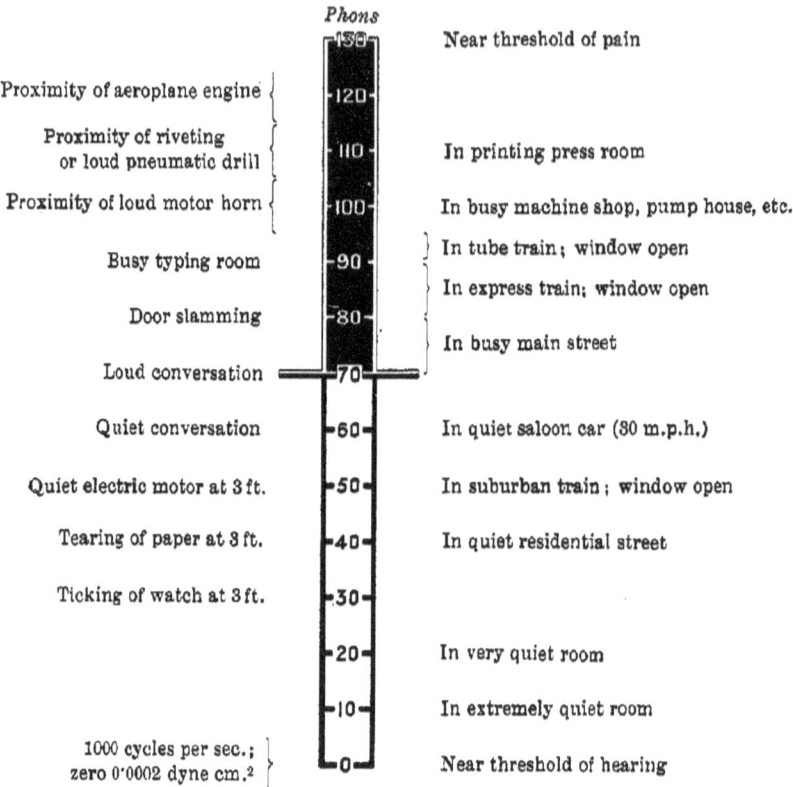

FIGURE 1. Kaye's phon scale. From George William Clarkson Kaye, "The Measurement of Noise," *Reports on Progress in Physics* 3 (1936): 130–42, https://doi.org/http://dx.doi.org/10.1088/0034-4885/3/1/309, 141. Used with permission of the Institute of Physics, conveyed through Copyright Clearance Center.

activists sought to shift the conversation about noise out of the realm of subjective distaste and recast it in terms that were objective, dangerous, and legislatable. Over time, however, loudness charts began to migrate into very different discursive spheres. Today they are a common sight in textbooks on physics and acoustics. Stripped of their political connotations, such charts now purport to illustrate fundamental truths about sound and the human hearing apparatus. While there are often small changes in their specific reference points, two nodes remain constant in nearly all versions: the limits. The lower end, at 0 phons, is labeled "near threshold of hearing." This level is perceived as silence, a point where no sound is experienced. Vibrations may be present, but they are too weak to be registered by the human ear. The upper limit is somewhat more intriguing. It is labeled "near threshold of pain."

Though the reference to pain certainly bolstered arguments against noise, the label was more than merely a rhetorical device. Fifteen years before Kaye, physicist R.L. Wegel observed that there was no maximum level at which a sound became too loud to hear. Instead, it simply passed a point at which hearing seemed to transform into something else entirely: "A sound much louder than [the ear's upper threshold] is painful. . . . *While this point of feeling probably has no relation to the auditory sense it does serve as a practical limit to the range of auditory sensation.*"[5] Although some researchers initially referred to this level as the "threshold of feeling," the term "threshold of pain" has gradually superseded it since the 1930s.[6] Today this has become the standard terminology to describe the limits of loudness in a wide range of contexts. Some clinicians also employ the slightly less polemical "uncomfortable loudness level" (or UCL) in a similar capacity.[7]

Pain. Feeling. Discomfort. However one terms it, such a threshold constitutes a curious upper limit to measurements of sonic loudness. Above this point sound waves are no longer experienced as intangible or detached objects of hearing but confront the body through an experience of direct physical touch, force, or torment. It represents, to borrow another phrase from Wegel, "a point where the hearing and feeling lines appear to intersect, [making it] difficult to distinguish between the sense of hearing and that of feeling."[8] Beyond the edge of the quantifiable, Wegel, Kaye, and their successors encountered a limit that was decidedly physical, experiential, and potent.

Loudness—a fundamental parameter of sound itself—exists as a continuum bounded on either side by silence and pain.

INTRODUCTION: INTENSITIES AND IN-BETWEEN-NESS

Just as amplitude is a necessary component of any wave, loudness is a necessary component of sound. Yet despite this fundamental role, the experiential and aesthetic potentials of loudness are rarely considered in music or sound studies literature. The omission is jarring, as loudness seems to impact our everyday listening practices in relatively intuitive ways. Imagine, for example, trying to fall asleep to a lullaby sung at the level of a jet engine or attending a sporting event where the stadium is as quiet as a library. Expectations of certain loudness experiences are built into the way we encounter sound on a daily basis and are closely intertwined with other aspects of aural perception. While these expectations may be tempered by interpretative frames that extend outside the sound-event as well (the quiet stadium, for example, may indicate a nervous crowd), it is through loudness that much of their impact is felt and registered.

The goal of this chapter is to explore the impact of loudness (and the associated, though not identical, concept of volume) as an undertheorized generator of sonic affect, particularly in musical settings.[9] In considering sonic encounters with loudness through their affective potential, I draw from models broadly outlined by Melissa Gregg and Gregory Seigworth, who refer to affect as the operation of "intensities that pass from body to body (human, nonhuman, part-body, and otherwise), in those resonances that circulate about, between, and sometimes stick to bodies and worlds, *and* in the very passages or variations between these intensities and resonances themselves."[10] Affective encounter arises in spaces of "in-betweenness,"[11] in forces that move into and through a range of corporeal and non-corporeal realms: aural and haptic, subjective and social, conceptual and embodied. Reports of powerful loudness experiences often draw upon strikingly similar language. Such descriptions depict moments in which normally distinct perceptual realms are merged and perforated, especially the division between sound and the body. Appreciating the impact of loudness requires attending to these transmissions into, through, and between bodies—to loudness's tenuous physicality between silence and pain.

These fascinating limits bounding loudness experience are especially instructive in the way that they point to such drastically different registers of sonic non/encounter. They are, in a sense, limits that sit *beyond the limits,* with neither conforming to what we commonly understand—and what Wegel identified—as the auditory sense. Composer Curtis Roads similarly describes them as sitting outside the realm of conventional audibility, instead referring to them as subsonic (below sound) and perisonic (dangerous sound) intensities.[12] Yet by emphasizing issues of touch and withdrawal, of presence and absence, silence and pain serve as reminders that the aural is always already physical. It is these moments when bodies reveal themselves—rather than a fetishistic concern with "pain" as such—that I wish to draw out. Silence and pain mark the limits of our ability to conceive of listening as detached or distant. In between the physical and the perceptual, loudness makes sound's presence felt.

. . .

The discussions that follow make no attempt at being comprehensive. Rather, they offer preliminary attempts at grappling with several specific loudness effects. The text is divided into two sections. The first explores various attempts at describing loudness experience, culled from a variety of perspectives. It begins with a very brief overview of the role of loudness in the field of psychophysics—a discipline rooted in studying the boundaries between physical and perceptual stimuli. I go on to consider listener accounts of experiencing loudness, drawn primarily from literature on rock and noise music. The discussion is structured around three commonly reported types of loudness effect, each of which centers around affective transfers of intensity across perceptual boundaries. Using the terminology developed here, the second section steps back to apply these effects to two theories of musical aesthetics: Michel Poizat's operatic "cry" and Fred Moten's discussion of "Aunt Hester's scream" in African American music.

PART I: LOUDNESS EFFECTS

The physical properties of sound were studied and systematized extensively by acousticians starting in the nineteenth century. During this time, scientists began to measure sound in terms of several basic properties of waves: frequency, waveform, and amplitude.[13] Introductory physics courses tend to portray each of these properties as mapping neatly onto a single parameter of how we hear: frequency corresponds to musical pitch, waveform to timbre, and amplitude to loudness. While this works in a rough sense, in practice the relationships between physical waveforms and perceptual experiences are complicated by a vast array of contextual factors. The study of relationships between how sound waves exist in the world and how they are perceived and made sense of by the ear and brain eventually blossomed into an entirely new field known as psychoacoustics—a subset of the larger discipline of psychophysics.[14]

Loudness played a germinal role in early psychophysics, due primarily to the work of Gustav Fechner. Like several predecessors, Fechner noted that increases in wave amplitude were interpreted by the ear as increases in perceived loudness. However, he also observed that the ratio between these increases was not linear. Two violins playing in unison, for example, do not strike us as sounding twice as loud as one. Fechner instead proposed that these increases were based on a base-ten logarithmic formula. Thus, to double the perceived loudness of one violin required the use of ten (10^1), tripling it required one hundred (10^2), quadrupling it required one thousand (10^3), and so on. The discovery, which became known as Fechner's Law, was a watershed moment in the field. Although later researchers would improve upon the exact formulation, the law's elegant approach to quantifying a relationship between physical and perceptual realities provided an important model for subsequent research. To the present day, the International Society of Psychophysics celebrates the discovery with a yearly "Fechner Day" celebration at their annual conference.[15]

In contrast to the quantifiable data sought by psychophysicists, nonscientific descriptions of loudness tend to rely on more qualitative accounts that oscillate between individual and social interpretations. In each of the examples below, the force of loudness is predicated on the interplay between direct material confrontations (bodies pressing against bodies) and culturally mediated expectations, with neither fully reducible to the other. By pointing to loudness's ability to transfer and transduce sonic intensity into various modes of physical and (pre)personal potentiality, these descriptions can begin to sketch the affective outlines of loudness as it confronts listening communities. For obvious reasons such accounts are more common within sonic traditions that foreground loudness as an aesthetic parameter, including rock and noise music.

To interrogate this idea further, I offer brief examinations of three commonly reported phenomena associated with loudness, which I refer to as "listener collapse," "imagined loudness," and "noise occupation."

Effect #1: Listener Collapse

> To be listening is to be at the same time outside and inside . . . the sharing of an inside/outside, division and participation, deconnection and contagion.
>
> —JEAN-LUC NANCY

Philosopher Jean-Luc Nancy shares a crucial insight with psychophysicists.[16] In his book *Listening*, he also describes how aurality acts as a meeting point between exterior/physical and interior/perceptual worlds. To listen is to encounter an exteriority, yet it elicits an experience that is located firmly within the body of the listener. Nancy conceives of sound as being identical with its emitter (be it instrument or person), whose vibrations not only create sound but in a real sense *are* sound. Source, space, and listener(s) are brought into intimate contact through a single shared vibration—a shimmering together that nevertheless is always experienced individually.

While Nancy's proposition is simple enough to understand in the abstract sense, the everyday act of listening often feels quite different. Vibrations may very well be conceived as a form of touch, but in practice sound tends to be experienced as traveling from a remote source to our ear. This process delineates a perceptual distinction between world and self by locating the sound source at a defined, distant point in space. It is this perception that has allowed researchers since Wegel to postulate on the boundary between the auditory and haptic senses, a boundary that only becomes recognizable at moments when it is transgressed. One of the most common ways to affect this transgression is through extreme loudness.

In his 2013 study of Japanese noise music, David Novak describes a conversation with a friend regarding the power of noise performance: "At the beginning of a good Noise show, [my friend] said, the volume 'just sucks all the air out of the room,' leaving the listener suspended in sound: 'You can feel your whole body react [he snapped his body back as if suddenly startled] when they start—the sound fills your mind completely and you can't think. At first you're just shrinking back, until you overcome that and let it go, and then you're in it and you're just being blown away.'"[17] This description provides an example of one of the most common effects associated with extreme loudness, an effect I refer to as "listener collapse."[18] An experience of listener collapse occurs when loud sound dissolves the ability to distinguish between interior and exterior worlds, especially in regard to sound and self. Sound does not only touch, it saturates and fills mental and physical consciousness, eliminating the possibility of detached listening. In a sense, listener collapse acts as a forced imposition of the type of sonic experience proposed by Nancy; it is a moment in which penetration erases our ability to distinguish between exterior/sound and interior/self, bringing both together in a single inescapable vibration.

In sonic communities that value extreme loudness, the experience of listener collapse can be a powerful source of pleasure. Describing rock music, Theodore Gracyk writes: "For a receptive audience, volume bridges the sense of distance between the audience and the performers by erasing the gap between the self and the music.... [L]oud music can break us out of our sense of detached observation and replace it with a sense of immersion, for it is literally around us (or, with headphones, seemingly inside our head). Where traditional aesthetic theories have often offered an ideal of disinterested contemplation of 'psychical distance,' the presence of noise can overcome the respectful, reverential aspects of distancing."[19] Here, loudness provides the basis of an alternative aesthetic that seeks out immersive physio-aural-haptic experience. This desire can be traced in numerous rock and noise music communities. We can see it in bands like My Bloody Valentine, whose fans gleefully describe them as "The Loudest Band In The World" and who often cap their performances with an extended high-loudness noise section dubbed—tellingly—the holocaust.[20] An even more stark example can be seen in the Seattle drone metal group Sunn O))), whose performances blast audiences with slow moving sub-bass frequencies at 120dB. Describing her experience at one of the group's concerts, Olivia Lucas writes: "The sound envelops my body, cutting me off from other sensations, making me safe. Closing my eyes, I sway slowly from side to side to the slow beat of the vibrational pulses. I am touching sound."[21]

But how does loudness initiate this powerful dissolution of boundaries between self and other, between the material and the reflective? I suggest that the process hinges upon a unique double-movement that simultaneously transforms how both sound and selfhood are processed. First, sound projected at high levels generates vibrations that resonate in bodily locations other than the ear. The feeling of sound rumbling in one's chest, for example, is a familiar sensation at rock concerts, operas, sporting events, lightning storms, and in any number of other contexts. Lucas's encounter with Sunn O))) makes repeated references to feeling sound in her stomach, her sternum, her sinus, her hands.[22] This somatosensory shift transforms sound into a tangible presence, reminding us of sound's identity as a tactile object that operates in, around, and through the body. While this is easy to forget in standard (low volume) contexts, loudness makes it impossible to ignore.

While this first movement emphasizes materiality by elevating the sonic to the level of the physical self, the second movement does the exact opposite. Here, high loudness works to destroy the experience of selfhood by approaching the upper limit of the loudness scale: physical pain. As Elaine Scarry details in her pathbreaking work on torture, experiences of extreme pain work to dissolve the most basic concepts of self and world. For the body in pain, neither self nor world nor choice exist, as torment becomes the only perceivable content of consciousness.[23] Scarry's account speaks to the ways that pain breaks down fundamental categories of sensory experience: "Although vision and hearing ordinarily reside close to objectification, if one experiences one's eyes or ears themselves—if the woman working looks up at the sun too suddenly and her eyes fill with blinding light—then vision falls back to the neighborhood of pain."[24] By approaching the threshold of pain, high-level sonic experience affects a similar collapse of interior and exterior, dissolving self and other into an undifferentiated experience of sound and/as pain.

The frighteningly destructive potentials of listener collapse are noted often in scholarship on musical torture and sonic weaponry.[25] However, it is also important to recognize that this powerful form of affect can provide an important source of fulfillment within some listening communities. Even references to pain are not always in opposition to such aesthetics. Novak comments on how many noise performers choose stage names that foreground pain and destruction, while positive descriptions of shows often use terms like "brutal" or "painful."[26] Lucas likewise analyses her experience in terms of "masochistic submission" and "ritual domination," drawing from the work of Fred Maus.[27] Both authors make reference to listener collapse's ability to evoke experiences of the sublime—an encounter with an object of such force and power that it defies attempts at measured or detached comprehension.

One final question might ask whether listener collapse functions primarily as an individual or as a social experience. Novak emphasizes the former, writing: "Volume flattens out the scene to foreground the idiosyncrasies of individual sensation.... This immersion in volume is not a moment of social collectivity, but a personal encounter with the overwhelming presence of sound."[28] In light of the preceding discussion, however, I suggest a somewhat different interpretation. Loudness's act of flattening is not simply a matter of drowning out the social in deference to the subjective. Rather, the flattening itself enacts an erasure of the basic line between individual and social. When one can no longer distinguish between interior and exterior worlds, parsing individual versus collective experience becomes a fruitless exercise. As Gracyk suggests, sound becomes a bridge that brings multiple actors (human and nonhuman) together in an experience that is profoundly personal but also profoundly shared. Reverberating Nancy's dictum, all vibrate together, connected by sound, unable to distinguish where my vibrations end and another's begin.

Effect #2: Imagined Loudness

"Imagined loudness" refers to listeners' ability to reinterpret the level of perceived sounds in order to meet certain requirements or expectations that are not fulfilled by a sound's physical characteristics. This allows the listener to compensate for sonic encounters that fail to meet the aesthetic demands of a particular tradition. Take, for example, this statement on heavy metal from Robert Walser: "The complete electronic control of sound reproduction that characterizes modern music allows metal to be reproduced, theoretically, at any level. However, the nature of metal and the needs and pleasures it addresses demand that it always be heard loud. Even when it is heard from a distance, or even sung softly to oneself, metal is imagined as loud, for volume is an important contributor to the heaviness of heavy metal."[29]

The ontological status of imagined loudness is somewhat unclear. Is it a desire? An association? A delusion? A projection? Although it cannot be described as physical, its phenomenological potency is sufficient to satisfy a metal fan's aesthetic requirement for loud experience (and perhaps listener collapse), even at moments where further amplification would be impractical. Once again, the observation finds loudness operating at the intersection between individual and social experience. Here, aesthetic expectations established by listening communities impinge upon the affective experience of individual listeners, even when those listeners are removed from social settings (e.g., "even sung softly to oneself").[30] To be precise, the effect described by Walser is not entirely imagined but results in part from other associations noted elsewhere in his text. Timbre, for example, is perceived as being closely intertwined with loudness, especially through the sound of distorted (overdriven) electric guitars. For much of rock's history, distortion was only obtainable by pushing amplifiers to the point of overloading their electronic components. Through this connection, distorted timbres can arouse a perceptual impression of loudness even when reproduced at softer levels, evoking the haptic memory of pleasurable listener collapse.[31]

As a critical tool, imagined loudness provides a productive way to unravel certain issues surrounding volume and electronic manipulation. For example, it may help to explain Gracyk's confusion regarding a quote from writer Sheila Whitely:

> Sheila Whitely says of "Purple Haze" that its "sheer volume of noise works towards the drowning of personal consciousness." This should give us pause; Whitely is discussing a recording, and *any* recording can be turned up to a level where it might "drown" personal consciousness through sheer volume. . . . Surely Whitely herself decided that high volume is particularly suitable for "Purple Haze," more so than for "Little Wing" or "Spanish Castle Music [sic]." Listening to recordings and the radio, the audience controls the volume level. Yet different musics seem to demand different volumes.[32]

Imagined loudness can help shed light on Whitely's quote. For her, "Purple Haze" can always be experienced phenomenologically as a loud event, even when the recording is turned down to low levels. The timbral effects of distortion again play a major role; it is not surprising that "Purple Haze" utilizes heavy guitar distortion, while Gracyk's two contrasting examples do not.

This should not imply that certain sounds intrinsically possess or imply a fixed loudness perception. The conditioning process that links sounds with expected loudness levels is undoubtedly established through repeated exposure and learned expectations within a given culture.[33] Yet we should also note that these associations, once established, are quite resilient, persisting long after technological change renders them outdated. Electronic effects pedals, for instance, have allowed guitarists to play distorted sounds at low levels for decades, yet their association with loudness remains largely intact—a notable phenomenological inertia. Eventually, however, all such associations are vulnerable to shifting, a disjuncture that is especially notable across generations. Whitely's imagined loudness experience of "Purple Haze," for example, might not resonate with a child of the 1990s whose musical upbringing affixed very different associations to the sound of Jimi Hendrix. For such a listener, the sound of Hendrix's guitar might evoke only the low-level playback of family car rides, not the overwhelming intensity of late 1960s rock bacchanalia.

Unlike listener collapse, imagined loudness does not only operate at extremely high levels. It can be attached to softer sounds as well. Take, for instance, John Szwed's description of Miles Davis's delicate trumpet sound, played through a Harmon mute:

> Miles ... pulled the tube out and played the mute straight, shoving the bell of his horn into the microphone to gain volume and resonance.
>
> The Harmon had a certain mystique to it because it was hard to record. It muted so well, in fact, that trumpet players blew harder, and it subdued the fundamental of the tone, as the engineers might say, giving off high-frequency transients.... The mute also allowed Miles to play the way he spoke, in that grainy whisper that compelled others to lean toward him—a wisp of a musical tone that could suggest delicate intimacy but also a force barely under control.[34]

This account offers a compelling inversion of the rock writers. Where Walser's volume knob allows him to turn down a record while still imagining it as loud, Davis's microphone and mute allow him to project tones that are loud enough to be audible while nevertheless suggesting intense softness. Timbre again plays a major role, as Szwed observes. By subduing the fundamental, the muted horn emulates a whisper, evoking low-volume associations of closeness and intimacy.

The paradoxical power that can be generated through low loudness (imagined or otherwise) is similarly explored by Anne Karpf in her writing on the human voice: "Among those who have been silenced historically ... volume can be a sign of defiance.... But volume can also be inversely related to status. To compel total attention some powerful people speak so softly that their listeners are obliged to lean forward to hear.... Reversing the norm can be powerful, too. Since loudness is traditionally associated with rage, and softness with intimacy and confidentiality, quietly expressed anger can be devastating."[35] Read in dialogue with Szwed, these observations allow for a provocative reading of Davis's musical allure. Note, for instance, how both accounts reference an audience's submissive need to "lean forward/toward" the soft utterances of dominant figures. What is striking about Szwed's image of "a force barely under control" and Karpf's suggestion of quietude's ability to "compel total attention" is the paradoxical intimation that low loudness can exert a power that rivals, if not mirrors, that of high loudness. As will be explored further, the impact wrought by the extremities of the loudness spectrum often commingle and converge in unexpected ways.

Effect #3: Noise Occupation

Noise is generally defined in one of two ways: (1) a sound that is not desired, or (2) a sound that distracts from another sound that is desired (a signal, or code).[36] Like a weed, its designation is rooted in a metaphysics of un/desire that is fluid and subjective. This fact has been well-known to experimental artists (rock, jazz, classical) since the early twentieth century, who have continuously worked to emancipate various sounds from the label of noisiness—to alter their meaning through the simple act of focusing attention upon them. As Paul Hegarty describes: "Noise itself constantly dissipates, as what is judged noise at one point is music or meaning at another. As well as this disruptive element, noise must also be thought of as constantly failing—failing to stay noise as it becomes familiar or acceptable practice."[37]

While noisiness and loudness might seem like very different properties of sound, in practice they are closely implicated. Studies of noise music, for example, frequently reference loudness as a technique used to provoke noise's sonic un/desire.[38] Though extreme loudness may not always be a necessary prerequisite for creating noise, it is certainly a powerful tool. By provoking physical responses that approach pain, loudness acts as a catalyst. It initiates the affective economies of desire, penetration, and resistance through which noise becomes (more) noisy. Perhaps not surprisingly, the political ramifications of noise have been a recurrent theme within the recent history of sound studies.[39] Debates over noisiness (both its nature and its presence) call our attention to the many ways that sound is assessed, valued, contested, and manipulated. An ever-shifting discursive construction, noise shines light on the ways that social power is articulated in the sonic realm. Karin Bijsterveld argues that "the right to make noise as well as the right to decide which sounds are allowed or forbidden has long been the privilege of the powerful, whereas those lower in rank (women, children, servants) were supposed to keep silent, or were under suspicion of intentionally disturbing social order by making noise."[40] By focusing attention on sound as a staging ground for debates over value, the study of noise highlights a central goal of the sound studies enterprise: examining what aurality has to teach us about social dynamics, mediation, control, and listening bodies.

A key foundational text in the contemporary study of noise is Jacques Attali's *Noise: A Political Economy of Music*. Attali argues that control over sound has long been essential to the operations of hegemonic power and that this control takes place through the imposition of various codes that "analyze, mark, restrain, train, repress, and channel the primitive sounds of language, of the body, of tools, of objects, of the relation to self and others."[41] For Attali, "noise" is defined as any sonic event that arises from outside of these codes—the sounds that are undesired by the powers in control. To make noise is therefore a deeply political act, since noises are, by definition, the sounds that hegemonies wish to suppress. The tendency of sound to expand outward into public space therefore provides a formidable tool for both the hegemon and its resistors. Noisiness offers a means for claiming and reclaiming public space in the interest of various competing sonic ideologies. I refer to this process as noise occupation.

Attali's theories have resonated strongly among certain rock music writers, including Gracyk. Although he takes issue with certain aspects of Attali's model, Gracyk connects with the theorist when discussing the political potentialities of music played at high levels. Through noise occupation, loudness and volume embolden music by enabling it to permeate more deeply into contested spaces. Loudness increases the distance that sound can travel, allowing it to impose itself upon others and (re)claim public space through the saturating force of sonic presence. Such deployment creates the potential for "turning music into a weapon" that can be used to either reinforce or resist systems of control.[42] Insofar as it emerged in postwar America as a high-loudness genre that self-consciously opposed mainstream power structures, rock music can perhaps therefore be considered "noisy" in the Attalian sense.

But other accounts may complicate this heroic countercultural narrative of hegemony and resistance. Instead of focusing exclusively on oppositional binaries, William Echard argues that rock's unique aesthetic systemization of sound (including the desire *for* loudness) makes it difficult to consider the music as pure noise in the manner outlined by Attali. Instead, Echard proposes a model of "relative" noise that operates by blurring the boundaries between noise and code:

> There are many ways in which the balance between noise-as-noise and noise-as-code may be enacted. For example, a performance may be understood as being *about* noise even when it is highly conventional. . . .

Or listeners may choose to pay special attention to features of the music which are more noisy and disregard factors that suggest regulation, in effect suspending their disbelief and allowing a temporary enactment of noise as a phenomenological event.... Or an event may be noisy relative to other kinds of events. Rock music may have conventionalized noise within its own practices, but it can still be noisy when compared to traditions which have not undergone this exercise.[43]

Echard's relativization of noise suggests a crucial corollary. While Attali's original text is concerned primarily with macro-level, post-Marxian models of late-capitalist hegemony, Echard deconstructs the model further by fragmenting noise and code into more localized networks. Within this decentered framework, questions regarding what types of sounds objectively constitute "noise" or "code" become meaningless. Rather, noise's discursive contours remain fluid, subjectively delineated by the preferences and cultural ingrained belief systems held by each listener. Expanding this idea outward, musical genres can likewise never be cast as solely oppositional to (or in alliance with) a single mainstream power—despite frequent attempts to frame them as such. Instead, they must be seen as possessing their own structuring, perhaps micro-hegemonic, principles.

Throughout such discussions loudness continues to function as a pivotal tool through which salvos of code and noise are volleyed by various constituencies. Amplifying loudness provides the most straightforward means of "weaponizing" sound in both literal and metaphorical ways. Through the effects of noise occupation, loudness allows sound to impose a sociosonic discipline upon the space in which it operates. It is no coincidence, for example, that military bands often comprise the loudest instruments in a given culture (Scottish pipers, European drum corps, Turkish janissary, etc.). Musical genres associated with protest have also tended toward high loudness—from the piercing trumpets of jazz to the booming bass of hip hop to the distorted guitars of rock. Even the American folk revival of the 1960s, despite its professed aversion to electric amplification, cultivated loudness (and volume) through mass sing-alongs and communal gatherings.[44]

The political power of noise occupation is more than simply a metaphorical display of solidarity. Instead—like listener collapse—it operates within the affective space in between individual and social experience. On the one hand, noise's un/desirability is negotiated by myriad cultural values and expectations. On the other, it operates via an uninvited penetration into the ears of individual subjects. In Foucauldian terms, one might say that noise occupation imposes social mandates through acts of discipline inflicted upon physical bodies. This becomes especially evident when considering the various weaponizations of sound that have arisen over the past several decades (LRADs, Operation Nifty Package, Guantanamo Detention Techniques, and so on). Loudness and volume empower noises to penetrate directly into the bodies of anyone close enough to hear—anyone within ear/shot.

PART II: THE CRY AND THE SCREAM

Thus far, the discussion in this chapter has focused on defining a series of reported effects that speak to loudness's affective impact. In this final section I attempt to apply the preceding ideas to two texts on musical aesthetics: Michel Poizat's concept of the operatic "cry" and Fred Moten's examination of "Aunt Hester's scream" in African American music. Though dealing with very different genres, the two writers share a concern with the immense force of nonlinguistic vocal utterances. Both stress the wordless nature of the sounds as the key to their power. Although this is certainly significant, I propose that additional sources of affect can be found in two other characteristics that go largely unexamined: their intense loudness and their paradoxical parallels to silence. It is no accident that both theorists focus on the extremities of human declamation (loudness and absence), rather than choosing among the many other forms of nonlinguistic sound (the gasp, the whimper, the sigh, etc.). This section reexamines both theories to consider how accounting for loudness may offer additional insight.

. . .

In his book *The Angel's Cry*, Poizat explores various relationships between speech, music, and silence in the realm of operatic singing. He begins with a historical account of the long-standing argument over which feature of opera is more important: music or text. The roots of this debate are traced to ancient accounts of unease surrounding the mysterious, unexplainable power of musical tones. For centuries, political and religious leaders sought to contain this power through the controlling restraint of intelligible sung texts. Despite their efforts, Poizat argues that opera has steadily moved away from intelligible speech and toward a less comprehensible style of singing, ultimately culminating in the emergence of the pure cry.[45]

Reflecting upon this trajectory, Poizat proposes a new way of thinking about the operatic voice that abandons the older binary of music versus text. Instead, he suggests a spectrum of possibilities derived from linguistic signification itself. On one side, the scale is bounded by the presence of linguistic signifiers as communicated in clear, intelligible speech. On the other, it is characterized by the absence of language, which can either occur through total silence or through the cry. This idea is illustrated through the following diagram:

Silence, cry   Singing   Speech, signifying
                                                      linguistic message[46]

The cry, in its position as both similar and directly opposed to silence, becomes a central element in Poizat's theory. He defines it as follows:

> [W]henever I speak of a *pure* or sheer cry, I mean specifically a paroxysmal vocal emission beyond the range of music and out of reach of the word. This cry is therefore not supported by the musical notation, nor can it be accommodated on the staff; and it is not supported by direct verbal notation in the text (at most, it is indicated by an "Ah!" in the libretto, though usually it is given in a stage direction such as "screams with horror" or "cries out in terror"). It is in this dual sense that the cry is literally unsupportable, unbearable, and untenable. Lulu makes us feel the horror of the cry that no human symbolic system can accommodate, and this is why the cry is so often called "inhuman."[47]

For Poizat, the potency of the cry is derived from its uncontainability in any linguistic or symbolic system. Instead, it generates affect by simulating "the cry of pain [that] preceded all speech."[48] He frames this idea via Jacques Lacan's theory of the "object voice," a prelinguistic form of utterance that is properly possessed only during infancy. The object voice has no recourse to meaning, and the infant speaker is unable to distinguish between his/her voice and his/her self. This experience of the voice is lost, however, as soon as the infant acquires the use of language.[49] For Poizat, the cry is opera's attempt to simulate the sublimity of the object voice by presenting an utterance that triggers affect without relying upon the word. It is this striving toward an unobtainable prelinguistic mimesis that gives the cry its chilling power.

Before returning to the question of loudness, one final aspect of Poizat's theory should be noted: its treatment of silence. The author conceives of silence in two separate ways. The first imagines it as a form of absence—a gap between sounds that allows them to be separated and differentiated from one another. This separating function allows sound to be molded into semiotic systems, and he therefore refers to it as "the silence that speaks." But Poizat dwells somewhat longer on a second formulation, which he refers to as "the silence that screams." Here, silence is not conceived as an absence but as a pervasive presence that underlies all sonic experience. It only becomes recognizable "when the verbal, the articulate, is cast back into nothingness . . . a silence that results from that destruction, a deadly silence, the unsevered and *absolute presence* of the pulsing of presence and absence."[50] Like the cry, the silence that screams derives its force by summoning a form of presence that reaches before and beyond systems of signification. By casting off semiotic meaning, the silence that screams imposes itself as a crushing presence due to the absence of (signifying) absence.[51]

It is in this overlap between silence and the cry that we find our first indication of possible loudness effects. Note that these two events embody the furthest ends of the loudness spectrum: silence and pain—those limits at which the listener can no longer listen. Although Poizat describes the cry primarily in terms of heightened pitch and lack of linguistic content, all of his primary examples (Berg's Lulu, Wagner's Kundry, Mozart's Commandant, etc.) occur at the loudest moments of opera. At such levels the performance becomes capable of evoking several crucial loudness effects. First, by presenting itself at extreme levels, the cry initiates the characteristic double-movement of listener collapse. Its loudness foregrounds sound's identity as a physical presence, while at the same time dissolving selfhood through the approach toward physical pain (or—in the related example of the silence that screams—psychological terror). This observation does not contradict Poizat's analysis but rather enhances it. As listener collapse dissolves the distinction between (exterior) sound and (interior) self, the cry becomes better equipped to perform its terrifying simulation of a Lacanian prelinguistic object voice.

One might protest that although the cry is presented as a dramatization of pain, orchestras and singers rarely reach levels loud enough to produce actual physical anguish in the opera audience. As such, listener collapse could never function in the way that it does for a genre like heavy metal (which, through amplification, is more than capable of reaching such levels). To this, I offer two responses. First, if the classical orchestra is unable to match metal's extreme loudness, it is certainly not for lack of trying. The continuous growth in the size of orchestras up through the nineteenth century can be read as a steady accumulation of loudness potential, even if they could never approach the levels attainable through electric amplification (due to the restrictions implicit in Fechner's logarithmic function). It is worth noting that the most influential figure in expanding the orchestra is also Poizat's central example in developing the cry: Richard Wagner. The desire for loudness effects may have been a common factor underlying both developments. Second, even when the orchestra's loudness does not approach the threshold of physical pain, listeners may be able to fill in the remainder through acts of imagined loudness. The timbral associations of the crying, straining, distorted voice work to create a phenomenological perception of loudness that is sufficient for the cry to have its crushing effect. Through imagined loudness, the aesthetic-affective impact of the cry can be experienced by those straining to hear from the highest balconies, just as it is by those who are engulfed in the front row.

Several related issues arise in Moten's analysis of Aunt Hester's scream, a reference to a passage from the first autobiography of Frederick Douglass. The scene relates an event from Douglass's youth in which he witnessed his aunt being beaten viciously by their enslaver. The piercing sound of her screams haunted Douglass throughout his life and, Moten argues, has continued to haunt African American artists, historians, and writers ever since. In this way, he conceives of the scream as a foundational moment for radical Black aesthetics. Where Poizat is concerned with spectrums, Moten highlights the significance of discursive gaps (breaks, cuts, etc.). The impact of Aunt Hester's scream stems from its position inside several such breaks. One of these closely resembles Poizat's emphasis on sounds that generate affect by operating outside of linguistic signification. In Moten's words, the scream constitutes "a radically exterior aurality that disrupts and resists certain formulations of identity and interpretation by challenging the reducibility of phonic matter to verbal meaning or conventional musical form."[52] Unlike Poizat—who stresses the cry's unidirectional movement away from significatory meaning—by conceiving of the scream in a conceptual gap, Moten proposes that it engages in its own double-movement *toward and away from* signification. The scream is powerful in the way that it symbolically conveys defiance as well as in its presence as a pure vocalization that transcends language. In this it defies any model that would attempt to position it as either signifier or signified. Aunt Hester's scream announces itself as both and neither, cleaving a deep rift in the structure of signification itself.[53]

The cut opened by the scream mirrors that engendered by the institution of slavery more broadly, in which lines between subject and object are obliterated through the perverse conceptualization of human chattel. In a reversal of Marx's concept of "exchange value," Moten argues that it is through speech acts that the enslaved person is able to resist commodification, namely by announcing one's own subjecthood. In the case of the scream, however, this act of defiance is not pure but functions as another treacherous double-movement. On the one hand, Aunt Hester's scream disrupts the logic of bondage through a subjective, improvisational, vocalized defiance of her commodification. But on the other, the scream, as a response to physical pain, reinforces the objectification that is intrinsic to the system of enslavement. The scream always conveys more and less than it intends; as Douglass notes, the enslaver "would whip her to make her scream, and whip her to make her hush."[54] Within the system of enslavement, where subject/object distinctions disintegrate and signification becomes bankrupt, the human voice is left with only the scream, or silence.

Considering loudness can once again illuminate the process through which Aunt Hester's scream cuts us. As with Poizat's cry, the voice's intensity again works to provoke an experience of listener collapse that arrives with crushing force. But simultaneously, as a form of active defiance, Aunt Hester's scream also taps into the potentialities of noise occupation through an Attalian reclamation of sonic space. Through its immense volume, the scream cuts into the bodies of those within earshot. The symbolic rape of Hester's beating is resisted and inverted as her scream functions as a sonic penetration against her attacker, a penetration the enslaver cannot control.

But of course, this penetration is turned not only on the enslaver but also onto young Douglass himself. Bearing witness to his aunt's pain, the young man is materially and conceptually torn open through the scream's terrifying affect. In Douglass's words: "I remember the first time I ever witnessed this horrible exhibition. . . . It struck me with awful force. It was the blood-stained gate, the entrance to the hell of slavery, through which I was about to pass."[55] Yet even as the moment marks a non-negotiable entrance into slavery, it simultaneously enables Douglass to position himself outside of it—a view of hell from beyond the gates. The pain of Aunt Hester's scream, as a jarring i(nte)rruption of the architecture of slavery, opens a space for questioning and resistance that becomes the groundwork for future Black radicalism. Moten goes on to describe several of her most resonant descendants:

> [Abbey] Lincoln hums and then screams over [Max] Roach's increasingly and insistently intense percussion, moving inexorably in a trajectory and toward a location that is in excess of or inaccessible to—words. You cannot help but hear the echo of Aunt Hester's scream. . . . That echo haunts, say, Albert Ayler's "Ghosts" or the fractured, fracturing climax of James Brown's "Cold Sweat." It's the re-engendering haint of an old negation: Ayler always screaming secretly to the very idea of mastery, "It's not about you"; Brown paying the price of such negation, a terrible, ecstatic, possessive, dispossessive transfer, a transcendental fade, an interminable songlike drag disrupting song.[56]

We should not be surprised that Moten's examples—Lincoln, Roach, Ayler, Brown—again draw upon extreme levels of loudness that push beyond linguistic meaning. Their sounds proliferate in multiple directions: connecting communities through interpersonal sonic touch and shared pain, staking a visceral claim to physical, political, conceptual, and spiritual spaces.

The loudness effects in Moten's theory reconnect with Poizat again at the end of his book, where the author analyzes an installation by artist Adrian Piper called *Untitled Performance for Max's Kansas City*. In the piece, Piper presents herself physically within the space of her artwork. She remains perfectly still, eyes and lips tightly closed, and refuses to interact with anyone in the room. Her charged silence functions as an active resistance to expectations of her speech. Like Aunt Hester, Piper conveys her message through a presence that refuses recourse to signification. Through Piper, Moten's theory comes full circle, identifying a descendant whose power is drawn from silence yet retains kinship to the scream.[57] Where Hester's subjectivity is enacted through a vocalization that rejects her designation as a silent commodity, Piper's is performed through a crushing silence that refuses the role of speaking collaborator. Where Hester penetrates by filling up sonic space, Piper castrates by stripping away symbolic systems. Where Hester's resistance is the soul-saturating loudness of the cry, Piper's is the equally devastating stillness of the silence that screams.

CONCLUSION

Given the numerous threads explored, it is useful to return to a central question: What is to be gained by considering loudness? How might we benefit from reexamining its role as a generator of sonic affect? To summarize, I present the following general points. First, loudness operates in the liminal space between multiple experiential registers. Especially at extreme levels, it draws its force from an oscillation that flattens and/or transgresses several perceptual binaries: interior/exterior, self/other, presence/meaning, individual/social, physical/reflective. In each of the examples of listener collapse, imagined loudness and noise occupation, we observe loudness cutting across categories, distorting and obscuring them, disorienting us by disrupting our most basic perceptual apparatuses. This in-between-ness speaks to its affective impact—its ability to transfer intensities across bodies and discourses. Unexpectedly, such a model provides compelling correspondences with loudness's germinal role in the history of psychophysics, a quantitative field that was predicated on interrogating the translation of experience across physical and perceptual realms.

Second, by shining light on loudness, we open new avenues for considering the impact of musical/sonic encounters. While other parameters of musical sound (pitch relations, rhythmic structures, textual settings) are perpetually analyzed and interpreted, loudness is often glossed over as obvious or self-evident. Yet any conductor can tell you that the dynamics of a passage have tremendous ramifications for its realization; any performer can relate the long hours spent developing a powerful sound on their instrument; any mixing engineer can describe how manipulating levels can make or break a recording. These nuances speak to loudness's importance for aural experience, but too often they go overlooked or unmentioned. Such was the case in the examples of Poizat and Moten. The loudness of both the cry and the scream seems so obvious that neither author dwells on them, but upon closer examination it can be seen as a powerful contributor to their affective poignancy.

While this chapter has focused on the furthest ends of the loudness spectrum, it is not only here that loudness is felt. I conclude with the hope that future work may continue such examinations on more moderate levels of intensity. Despite our perceiving them as unique moments, silence and pain are not alien entities; they are not detached from other registers of sonic encounter. By mapping the edges of listening, they remind us of aurality's broader affective potentials. In the sounds between silence and pain, our ears touch a world beyond.

2   Let's Listen to Nothing
Silence and the Anechoic Chamber

PROLOGUE

Let's listen to planes.

The device pictured on the opposite page is called an acoustic locator (Figure 2). It was an early warning technology used by militaries in the early twentieth century to detect enemy aircraft before the widespread adoption of radar. As you might guess, it functions as a prosthesis—an enlarged supplemental ear designed to increase the reach of human audition. The curve of the cones focuses and amplifies minute sound waves, allowing the wearer to hear distant sounds that would not be audible to the ear alone. By pointing the device in the direction of the enemy, human operators could hear the engines of approaching aircraft long before they came into view.

Locators were built in many designs by different militaries, some appearing like straightforward extensions of the body, others as enormous stone amphitheaters nestled in the countryside. Some of these larger structures still stand today, including several in southern England. These simple devices represent an early attempt to use listening—not just sound, but the actual human cognitive processing of that sound—as a technology of war. This distinction is important, since the term "acoustic locator" does not only refer to the prosthetic. It also refers to our own fleshy, living bodies, straining to hear vibrations that the prosthesis places within our reach, noting them, measuring them, and using them to construct an image of the world around us.[1]

Let's listen to boats.

Again, we strive to hear our enemies, but this time let's use a more complex prosthesis. Around the end of World War I, military physicists began

FIGURE 2. Acoustic locator, circa 1930s. Courtesy of Museum Waalsdoorp, The Hague.

FIGURE 3. SONAR operator and display monitor. Photo by Trenton James.

developing active SONAR, a more sophisticated form of sonic detection. A sonar operator can be seen in Figure 3. The basic premise of the technology is well known. The device releases a short pulse of sound (a "ping") that careens out through the open water. When the sound waves meet an object—an enemy submarine, a school of fish, and so on—some of them are reflected back to the original source. By measuring the time and direction of the returning echoes, the device can pinpoint the location of the distant object. Eventually machines were capable of translating this information into a visual display to be read by human operators.

Again, sound is key, but listening functions quite differently here. For one thing, it is no longer the human operator who does the listening but the machine itself, through calibrated microphones. The machine's goal is not to hear something that sounds like a boat, but something that sounds like a ping. That is the only sound the machine is interested in processing (indeed, other sounds must be filtered out). In fact, one of the challenges to SONAR developers through the 1940s wasn't in getting the machines to hear, but getting them *not* to hear—that is, to filter out all of the underwater world's excess "noise" so that the machine could accurately detect and cull data from the pings.[2] The only sound that matters is the sound that the machine itself creates. Here, sound has been thoroughly instrumentalized to create a spatial map, conveyed to an operator not through the ears but through the eyes on a flickering screen. In the process, the outside world is no longer heard at all; by transducing the data from ping to screen, listening (aurally) becomes little more than another way of seeing (visually). The exterior world is reconceived not as a source of sound, but only as a material surface to reflect the sounds that we put into it.

Let's listen to nothing.

But as we do, let us not divert attention from the enemy that militaries always imagine to be just beyond technology's horizons. By World War II the success of SONAR had sparked something of an acoustic arms race, and military-funded research centers in the United States sought new ways of harnessing sound for the war effort. In fact, three of the earliest government-funded research laboratories at American universities were acoustics labs established at Harvard University by the Department of Defense.[3] The first, dubbed the Harvard Underwater Sound Lab, focused primarily on refining SONAR and creating new types of "listening torpedoes."[4] The second, the Psycho-Acoustic Lab, studied the effects of high-noise environments (like airplane cockpits) on soldiers. And the third, the Electro-Acoustic Laboratory, was tasked with inventing new devices for transmitting and controlling sound on the battlefield, including higher fidelity headphones, speakers, and communications equipment. It is the third of these laboratories—the Electro-Acoustic Lab—that I follow briefly here.

The lab was run by a somewhat young physicist named Leo Beranek (b. 1914), who had just completed a doctorate in applied physics in 1940. He expected to go on to a career in radio and architectural acoustics, but instead was recruited by the military to take leadership of the new lab.[5] Among other assignments, the military commissioned the lab in 1942 to develop a new type of high-output loudspeaker, the loudest speaker that had ever been created. Unlike the more recent LRADs (long range acoustic devices) of the twenty-first century—which can use loudness to directly inflict physical damage—the purpose of these speakers was not assault but deception.[6] They were intended to travel alongside a decoy unit of inflatable rubber tanks, known colloquially as the "ghost army." The idea was that the decoys would trick German reconnaissance pilots, who would see them from the skies and relay back false information about allied troop locations. The "tanks" were supplemented with staged radio communication, which was designed to be intercepted. To complete the effect, the military wanted Beranek's loudspeakers to blast prerecorded tank and troop sounds throughout the countryside, to be picked up by enemy scouts. It would be the finishing touch on a multisensory ruse. The ghost army was eventually

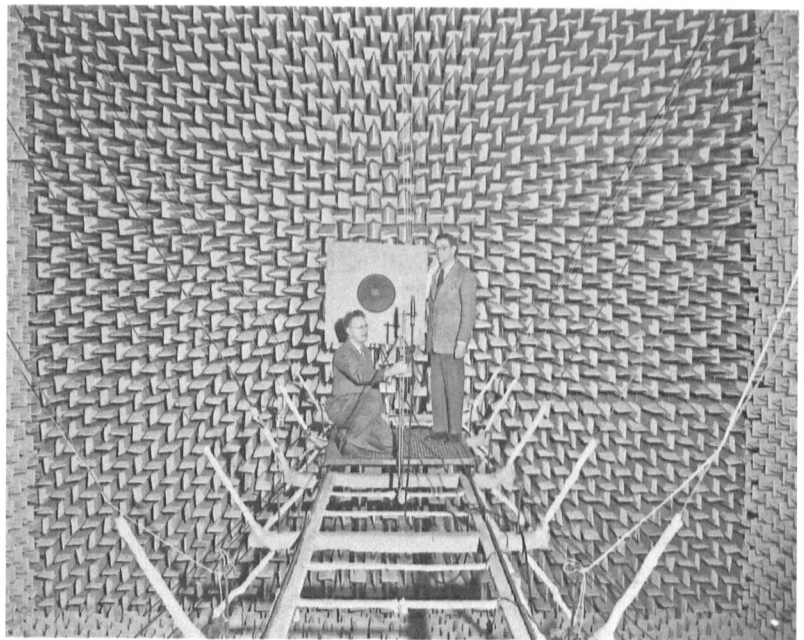

FIGURE 4. Interior of the Harvard anechoic chamber with scientists Edward R. Myrbeck and Arthur A. Janszen, 1948. Courtesy of the Harvard University Archives. Item UAV 605.270.1, Box 8 (SC 1978).

deployed on the western front a week after the invasion of Normandy and continued their operations through the end of the war.[7]

Developing the speakers required Beranek to build a new kind of space to test them. He needed a test site that could both (A) allow for ultra-precise calculations of sound output, while also (B) preventing noise from the tests from spilling into the outside world (after all, they didn't want the top-secret tests thundering through Harvard Yard). To accomplish both goals, Beranek designed and built a massive new testing facility on the Harvard campus. It was three stories high, surrounded by foot-thick concrete walls. The interior consisted of a single enormous room, with all four walls, the floor, and the ceiling blanketed in forty-eight-inch-long, sound-absorbing fiberglass wedges (researched and created specially by Beranek's team). In the center of the space, a four-foot-wide track was suspended in midair to hold any equipment being tested. The interior of the space can be seen in Figure 4. Designed to absorb all sound and allow no reverberation, Beranek dubbed the structure the "anechoic chamber," meaning "without echo."[8] Among researchers on campus, however, it became known informally as

"Beranek's Box."[9] Although it was designed to test incredibly loud equipment, the room's vibration-absorbing properties had a remarkable side-effect. When the military's ear-splitting technology was removed, Beranek's vibrationless box became the most silent space the world had ever known.

INTRODUCTION: ABSENCE MEASURED, ABSENCE FELT

This chapter and the next aim to think about various types of silence, silences, and silencings in the mid- to late twentieth century. They ask what silence has meant for a range of individuals who have created, received, or been denied access to it. Although I begin with a consideration of scientific silence as constructed and instrumentalized by figures like Beranek, the discussion turns toward aesthetic deployments in the work of three composers. In parallel to the previous chapter's focus on the extremely loud, much of what follows centers on the diverse ways that silence can function for different constituencies at particular moments. At the center of this argument is the suggestion that silence might be understood not merely as a physical, acoustic state (an absence of objectively measurable vibrations) but as a unique mode of sonic encounter between a listener and a world outside. Though I say "listener," the topic (like the other case studies in this book) extends beyond a standard account of listening in which a pressure wave meets/touches/presses against a perceiving ear. Instead, in thinking through what it means to hear silence, it becomes useful to again consider it as a type of affective state. That is: silence is one's condition of being at the moment of encountering and contending with (sonic) absence.

In exploring silence's varied resonances, I draw from descriptions suggested by Ana María Ochoa Gautier in her contribution to the collection *Keywords in Sound*. Ochoa Gautier reminds us that silence can reference a range of physical states as well as lived experiences. She takes special care to remind us of the term's verb form—*to silence*—which she notes is "used in political language to imply an active politics of domination and nonparticipation." This "biopolitics of silence" not only involves actively silencing certain modes of expression but also policing acceptable modes of engagement with aesthetic objects. This includes "listening constituted by silent attention, understood as a crucial dimension of an ideal, rational subject that is in control of the production of meaning."[10] Although political resonances bubble up in various ways in this chapter, my main examples focus on deliberate constructions of silence by figures in the scientific and artistic community. In other words, I focus more on those who intentionally sought out and developed theories of silence, rather than those who had silence imposed on them from the outside. As we will see, however, there are also occasions where both things happen at once—where one individual's silence is used as a way of silencing another.

Chapters 2 and 3 revolve around a series of interconnected themes, each of which considers silence in a different form. The remainder of chapter 2 follows the thread of Beranek, the three World War II acoustics labs at Harvard, and broader questions regarding military applications of sonic research. These applications tended to approach silence from a vibrational/computational perspective: silence was merely the measurable absence of vibration. I then pivot to the work of composer John Cage, whose well-chronicled engagements with silence were informed by an oft-retold visit to the very same Harvard anechoic chamber. Though Cage initially appears to pose very different types of questions from the scientists, I argue that his ensuing ideas about silence retain a number of scientific inflections that echo the work of Beranek and his colleagues. In doing so, they limit the possibilities of how one might understand or encounter silence as an affective force (and not a measurable quantity).

Chapter 3 delves further into these limitations by inquiring what other artists and theories have been overlooked by a common music historical tendency to frame Cage as the twentieth century's foremost theorist of musical silence. After a pivot that considers several problematic rhetorics that emerged in a series of collaborations between Cage and jazz artists, I consider contrasting understandings of silence, quietness, and space in works by Wadada Leo Smith and Pauline Oliveros. These two composers are not meant to be exhaustive of the topic but provide two (out of many) contrasting examples. By examining their work, the discussion is concerned with questions over who is granted access to silence in the artistic sphere, who is given the power to define it, and how the use of silence was/is received in both African American and Euro-American concert traditions.

BERANEK'S BOX AND SCIENCE'S SILENCES

For the scientists who designed and used the anechoic chamber, silence operated primarily as a tool. It provided a sonic baseline, a blank canvas that could allow acoustic instruments of increasing complexity to make measurements of increasing precision. Sonic isolation became a way of isolating the variables of their experiments, to avoid the interference of "noisy data." In the decades that followed the war, the Harvard anechoic chamber was used for countless studies, and similar chambers continue to be built and used into the present. The tests conducted in the chambers are generally not concerned with the sound of the space itself but with testing the properties of various sound-generating materials and/or listening systems. The chamber's silence is merely an absence that allows researchers to better hear, record, and measure the sonic presences that they bring into it. This instrumentalizing of silence echoes (and follows closely on the heels of) the aforementioned instrumentalizing of sound that was already ongoing in military research. It should be no surprise that such an understanding of sound tends to be decidedly nonmusical, nonaesthetic, nonaffective. Here sound (and silence) is not something to be desired, pondered, or savored but is useful only insofar as it can help to generate some other form of knowledge.

Though it might seem obvious that a military research lab would be concerned with practical, war-driven applications rather than aesthetic/affective engagements, the point comes into particular clarity when delving into the archives of the three Harvard labs. Today the university maintains a particular abundance of records relating to the Harvard Underwater Sound Lab (HUSL). This was largest of the three laboratories, at its peak employing some three hundred workers. Led by physicist Frederick Hunt (who had been Beranek's doctoral adviser), the lab was tasked with three interrelated projects: "Improvement of existing underwater sound equipment, particularly active sonar . . . development of a new scanning sonar . . . [and] torpedo/mine development."[11] Whereas at the beginning of the war American torpedo technology lagged far behind that of Germany and Japan, the lab helped to significantly narrow that gap. It made particular advances in creating tools to battle German submarines, which had ravaged the allies in the early years of the war.[12]

A great deal of the HUSL's efforts focused on using sound to create more accurate mappings of physical space and using those maps to guide automated homing torpedoes. This not only required teaching machines how to hear but also teaching them what *not* to hear, in order to avoid false signals. The underwater world, after all, is very different from an anechoic chamber. It is not an empty medium in which pings travel directly from the vessel to the enemy and back in a straightforward way. It is a teeming ec(h)osystem, rife with potential interference from other vessels, wildlife, water itself, and even the ocean floor. Instrumentalizing the system required constructing mechanisms and techniques for the machines to distinguish (to use one memo's phrasing) the "true echoes, i.e., the desired echos" from the "'false' echoes from bodies dispersed through the water and on the bottom."[13]

We might say, then, that the goal of the scientists was to construct a sort of sonic ontology. I use the term not so much in the broad sense employed by philosophers but in the somewhat more limited usage developed by information theorists.[14] In the context of machine-reading applications (i.e., computers designed to read text or other files and extract certain types of data), an ontology refers to what factors a machine is trained to seek out from a file and, conversely, what factors it is trained to ignore. In an information-rich context, clearly delimiting how a machine's ontologies are defined becomes a crucial element in having that machine perform a given task.[15] The searched-for parameters are, in a very literal sense, all that exist for the machine—it is all that the programmers have trained it to comprehend or process. The scientists of the HUSL were in this sense acting as sonic information ontologists. Their goal was not so much to train the machines to hear more and more but to hear less and less, and to filter and analyze that information in highly specific ways.

This is not to say that lab employees lacked any aesthetic or narrative sense surrounding their work (I certainly don't want to portray them as cartoonish data miners). To the contrary, archival materials show how much of their sense of mission was undergirded with heroic narratives about the war effort and their place within it. The sense of national duty is particularly apparent in the HUSL's internal newsletter *The Lab Echo,* which published twelve issues between February 1944 and June 1945. The 10-inch × 13-inch publication was laid out like a newspaper and featured a fascinating mix of updates from the front, internal lab news and announcements, employee profiles, and light humor. The front page of the debut issue, for example, juxtaposes a headline about lab members enjoying a ski outing in New Hampshire, a photo of naval sailors sleeping above a torpedo on a submarine, a piece about lab employees donating blood, a news item about a new glider for troop transport, and a reminder to employees to display their ID badges when entering the building. The back page of every issue carried a feature called "So Proudly We Hail," which printed "news and notes of our boys in the service," which for a time appeared above a cheeky humor feature called "Dots and Dashes" (Figure 5). In total, *The Lab Echo* offered a disjointed combination of light and heavy subject matter, which reinforces both the workaday operations of the lab (including the highly gendered nature of such workplaces in the 1940s) as well as the staff's ongoing sense of underlying patriotic duty.[16]

Yet this sense of mission often seemed a level removed from the day-to-day calculations of their scientific and acoustic work. A particularly striking example contrasting the role of science with that of mission/narrative/aesthetics can be found in the log reports of the USS *Galaxy,* a Navy research vessel tasked with testing the lab's inventions in Boston Harbor. The reports

FIGURE 5. *The Lab Echo*, 1944, no. 1 (front and back cover). Courtesy of the Harvard University Archives. Item HUF 859.822.

provide a daily account of the activities of the ship, and nearly a hundred pages are preserved. The vast majority of the entries are brief, noneventful, and formulaic:

August 4

Military inspection; no civilians aboard. Ship returned to dock at 2 p.m. At 4 p.m. Schuck, Watson, Morton, and Lane aboard. Test bearing recorder to be installed on SYLPH . . .

August 7

At dock—Sebring, Nolle, Chernosky, and Lane aboard. Continue installation of SYLPH's ATT, ERB gear . . .

August 12

Sailed for Fairhaven at 8 a.m. Sebring and Nolle aboard. Continued adjustment and tests on SYLPH's gear. Arrived Fairhaven at 3:30 p.m.[17]

Pages upon pages of such entries populate the files, a testimony to both the everyday routine of scientific work as well as to a military mandate to maintain protocol, order, and regular reporting.

But then one day, the tone takes a dramatic shift. The date is May 8, 1945: VE-Day, marking the end of the war with Germany. In the Atlantic one of the formal locations where the surrender would take place was located off the coast of Portland, Maine. As a vessel with sound-recording equipment, the *Galaxy* was called in to record the proceedings. Here is the beginning of the log entry for that day:

> May 8
>
> This date was the start of what for the GALAXY turned out to be a strange interlude. Strange in that it had nothing to do with research—by intent, that is . . . [T]he task of organizing the morning's operations was proceeding when Captain Hodges stepped from his office and said, "Henry, you've got to help me out! The District just called and asked us to proceed to Portland, Maine, to record the surrender point off that port."
>
> Now there was an intriguing idea, if ever we heard one. Consider our frame of mind. We had just listened to President Truman's VE day proclamation over the shipping room's radio. We knew through the scuttlebutt that the Navy had for the past week been broadcasting surrender instructions to German U-boats in the Atlantic. Subs were probably popping up all over the place at that very moment. Would we go? Hell, yes! Myrbeck's repeater could wait.[18]

"Strange interlude" indeed—the shift in tone is staggering. At the moment that the ship's assignment changes from a scientific one to a documentary one, the entire thrust of the log transforms completely. The text suddenly takes on an evocative, novelistic, and at times jokey tone, beginning from the very first sentence. Quotes appear—actual speaking humans!—bubbling over with emotions and opinions: "Would we go? Hell yes! Myrbeck's repeater could wait." Science, in other words, could wait, as the crew embarked on a more heroic expedition that seemed to demand more colorfully-inflected prose. This style of writing continues for nearly nine pages, culminating in a scene of light tragedy when the ship is reassigned to other duties and its Captain Hodges is removed from command: "We watched the great guy die a little. He loved that ship and his job in her."[19]

Like many developments in wartime technology, the nobility and importance of contributing to a broader, humanistic war effort seemed integral to justifying the day-to-day work of the lab. War was conceived as humanistic, striving, aestheticized, while science was pursued primarily to provide data to support that effort. Sounds, likewise, were not noteworthy in and of themselves, but merely insofar as they could be used as tools within a larger national mission. And this mission was believed to be ongoing. As one speaker intoned in a speech given at HUSL near the end of the war: "There is no such thing as postwar research. It is all prewar research."[20]

. . .

In tracing what silence meant or didn't mean for the scientists developing the anechoic chamber, this broader instrumentalizing of sound (one could even say "weaponizing," though in a somewhat abstract sense) for the war effort provides crucial background. Beranek's creation of the anechoic chamber was similarly instrumental. That is to say, the chamber's silence was developed to answer specific questions and solve specific types of engineering challenges. Despite Beranek's own lifelong interest in music and performance acoustics, his numerous descriptions of the chamber convey very little in the way of any aesthetic or affective interest in the space or its silence. Instead, they focus more on it as (A) a solution to a certain mathematical problem, and (B) a tool to enable the solution of subsequent problems. This seems to have been the case in at least three separate pieces of writing, made at different points in his life.

Beranek's first published writing on the chamber appears in an article in the *Journal of the Acoustical Society of America (JASA)* from 1946. The piece goes into immense detail surrounding the research, construction, and acoustic performance of the chamber, noting that it far exceeded the capabilities of previous rooms built in Berlin and at Bell Telephone Laboratories. Although the article does briefly trace the origin story of why Beranek's team built such a chamber, the bulk of it is decidedly technical. It traces the precise specifications of the chamber, the research that went into its construction, its performance in testing, and its measurable advantages over previous similar testing sites. None of this is at all surprising for a journal like the *JASA*, whose readership would have been interested in such technical details. To the contrary, an account stressing the profundity of the space's silence would have seemed decidedly out of place.[21]

What if we instead consider the account given by Beranek in his 2008 autobiography, *Riding the Waves*? Here we find a genre much more conducive to broader humanistic accounts. Even the overall thrust of the book carries a somewhat novelistic tone, framing Beranek as a small-town Iowa kid whose life progresses "From Bumblebees to Ivy."[22] Yet despite having greater poetic license, Beranek's description of the anechoic chamber proceeds along similar lines. It focuses on the space as a feat of engineering, rather than a setting that enabled a certain kind of listening experience:

> We completed the chamber in record time. Our measurements showed the wedge-covered surfaces reflecting hardly any sound and nothing could be heard outside. The first loudspeaker tests were carried out in the summer of 1943. The chamber became known in the Harvard

community as "Beranek's Box." I coined the term "anechoic," meaning "without echo," and, after I used the adjective in a published paper, it eventually (1962) appeared in *Webster's Third International Dictionary*. Since then, thousands of anechoic chambers have been built around the world, most using my pioneering wedge structure or a slight modification of it.[23]

The description here appears in the midst of a chapter outlining a string of Beranek's wartime accomplishments and inventions at the Electro-Acoustic Lab. Once again, however, the experience of being in the space is minimized, with the account stressing technological innovations to advance a broader war effort.

This is not to say that Beranek was unconcerned with acoustic aesthetics or the affective power of sonic spaces. Quite to the contrary: following his time in military research, Beranek's biggest professional accomplishments came via a decades-long career as an acoustic consultant for concert halls through his architectural firm Bolt, Beranek, and Newman. Many later chapters of his memoir describe the firm's ongoing efforts to improve the acoustics of musical spaces, including Lincoln Center's Avery Fisher Hall, Tanglewood's Koussevitzky Music Shed, and the Tokyo Opera City Concert Hall. Often the efforts stressed finding the optimal reverberation time (according to Beranek, "1.4 to 1.6 seconds, for an opera house").[24] This is obviously very different from the bone-dry soundscape of an anechoic chamber, which simply sought to eliminate reverberation altogether. In its deviation from what Beranek saw as an acoustic ideal, the chamber remains depicted firmly as a clinical/scientific space and decidedly not an affective/aesthetic one.

For a third account of the chamber, I had the privilege (along with my colleague Peter McMurray) of conducting an interview with Beranek at his home in 2014. The conversation followed similar lines, with Beranek emphasizing the herculean task of confronting discrete, on-the-ground problems and coming up with practical, realizable solutions that could be deployed to soldiers as soon as possible. This came up, for instance, when we discussed the initial founding of the Electro-Acoustic Lab, whose first assignment was to invent and install new acoustic shielding and communication devices for airplane cockpits. When we asked why the military was so interested in acoustics, Beranek replied simply: "Well, we had to solve this communication problem. They had to talk and they weren't able to do it. We had to solve that problem. That was our big job."[25] His descriptions tended to focus on a mix of entertaining interactions with military brass, punctuated by a series of technological triumphs (the chamber, new forms of headphones, a fiberglass material that remains in use until today, etc.). Although Beranek did describe the experience of stepping into the chamber, its deep silence factored primarily as an aside within his more compelling narratives of military intrigue and engineering ingenuity.

HEARING AS AFFECT, OR, WHAT DOES IT MEAN TO LISTEN WITHOUT HEARING?

In considering how to hear silence through the ears of Beranek and his colleagues, we might first ask the broader question of how to grapple with the forms of sonic encounter advanced by the military's decades-long project of instrumentalizing sound for war. Thinking through this question requires looking beyond the perspective of human listeners alone. To the contrary, a recurrent theme in military acoustics involved developing increasingly sophisticated techniques for severing the ties between audition and the human body. Much military research on sound has involved creating increasingly complex types of mechanical ears and/or mechanical auditory cortexes—resonating machines that could overcome the clumsiness of fleshy bodies. In the military this theme can be traced at least as far back as World War I (e.g., the aforementioned acoustic locators).[26]

Not all of these devices outwardly resembled extensions of the ear. For example, in 1916, William Sansome Tucker, one of the British military's foremost acoustics researchers, developed a new type of microphone capable of registering the difference between two parts of the sound created by artillery fire: the "gun wave" (the shock wave created when a gun fires) and the "shell wave" (created by the speed of the shell in motion that follows). Aurally, the noisier, higher-pitched shell wave tended to mask the sound of the gun wave, but the Tucker microphone's ability to distinguish them made it possible to more accurately judge the distance of enemy guns.[27] This would be the first of numerous mechanical ears that Tucker experimented with. On February 18, 1918, he wrote a memo describing a new research facility that included the following description: "[The facility includes] all that could be desired for Acoustic Research. Equipment makes it possible to experiment with electrical instruments replacing the human ear and measurement of sound at all pitches."[28]

Rather than relying on our own faulty bodies, Tucker and others sought ways to outsource listening to machines. Sound was useful only insofar as it could be transduced into data, and machines offered the most expedient means for doing so. In excising flesh from the sonic realm, such machines may prompt us to question commonly held assumptions about sound, affect, and auditory practice. This in turn can lead back to other insights about human listening processes. In many accounts of human aurality, audition is conceived as occurring in two stages. The first stage—hearing—is usually couched in the language of sensation, the moment of raw physical touch with the outside world. The second stage—listening—is described not as sensation but as perception. Listening is the *processing* of the sounds we encounter; it is attentive, reflective, focused, directed. It therefore acts as a form of doubling, creating a reflected image in the mind, of sounds that were already felt by the body.[29]

In certain ways this model resembles Brian Massumi's distinction between affect and emotion, which he emphatically distinguishes as unique realms. Massumi writes:

> Emotion and affect—if affect is intensity—follow different logics and pertain to different orders.
>
> An emotion is a subjective content, the socio-linguistic fixing of the quality of an experience which is from that point onward defined as personal. Emotion is qualified intensity, the conventional, consensual point of insertion of intensity into semantically and semiotically formed progressions, into narrativizable action-reaction circuits, into function and meaning. It is intensity owned and recognized.[30]

To proceed with a somewhat crude hypothesis, what would happen if we simply rewrote this excerpt substituting the term "listening" for "emotion," and "hearing" for "affect" or "intensity?" We would get something like the following:

> Listening and hearing—if hearing is [allied with] affect—follow different logics and pertain to different orders.
>
> Listening [involves the generation of] subjective content, the socio-[auditory] fixing of the quality of an experience which is from that point onward defined as personal. Listening is qualified hearing, the conventional, consensual point of insertion of the heard into semantically and semiotically formed progressions, into narrativizable action-reaction circuits, into function and meaning. It is hearing owned and recognized.

Rough around the edges, perhaps, but a relatively legible account in which hearing is understood as the affective register of audition, whereas listening is the act of placing that audition into semantic and semiotic contexts. I should note that using "hearing" to describe these affective responses diverges somewhat from the terminology chosen by some previous authors, who have pursued similar ideas using terms such as affective listening, drastic listening, or sympathetic listening.[31] All of these models seek to describe and/or advocate for a mode of audition that foregrounds the shimmering, shivering moment of felt impact, rather than a listening practice that immediately places the heard into a semantic/semiotic field.

Considering the affective potentials of hearing can work to disrupt the presumed linearity of the hearing-listening model. Too often, hearing is characterized as a precursor, a necessary but not sufficient condition for a higher-level experience of listening. It's not uncommon to come across accounts of subjects who "hear but don't listen," usually snidely framed as someone who registers the presence of a given sound but is incapable of truly comprehending it.[32] Tom Rice notes how many such accounts hinge on a distinction between listening as active, and hearing as passive, which includes a notion of hearing as "a kind of sensory substrate in which listening is grounded." But if we follow the affective thread, we can begin to see this linearity break down. Instead, as Ben Anderson writes regarding affect and thought: "Modalities slide into and out of one another to disrupt their neat analytic distinction. Diverse feedforward and feedback loops take place to create such hybrids as 'affectively imbued thoughts,' and 'thought imbued intensities.'"[33] In other words, by reattending to hearing as a point of intimate contact, audition can be understood not merely as a process that begins in the ear and ends in the brain (or, perhaps, the soul?), but as a multidirectional flow of intensities between subjects, objects, and bodies in motion.

Such an observation does not undermine the possibility of hearing without listening. It does, however, enable us to think about its opposite: *listening without hearing*. This is a difficult notion to conceptualize in terms of human audition but can become clearer when thinking about the military's mechanical ears. What is SONAR, for example, if not an attempt to achieve listening without hearing? Sound becomes nothing more than a data point to be understood, placed in a context, or transduced into other types of outputs. But the actual moment of "hearing" is rendered irrelevant. The point of contact must be *explained away*, even if it can never be fully erased. It is not quite that the moment of sonic impact (where sound strikes a receiver) doesn't exist, but more that it doesn't matter, except insofar as it registers some other, more useful quantitative data. The vibrational instantiation of the ping is meaningless; it always just sounds like a ping. All that matters to the machine is the data that the ping provides. The machine is certainly listening—placing sound in a meaningful, externally situated context—but it is not hearing in any affective sense.

Yet we should be wary of falling into a reductive binary of the human ear versus the machine. The process is always more complex. As Stefan

Helmreich reminds us in his ethnographic account of descending in a submarine (which itself uses SONAR among myriad other technologies): "The assemblage of the sub and its encapsulated scientists is clearly a cyborg, a combination of the organic and technical kept in tune and on track through the self-correcting dynamics of visual, audio, and tactile feedback."[34] As so much posthumanist scholarship reminds us, machines and humans cannot be clearly demarcated but are continually networked into systems in which each conditions the other.

Following posthumanisim in another direction might also lead us to consider a third type of ear: that of the bat. Bats are, of course, also echolocators but with fleshy bodies like our own. Their auditory systems process both the reflections of their own calls, as well as sounds penetrating them from the outside. When we refer to bats as "having SONAR," it is more than an innocuous figure of speech. As happens so often, new technologies provide us with metaphors that alter the ways that we conceive of how living bodies function.[35] And perhaps not incidentally, significant research on bat echolocation also took place inside another anechoic chamber at Harvard, also designed by Beranek.[36]

CAGE AND THE ENGINEER

The anechoic chamber's profound quietness became central to the lore surrounding the structure in the years after the war. Sometime around 1950, word of the chamber reached the composer John Cage. Cage was already interested in the aesthetic potentials of silence, and he contacted the lab to request a visit. Beranek was not there at the time—he had by then accepted a faculty position at MIT—but he heard about the request and directed Cage to contact Frederick Hunt, who had taken over management of the chamber. By Beranek's recollection, such requests were not uncommon. The chamber had been mentioned in several newspaper articles, and as a result the lab received occasional requests for tours from university officials and other interested parties.[37]

The encounter that followed has reached legendary status in twentieth-century music history. It was retold frequently by Cage himself. Here's a commonly quoted version from 1958:

> It was after I got to Boston that I went into the anechoic chamber at Harvard University. Anybody who knows me knows this story. I am constantly telling it. Anyway, in that silent room, I heard two sounds, one high and one low. Afterward I asked the engineer in charge why, if the room was so silent, I had heard two sounds. He said, "Describe

them." I did. He said, "The high one was your nervous system in operation. The low one was your blood in circulation.[38]

Cage took this episode to mean that to experience silence—absolute silence—was impossible for a living human. To live meant to hear; sound is inescapable. Reading from today's perspective, it is easy to note more than a little ableism embedded in this account. Cage never seems to consider the experience of those whose bodies might process sounds differently from himself. This omission is made all-the-more jarring by the fact that some biographers have suggested the "high" sound he heard may have been the onset of tinnitus (thus Cage was hearing his own distinctive [dis]ability and using it to assert a universal truth).[39]

Nevertheless, Cage's experience in the chamber famously influenced what would become his most famous work: the "silent" composition 4'33". Retellings of the story generally center around Cage receiving the insight that "there is no such thing as silence" and that a new conception of music could consist of seeking beauty in the sounds that always already surround us.[40] In his music that followed, one of Cage's central goals was to "let sounds be just sounds."[41] On the surface, this engagement with the chamber's silence seems quite different from that of Beranek and his colleagues. One might suggest that while scientists viewed the space's silence as an absence, Cage was more concerned with silence as a type of presence. It was not a tool or a blank canvas to be filled, but a weight, an aesthetic potentiality, a substance that can touch and be touched. We might even imagine this binary of perspectives—between Beranek's instrumentalized/data-driven silence and Cage's aesthetic/affective silence—as an extension of Michel Poizat's distinction between a "silence that speaks" and a "silence that screams," as outlined chapter 1.[42] In the decades after 4'33", Cage would become the most frequently cited composer in the Euro-American tradition regarding issues of silence. "Silence" even became the title of Cage's first and most famous book, published about a decade after the visit.[43]

The visit to the chamber was by no means Cage's first attempt at grappling with silence on both aesthetic and philosophical terms. As numerous studies have pointed out, Cage's interest in silence came from multiple sources. Commonly given inspirations included Zen Buddhism, the *I Ching* and chance operations, the study of Indian classical music and its religious underpinnings, the writings of art historian Ananda Coomaraswamy, and the white paintings of Robert Rauschenberg.[44] Douglas Kahn points out that Cage's ideas of silence went through a particular evolution in the years between 1948 and 1952: "[In previous years, Cage] was still thinking of sound and silence as being conventionally distinct from one another, a presence and an absence of sound. By the time of *4′33″*, silence became only the absence of an intentional sound, whereas musical sound had become ever-present and omnipresent, filled with intentional or unintentional sound."[45] In other words, earlier in his career Cage had viewed silence as a form of quietude or escape from the world, a perspective Kahn characterizes as akin to "noise abatement."[46] But by the time of *4′33″*, Cage's perspective shifted to conceive of sound as fundamentally unavoidable, and thus silence as a physical impossibility.

The visit to the chamber therefore provides a pivotal turning point—the *eureka!* moment that crystalizes both his intentions for *4′33″* and an understanding of silence that he would profess for the remainder of his life. The anechoic chamber became, to borrow another phrase from Kahn, "the technological emblem for Cage's class of silencing techniques."[47] Although he sometimes described silence as existing as a matter of intention ("It's simply a question of what sounds we intend and what sounds we don't intend"[48]), he more frequently gave a simpler, more quotable formulation: "There is no such thing as silence."[49] Cage's analysis of what he had created in *4′33″* also remained relatively consistent: as the performer remains still, the audience is free to attune to any other sounds present in the performance space (a cough, a chair scoot, an air-conditioning vent, a page turn, etc.). This has continued to be the dominant interpretation of the piece.

What I wish to ask, however, is what happens if we engage with the chamber story not through the perspective of Cage's career preceding it (which Cage scholars have done exhaustively), but instead through the perspective of the chamber itself. In other words, what happens if instead of tracing the story of a composer who stumbles across a chamber, we instead follow a chamber that has a composer stumble across it. Indeed, that is precisely how the episode was related by Beranek, who viewed the Cage visit not as a momentous episode in the chamber's history (in our conversation he couldn't even recall Cage's name initially), but as simply one of many visits from curious onlookers: "Well mainly these outsiders just came in to listen. Now if you brought in a research[er], well you would talk about how we could send sound from a loudspeaker here to this point and have just the sound from the speaker come [with] no reflections from any walls, you see. . . . [T]here were no reflections, so anything you're measuring is only what was causing the sound. And that's why it was setup originally."[50]

Here, Cage is not the protagonist, and the chamber a side note. The chamber is at the center of Beranek's telling, and Cage's arrival is merely a humorous aside. Although both accounts create a disconnect between "research[ers]" and "outsiders," there is a distinct inversion in how those roles are valued. Cage's version frames himself—the artist/humanist/philosopher—as the true receiver of a quasi-spiritual revelation and the (forever unnamed) engineer as a naïve literalist who cannot understand silence's true meaning; Beranek's version frames the researchers as the one possessing real understanding, while the (forever unnamed) visitors who "just came to listen" are well-intentioned but untrained onlookers who are incapable of grasping its full scientific value.

Other aspects of Cage's account also call out for closer reading. One thing to observe is that Cage's moment of insight happens not *while* he is in the chamber but immediately *afterward*, when he speaks to the engineer. In most versions of the story (including the one quoted earlier), Cage takes significantly more time relating this conversation then he does in describing his time in the chamber itself. This seems somewhat odd, especially for a figure so invested in the idea of reimagining the parameters of aurality. What did it feel like in the chamber? How long did he stay? Did his mind remain focused on the two tones or did it wander? Was the experience comfortable? How did the "silent space" affect him physically, mentally, aesthetically, spiritually?

What makes this omission particularly odd is that other people's descriptions of being inside anechoic chambers tend to have *so much* to say about the experience. Take, for instance, a quote from sound engineer Steven Orfield, whose Minnesota laboratory houses one of the quietest chambers in existence today:

> How you [normally] orient yourself is through sounds you hear when you walk. In the anechoic chamber, you don't have any cues. You take away the perceptual cues that allow you to balance and manoeuvre. If you're in there for half an hour, you have to be in a chair.
>
> When it's quiet, ears will adapt. The quieter the room, the more things you hear. You'll hear your heart beating, sometimes you can hear your lungs, hear your stomach gurgling loudly.
>
> In the anechoic chamber, you become the sound.[51]

Orfield is not alone in offering such descriptions. It's actually somewhat common to read similar accounts in newspaper, periodical, or other anecdotal sources published each year.[52] Some subjects report experiencing pressure in their head, auditory hallucinations, or feelings of intense discomfort.[53] On YouTube there is practically an entire genre of videos devoted to people visiting anechoic chambers and describing their experiences.[54] Chambers have even given rise to their own urban legends, such as the idea that remaining too long in an anechoic chamber "will drive you crazy in 45 minutes" or that a violinist once entered and "hammered on the door after a few seconds, demanding to be let out because he was so disturbed by the silence."[55] Most recently, in November 2022 the *New York Times Magazine* featured an extended story by Caity Weaver beautifully describing her experience during a three-hour visit to the Orfield chamber (while simultaneously debunking some of the more outlandish claims found in other accounts).[56]

These transfers of sound-becoming-body and body-becoming-sound point toward a deeply affective register that is reported by many visitors to anechoic chambers, a shimmering breakdown in the categories of inside and outside.[57] Yet Cage himself relates none of this. Instead, he limits his description to a (rather unsatisfying) one sentence musical transcription: "I heard two sounds, one high and one low." For such a pivotal encounter it's striking how little he actually says about it. Instead, he proceeds swiftly to the conversation with the engineer, and his newfound realization that "there is no such thing as silence."[58] For all of Cage's reputation as art music's most celebrated practitioner of silence, one could argue that he is actually quite *opposed* to the very idea of it. We might read Cage's account not as a desire to engage with the affective register of silence—to *hear* silence in the sense outlined earlier—but rather to *explain it away*, and to do so using language nearly as positivistic as the scientists that preceded him within the chamber's walls. I heard sounds; therefore there is no silence.

One might object that this interpretation takes Cage's exhortation "there is no such thing as silence" too literally. Some Cage scholars suggest a broader conclusion that Cage's findings are more in the mold of a paradox: through silence, one arrives back at sound—the two are really just two sides of the same coin. Cage certainly delighted in such paradoxes and aphorisms in his writings (such as "I have nothing to say, and I am saying it"). Kyle Gann connects this interest to the Buddhist tradition of koans and mondos, which include riddles such as "What is the sound of one hand clapping?"[59] Perhaps Cage's accounts of silence should be read in a similar vein. Silence is impossible, and yet here it is, for the next four-and-a-half minutes. Yet if Cage is invested in accepting sounds as sounds—as vibrational presences to be experienced and sat with, not judged or placed into hierarchies, harmonic settings, or semiotic models—then why is his account of the chamber so antithetical to this ideal? He achieves no insight while inside, but only afterward, only through conversation with the engineer, only when he is offered an *explanation* that puts that experience into a *framework* that he can understand.

Even the basic observation that "absolute silence" is impossible isn't really Cage's insight at all. This was already well-known to the community of scientists who worked on/in the chamber. Beranek's very first published paper about the chamber from 1946 goes so far as to report the vibrations measured in the room, noting that while they are still not zero (complete absence of vibration is impossible, as the scientists knew long before Cage "discovered" it), they were more minuscule than any previous attempt had yielded.[60] This recognition remains interwoven with scientific studies using chambers to this day. The *Guinness Book of World Records* even measures and maintains a record for the "Quietest Place on Earth," a record that most recently changed hands in 2015.[61]

Cage's account, rather than framing the chamber as a technological emblem that can be understood within a discourse of Zen practice, can therefore equally be seen as the substitution of a scientific/technological mode of understanding for any form of experiential or spiritual practice. It is an account that is both inextricably scientific (in that it explains a phenomenon) and scientistic (in that it depicts silence as a phenomenon that can *only* be explained through scientific principles). Rather than seeking silence as a profound register of experience, Cage instead attempts to explain it away through an appeal to a predominantly scientific understanding of the world around us.

. . .

Is there an alternative? What other accounts of silence might be possible once we know that vibrations are be present? Echoing chapter 1's examination of loudness, I suggest that one might arrive at a very different outcome if we think of silence not as a function of physical vibration but as a type of affective sonic encounter. Specifically, silence is experienced as a moment of confrontation between a subject and a (sonic) absence. It is not a measurement but a mode of lived experience.

In some ways this description resembles a model advanced in some of Cage's other statements. For example, in another interview, he says: "Silence is all of the sound we don't intend. There is no such thing as absolute silence. Therefore silence may very well include loud sounds and more and more in the twentieth century does. The sound of jet planes, of sirens, et cetera. For instance now, if we heard sounds coming from the house next door, and we weren't saying anything for the moment, we would say that was part of the silence, wouldn't we?"[62] A related quote has Cage noting that "silence is not acoustic. It is a change of mind. A turning around."[63] This provides a bit more nuance than the "no such thing" formulation (and, to be fair, Cage gave slightly varying descriptions throughout his career). They have even become the basis for significant secondary writing. John

Mowitt, for instance, points to the latter quote as purposefully distancing Cage's position from the discipline of acoustics, particularly the way the field "gives form to our intentions such that one might go about 'making' silence precisely by defeating echoes."[64]

Yet I would argue that such statements fall short of in several respects and still demonstrate a closer adherence to a scientistic model than Mowitt and others suggest. First, in drawing a distinction between "silence" and "absolute silence," Cage continues to privilege a positivistic understanding of silence—he merely recasts it as "absolute." Priority ("absoluteness") in defining silence is still granted to the vibrational component, while the lived experience of silence is presented as something akin to an illusion. Or perhaps the right word is "delusion," since Cage's descriptions of 4′33″ sometimes berate those listeners who hear "what they thought was silence, because they didn't know how to listen."[65]

This, then, points to a second shortcoming, that despite the potential for these statements to open up the conversation toward a richer understanding of silence, Cage never seems to use them in that way (even if others do, with fruitful results as we will see in chapter 3). Instead, Cage consistently uses his definition as a road back toward talking about sounds, now resting in the comfortable assuredness that sound will always be present. It isn't so much an effort to glean a more detailed understanding of silence. It's more of an excuse to never have to talk about silence again, simply writing it off as a phenomenological misinterpretation by the unenlightened. Finally, a third critique would note that speaking in the language of "intent" fails to account for how silence can arise at unexpected or unwanted moments, often explicitly without the listener's intention. Such a description particularly overlooks instances of *silencing*—when subjects are denied their right to voice, or their right to listen.

Among other ramifications, an affective model can also enable a very different interpretation of 4′33″ itself, one that profoundly diverges from Cage's own analysis. To witness a performance of 4′33″ is, in a very real way, to open oneself to an encounter with sonic absence. The encounter is even more striking because it is (most frequently) staged in settings where we are deeply conditioned to experience sonic presence. We sit in a concert hall or performance space, a performer sits at a piano, they open the lid, the piece begins and . . . nothing. In my own experiences witnessing the piece, the passage of time during the performance is not one of serenity and acceptance but of profound (and, in the best cases, aesthetically gratifying) unease. I feel myself squirm, my breathing suddenly seems louder, a need to cough arises that I hadn't felt before (and that never seems to arise in conventional concerts). I feel silenced, trapped, yet duty-bound to participate in the ritual at hand.[66]

Such a description resonates with accounts that describe 4'33" as fundamentally theatrical.[67] Here a key element can be found in the presentational frames that surround the performance: the stage, the performer's entrance, the lifting of the piano lid, and so forth.[68] If Cage's analysis foregrounds the presence of sound where one expects silence, a theatrical analysis suggests the exact opposite: the presence of silence where one expects sound. If this wasn't important, why bother to include so many bells and whistles to convince the audience that someone is about to play? Everything is carefully arranged to prepare us for sound through the repetition of concert rituals we have witnessed countless times before. Yet in the end we are left with nothing but absence. Watch, for example, the recording of the BBC Orchestra performing the piece from 2004.[69] The audience maintains a taut tension throughout, released only during the breaks between the movements. These breaks—signaled only by the conductor lowering his baton—are met with an audible outpouring of coughs and sighs. *That* is the moment of comfort, the release from the silencing bonds of Cage's composition. During the movements themselves, silence seems to bind the room together, the audience awash in a sublimely odd yet strangely compelling shared moment of absence. It is such an unusual experience to sit quietly in a room with strangers. This silence is anything but illusory—it is no happenstance chair scoot that arouses my appreciation—but a profound experience of nothingness in the moment.

. . .

In summary, if we think of silence as a form of affective encounter rather than an absence of vibration, we can arrive at very different interpretations from Cage of both the anechoic chamber and of 4'33". Silence becomes not an opportunity to foreground unintentional sounds but a moment when we confront the challenge of engaging with (and perhaps embracing) absence. In other accounts of visitors to anechoic chambers, this confrontation is saturated with all manners of physical, perceptual, and somatic pressure. Yet this is an experience of anechoic silence that Cage seems to miss in his cursory "two sounds" description. A successful performance of 4'33" can provoke similar responses: disorientation, rapid shifts in attention, hyperawareness of one's own body. This isn't because silence is impossible; it is because it is all too starkly present, and our perceptual apparatus has little framework to suggest how we should react. The piece does not disprove silence; it challenges us to confront it and wrestle with its power.

This description of the piece may also be aided by the affectively-inflected conception of hearing (as opposed to listening) suggested earlier. This time, such a model disrupts not the linearity of hearing/listening but the *hierarchy* presumed in such discussions. Hearing is too often portrayed as listening's easily distractible kid sibling. Anyone can hear, but to truly listen requires training, understanding, intellect, empathy, depth. Even Cage falls into such tropes. As he stated in an interview about negative reactions to the piece's premiere: "[The audience] missed the point. There's no such thing as silence. What they thought was silence, because they didn't know how to listen, was full of accidental sounds. . . . [T]he people themselves made all kinds of interesting sounds as they talked or walked out."[70] One might presume that these sounds were *heard* by the audience, but by failing to *listen* to them, Cage suggests that they missed the broader point. Yet the piece's bare, unadorned confrontation with silence is, I suggest, not something that can truly be experienced through "listening" at all. For listening—the interpretive/intellectual act of placing sound in a context—is already an exercise in avoiding this confrontation. By insisting on a context, a rationale, an explaining away, one moves away from the affective impact of hearing, rendering it toothless. The disorienting power of silence goes away the minute one accepts an explanation.

A personal example can reinforce this last point: for several years while teaching introductory undergraduate courses, I used a global music textbook that began with an account of *4'33"*, drawing mostly on Cage's own analysis. I would often begin the lesson by playing the BBC performance without an explanation. It got the occasional laugh (of course), but in general the reaction was one of tension, of not knowing what to do when confronted with several minutes of silence in a setting (this time a classroom) in which they were accustomed to receiving sound. But once I explained the piece in Cage's terms, as promoted by the textbook (i.e., listen to the sounds around you), there would be—aside from a certain degree of incredulity—a noticeable easing of tension, an exhalation that echoed that of the audience between movements. The students could now rest assured in their comfortable understanding of what exactly they had just experienced. As an educator, this was a welcome release. I certainly don't want students to feel excessively uncomfortable or disoriented. But as an aesthetic account, it often felt like something was lost at this moment of explanation. The curtain is pulled back and the mystery revealed, but in the process the thickness, the potency, dissipates. Cage's explanation saps the power of Cage's own piece.

CONCLUSION

In this chapter I have traced a number of themes, beginning with the understandings and applications of silence emerging from the US military's decades-long engagement with acoustic research. Just as these efforts sought to instrumentalize sound to aid military power, so silence was also instrumentalized not as an object for affective reflection, but rather as a measurable condition that enabled specific engineering applications. Silence was understood within a certain computational context, but researchers had little interest in the direct points of contact between a listener and a silent experience. After John Cage experienced the anechoic chamber during his visit in the early 1950s, he sought to deploy silence somewhat differently, leading to the composition of 4'33". Yet even in this piece, the tendency to view silence as an impossibility rather than a form of affective sonic encounter limited the extent to which Cage or his listeners could fully engage with silence's power.

Chapter 3 expands on these points by asking how Cagean silence impacted his interactions with others as well as exploring two alternative deployments of silence by practitioners from other experimental music traditions.

3   Silencing and Alternative Silences

Where chapter 2 dealt primarily with considerations of silence as a noun, this one shifts to the verb form by thinking about various forms of silencing and ways of cultivating silence. In particular, I consider how John Cage's too often assumed position as the foremost theorist of silence led to instances of other artists being bypassed, or overlooked, despite developing theories of silence that were sometimes far more detailed than Cage's own. I begin with a trend of more direct silencing—namely Cage's own tendency to use rhetorics of silence or quietness to dismissively distance himself from jazz musicians. I then move to consider two other artists—Wadada Leo Smith and Pauline Oliveros—who developed somewhat different understandings of silence in their work.

THE SILENT CUDGEL: CAGE SILENCING JAZZ

Cage's invocation of Zen and his accompanying rhetoric denying the influence of a composer's ego—both of which were central to his understanding of silence—were also embedded in another recurrent theme in Cage's writing: his distaste for jazz. Cage's critique stemmed mostly from a contention that jazz's use of improvisation placed too much emphasis on intentionality, virtuosity, and individual voice. Cage considered these themes to be antithetical to his own interests in nonintentionality, aleatoricism, and environmental sound.

The long history of Cage's dis/engagement with jazz has been chronicled in research by Rebecca K. Kim, who describes how Cage progressed from an early interest and engagement with the genre to decrying it in later writings. Observing jazz's connection to indeterminacy (a connection that Cage often worked to undercut), Kim characterizes the composer's overall relationship with the genre as vexed: "No stable view of jazz is possible with Cage except perhaps that jazz was consistently the exception to the rule, singled out for its timbre, regularity of beat, conversational discourse, lack of disciplined action, or questionable use in the future of music. In spite of efforts to ascertain a realm beyond the imagination, Cage's rhetoric and actions often revealed that indeterminacy served to fulfill rather than transgress his imaginings about the future, which involved a tensely separate togetherness with jazz."[1] Kim's work further points to other scholars who have critiqued Cage's repeated distancing from jazz, including Georgina Born and David Hesmondhalgh, John Corbett, and George Lewis.[2]

For someone who claimed little affinity for the music, however, Cage participated in at least three collaborations with artists from jazz and/or Black experimental traditions. Rather than revisiting Kim's overall arguments surrounding the relationship between Cage and jazz, I wish here to pursue the narrower question of how issues of quietness and silence came into play in all three of these interactions. Specifically, I suggest that Cage's discursive matrix connecting silence, indeterminacy and anti-/improvisational rhetoric comes to bear strongly in these meetings. In all three occasions Cage uses silence as a sort of cudgel; Cagean silence is employed (perhaps unintentionally) as a way to silence the voices of his Black collaborators.

The first such meeting was a performance with saxophonist Joseph Jarman's ensemble in Chicago in late 1965. At the time of the meeting, Jarman was integrally involved in the formation of Chicago's Association for the Advancement of Creative Musicians (AACM), the landmark collective that became a wellspring of creative music in the decades that followed. The group was deeply influential in both its organizational model (a jointly run collective) and also in its musical output, which explored a range of contemporary compositional and improvisational techniques while consistently reaffirming its ties to Black performance traditions.[3]

Though no recording survives, many details of the meeting have been documented in research by Kim and Lewis. As Lewis notes, although contemporary reporting described Cage's work and the AACM's as independent parallel streams of experimentalism, Cage's account in a later interview portrays himself in more of a teacherly role:

[Interviewer:] Are young people active in popular musics eager to have contact with you and know what you think of their kind of music?

[Cage:] Very rarely. Mostly when that question is put, it is hoped that I will say that I like it, but I don't have much experience of it. The last direct experience I had of it was in Chicago in '67, '68, or '69, when I was invited by a group of black musicians to come and play with them. And they also asked me to criticize what they were doing. I said, "Well, play," and they did.

And I said to them that one of the troubles was that when they got loud, they all got loud. And they said, "How could we change that?" They were willing to change. I said that perhaps if they didn't sit together, those of them who could move through space should get away from one another. Some of them couldn't carry their instruments—the double bass was too big, and, of course, the piano—so that when one of them got loud, the others wouldn't be impelled to be so loud. That day, when we practiced together, and I played with them too, they did very well, and they enjoyed what happened—a kind of independence of a plurality of jazz spirits, and an extension of that idea of freedom of the soloists to all members of the group.[4]

Lewis rightly takes issue with the paternalism in Cage's description. It differs significantly from Lewis's own interview with Jarman, who portrayed the event as much more collaborative and recalled Cage offering gentler, more minimal suggestions: "He just said [imitates], 'I'm setting up this ... [pause] ... Do as you feel.' [Laughs.] And he just started playing. And because of my experience with the AACM concerts, I just started playing, and moved all over and blended horns."[5]

There's certainly a lot of privilege to unpack in Cage's account of the story: from his disinterest in recalling the names of the "black musicians," to casually lumping the work of the AACM into the category of "popular musics," to the suggestion that his instruction was somehow the first time the musicians had encountered non-solo-based collective improvisation (which had a long history in jazz, particularly in the jazz avant-garde). Kim also notes that Cage misremembers the group as being made up solely of "black musicians," as the three other members of Jarman's quartet (aside from Jarman himself) were white.[6]

Yet note as well how Cage couches his critique primarily through the parameter of loudness. Though ostensibly his argument is about independence of musical line (avoiding a "follow-the-leader" approach), loudness is the only area in which he raises this critique. He never says, "When they got soft, they all got soft," or, "When they got fast, they all got fast," or "When they got impressionistic, they all got impressionistic," even though any of these would be equally viable ways to make the point. Instead, the impression of loud Black (instrumental) voices was all that he retained. He saw his role as teacher—and it's hard to not read *white male* teacher into this context—as to teach quietness, silence, restraint. Though couched in the language of a Zen universalism, the description takes on oppressive and stereotypical undertones that portray Black sonic practice as loudness/noise/uncontrolled impulse that must be tamped down by the influence of a white authority figure.[7] The fact that the remainder of the interview continues to criticize jazz along familiar lines—while utterly failing to acknowledge the experimentalist intervention that Jarman and his AACM colleagues were making *at that precise historical moment*—reinforces such a reading. To Cage, Jarman and his colleagues were simply unnamed loud/Black/jazz/popular musicians, not contemplative artists pursuing the same innovative forms of critique (within Black music traditions) that Cage was seeking himself (in the European concert tradition).

Less than two years later, Cage was involved in a second jazz collaboration, this time with the saxophonist Rahsaan Roland Kirk. The two did not perform on stage but were juxtaposed via film, in a twenty-seven-minute documentary titled *Sound??*, directed by Dick Fontaine. Kirk and Cage never appear together in the film. Instead, scenes alternate between performance footage of Kirk playing in a nightclub and footage of Cage walking through different locations and reading excerpts from his writings (mostly drawn from his 1958 essay, "Composition As Process").[8] This separation was apparently done at the request of Cage himself. Fontaine's original concept had been to organize a meeting between the two artists, but Cage vetoed that idea.[9] Fontaine also intersperses environmental footage of various themes evoked by either Cage's reading or Kirk's playing: hectic machines in the modern city, animals emitting cries, children playing with whistles, and so on. Still other scenes show a Cage rehearsal and footage of Kirk listening to the music of Edgard Varèse.

In its intent the film remains outwardly respectful of both artists. The footage of Kirk is breathtaking, while Cage is painted as a sort of Svengali hipster speaking in riddles as he gallivants through the city in a long black coat. Nevertheless, the constructed dichotomy between Cage as essayist/philosopher/thinker and Kirk as performer/craftsman remains somewhat troubling. Despite Fontaine's goal of putting the artists in dialogue, in many ways the film's structure places them in starkly separate spheres, highlighting more about their differences than their commonalities. Perhaps the most overt example of contrast comes from the mouth of Cage himself in the film, when he recites a particular excerpt from his text:

> But music, do we have any music?
> Wouldn't it be better to just drop music too?
> Then what would we have?
> Jazz?
> What's left?[10]

It's delivered a bit tongue-in-cheek, as Cage obviously knew the nature of the project. Yet in the larger context of the film, the quote takes on a somewhat pointed character. Jazz is once again marked as a distinct realm from the interests that Cage is pursuing, despite Fontaine's efforts to place them in dialogue.[11]

The film concludes with Cage again returning to spaces of silence. About six minutes before the conclusion, Cage poses the question: "Is there such a thing as silence?" As he continues reading, he walks through a *hyperechoic chamber*—a sort of antithesis to the anechoic chamber that amplifies echoes, causing Cage's voice to boom around the room. Meanwhile, Kirk's high-energy performance of his composition "Rip, Rig, and Panic" plays behind him. As the performance reaches a climax, Cage is shown manically running around the chamber. We see Cage, but we hear Kirk, with the sound of the chamber now inaudible. When the instruments decrescendo and the piece comes to its electronic conclusion, Cage can be seen—without audio initially—standing in the chamber and emphatically shouting: "THERE IS NO SUCH THING AS SILENCE." This is followed by a voiceover of him reciting this passage from the printed essay: "THERE IS NO SUCH THING AS SILENCE. GET THEE TO AN ANECHOIC CHAMBER AND HEAR THERE THY NERVOUS SYSTEM IN OPERATION AND HEAR THERE THY BLOOD IN CIRCULATION."[12]

That's how the passage appears in the published version anyway, in emphatic capital letters. But here, Cage intones it softly and calmly. As the film concludes, we shift locations to an anechoic chamber, its doors swinging shut to leave Cage (and the viewer) inside. The sound of a heartbeat accompanies the final words, evoking the sounds of the body that Cage asks us to hear. Musically it's easy to read this final section as a resolution, a coming down from the intensity of Kirk's performance. But as an aesthetic statement, Fontaine gives Cage the final word. Silence—impossible or not—is again used as a sort of foil to the loudness of a Black artist. Kirk provides sublimity of performance, embodied practice, and is clearly shown throughout the film as a certain emblem of modernity and sonic openness. But it is Cage who provides the film's profundity of thought, with a retreat to silence (and away from Kirk) providing the final image.

Cage's third jazz collaboration came nearly twenty years later. On June 6, 1986, the composer took part in a performance with bandleader and Afrofuturist trailblazer Sun Ra.[13] Like the Kirk film, the event was structured not as a collaboration but as a juxtaposition. Although this time the two artists did share the stage, the concert consisted almost entirely of them trading off segments. Ra's portions featured him playing unaccompanied keyboard improvisations on his Yamaha DX7, or reading poetry, while Cage's consisted of excerpts from his unaccompanied vocal piece "Empty Words IV." The two artists had never met until two days before the concert, when they convened at Cage's loft for a *New York Times* photo shoot to promote the event. Ra did vaguely recall, however, that he had previously read portions of Cage's book *Silence*.[14]

Like Fontaine, the organizers of the event—record producers Rick Russo and Bronwyn Rucker—again pitched the idea of the two artists creating a piece together. Cage pushed back once again, as Russo recalled: "After the photo shoot, I talked to them about doing a piece together. Cage was very concerned that it would appear to be a publicity stunt. Sun Ra sort of reluctantly agreed, though Sun Ra seemed to be more open to doing a planned piece together."[15] In a quote from the *New York Times* preview of the event, Cage stresses the fact that the performance will not be a jointly conceived piece: "'I don't know what I'm going to do yet,' said Mr. Cage. As for working with Mr. Ra, he added, 'It's not a collaboration, it's a meeting, and if there is a collaboration it will develop there.'"[16] The article contains no quotes from Ra.

It's somewhat unclear what Cage might have meant by "publicity stunt" in this context. After all, the two had just completed a specially arranged newspaper photo shoot, so attracting publicity was clearly a goal of all parties. Even the venue for the concert—a former penny arcade near the Coney Island Boardwalk called "Sideshows By The Seashore"—seemed geared toward creating a sort of spectacle. Cage doesn't provide any further details on why a more carefully considered collaboration would have been more of a "stunt" than an unplanned meeting. One could read the statement as a distancing device to distinguish his work from jazz improvisation—a "defensive maneuver against the vitality of those popular forms" in the sense suggested by Born and Hesmondhalgh.[17] By avoiding the language of collaboration, Cage could claim that this "meeting" somehow didn't count as part of his true "composerly" output but was merely a casual get-together and sharing of ideas.

In the film footage that survives of the concert, the separation between the two artists is palpable. Though the original album liner notes depict a grand entrance by the pair, the footage shows the two walking out somewhat haphazardly, punctuated by an awkward handshake initiated by Ra.[18] The two occupy different areas of the stage, separated both spatially and visually by a long table. To the audience's left, Ra sits with his keyboard, in full cosmic regalia and flanked by several members of his Arkestra. On the right Cage sits alone in a denim work shirt, reading from a set of stray papers strewn upon the table. The two ultimately do end up playing together briefly for a few short minutes near the end of the performance. In Ra biographer John Szwed's account, however, even this moment might not have been fully welcomed on both sides: "Only once, for the briefest of seconds, did they play together, when Sonny added some soft bell tones behind Cage, but then quit, perhaps feeling a draft, sensing that Cage was somewhere else."[19]

A recent reissue of the full concert shows the joint piece lasting about five minutes, with Ra offering minimal accompaniment to Cage's continued performance of "Empty Words." Even this moment has the feeling of a supplement to Cage's piece, rather than a fully fleshed-out collaboration. Though by all accounts Cage was friendly with Ra throughout the process of organizing the concert (at one point he told Ra that "a writer friend had said to him that if he wanted to take another step in music and didn't want to be behind the times he ought to listen to Sun Ra"[20]), there seems to be a consistent desire to maintain a level of distance.

Silence also played a role in the way Cage structured his portions of the concert. Much of this silence is embedded in Cage's choice to perform "Empty Words," a composition he had written in 1978. "Empty Words" is a solo vocal piece that contains no recognizable language but instead only individual letters and sounds. In many ways the piece was a somewhat natural selection for Cage to present in a solo setting; it requires only a single microphone and no external performers. Cage performed it on numerous occasions in the years following its completion.[21] The full version is designed as a marathon affair, with part four alone taking approximately two-and-a-half hours. Importantly, the words and stray syllables of the piece are interspersed with long extended silences, often lasting several minutes. Cage described this sparsity of material as designed to create room and opportunities for meditation or for the mind to wander.[22] These long gaps make "Empty Words IV" a particularly notable example of Cage returning to questions of silence within his late oeuvre.

For the Coney Island performance, time restrictions meant that the piece had to be pared down extensively. Thus, for each of Cage's turns, he performs a segment of "Empty Words IV" in a sort of binary form: first, a section of the text, then a long interlude of silence (lasting two to three minutes), and then concluding with a second section of the text. On the most recent reissue these interludes are labeled "silent solos," purposefully echoing the structure of a straight-ahead jazz performance (head-solos-head). Ironically, this structure bears little resemblance to what Ra does in the concert, since the keyboardist (like many in the jazz avant-garde) had expanded far beyond only using head-solos-head structures, and he does not employ them at all here. It should be noted that the "silent solo" designation does not exist on the original LP version, and it's unlikely that the description came from Cage himself. Still, in light of Cage's ongoing distaste for the jazz solo as emblematic of ego, this idea of the oxymoronic, perhaps cheeky "silent solo" is an intriguing one to consider.

Could this be read as yet another critique of jazz performance practice? A comment along the lines of "Why would one bother playing complex solos rather than simply listening to the sounds around us or letting the mind wander?" Without over-reading the gesture, we might simply observe that such a reading would fall neatly in line with Cage's ongoing critiques of jazz. This extends the possibility of reading the concert alongside Cage's earlier interactions with Jarman and Kirk. In all three instances Cage structures his contributions around some form of silence, framing it as something the jazz musicians would not (or could not) do.

At the same time, by appealing to silence, Cage is able to bypass the types of improvisation favored by jazz artists, which he was ill-equipped to engage with regardless. Cage, of course, would have been out of his element in such settings—he's certainly no improviser at the level of Ra, Kirk, or Jarman—and would have been perhaps further disadvantaged by the fact that he (by his own admission) knew next to nothing about his collaborators before their meetings. By falling back upon the notion of silence, Cage recuses himself from actually engaging with either the jazz/Black music tradition writ large or with these artists in particular. And this becomes particularly stark in the Kirk and Ra examples when Cage refuses to collaborate on a joint piece. Silence becomes not a way for Cage to listen to the world around him—that is, listen to these fellow artists, who had read his work and arrived open to collaborate—but to shut it out, instead assuming that he possessed something that the jazz artists did not.

It's also instructive to note how the political undertones of Cage's silence change in these contexts. Even if we accept the narrative that Cage's original invocation of silence in *4'33"* was intended as a sort of insurrection—a rebellion from below against a music(ologic)al power structure that had grown stagnant—we can see that in these interactions silence plays a very different role. Here it is not a form of insurrectionist protest but a way of maintaining a certain status quo, a defense mechanism against Black artists whose work (both as improvisers and as experimentalists) posed a profound challenge to Cage's status as the avatar of the aleatoric. The same silence that had been used to break down the gates of the concert music hierarchy was now being used as a form of even more stringent gatekeeping. Cage, who had no trouble mixing it up in debates with both staid longhairs and countercultural youths, seems not only ill-equipped but utterly uninterested in exchanging ideas with artists that seemed too radically distant from himself.

WADADA LEO SMITH'S *SILENCE*

Throughout these interactions Cage's reductivism falls in line with common limiting discourses surrounding expressivity and Black culture. Kevin Quashie has noted how these discourses often characterize Blackness "as expressive, dramatic, or loud," and tend to think of it purely in terms of narratives of public resistance, rather than considering aspects of interiority, intimacy, and humanity.[23] Without dismissing the importance of resistance, Quashie's writing shifts to consider what is gained by considering registers of Black quiet within artistic and literary practice:

> Quiet is antithetical to how we think about black culture, and by extension, black people. So much of the discourse of racial blackness imagines black people as public subjects with identities formed and articulated and resisted in public. Such blackness is dramatic, symbolic, never for its own vagary, always representative and engaged with how it is imagined publicly. These characterizations are the legacy of racism and they become the common way we understand and represent blackness; literally they become a lingua franca. The idea of quiet, then, can shift attention to what is interior. This shift can feel like a kind of heresy if the interior is thought of as apolitical or inexpressive, which it is not: one's inner life is raucous and full of expression, especially if we distinguish the term "expressive" from the notion of public. Indeed the interior could be understood as the source of human action—that anything we do is shaped by the range of desires and capacities of our inner life.[24]

Like the artists discussed by Quashie, jazz musicians since the 1960s (and undoubtedly before) have indeed thought about silence, quietness, sound, and sonic presence in ways that were more complex than Cage would ever acknowledge. Nowhere was this more clear than in the movement dubbed "free jazz" and especially in the compositional work of the AACM. Whereas Cage tended to perceive jazz artists as purveyors of a particular brand of musical taste (which he seems to have conceived primarily through idiomatic, so-called "straight-ahead" approaches), in actuality free jazz artists of the 1960s were deeply invested in deconstructing the jazz language itself, all the way down to basic features such as pulse, harmonic progression, swing, and the relationships between soloist and ensemble.

In particular, AACM artists provide an instructive counterexample in how one could approach silence from another direction entirely, distinctly different from either Cage or the creators of the anechoic chamber. While the diversity of approaches within the AACM makes it difficult to paint the collective's work in broad strokes, a number of its members created work that meticulously explored soundscapes of silence and quietude. This diverged noticeably from some of their free jazz peers, such as the "energy music" approach associated with New York improvisors. Many AACM artists bypassed (though usually without disparaging) energy music's dense "fill-up-the-canvas" approach, in which performances were grounded by a constant, high-energy, collectively improvised accompaniment. While free/energy approaches can be heard occasionally on AACM albums, many members equally explored more sparse textures, in which pointed silence took the place of energy music's rumbling earthquakes of sound.

Here I explore one particularly direct example: trumpeter Wadada Leo Smith's aptly named composition *Silence*. The piece was the title track for an album nominally under the leadership of saxophonist Anthony Braxton, which featured a trio of Braxton, Smith, and violinist Leroy Jenkins. The album was recorded in 1969 but not released until 1974.[25] It's not hard to discern how the piece gets its name. The bulk of the performance consists of isolated, minimalist, often single note statements by individual members of the group, interspersed with long empty pauses lasting as long as ninety seconds. A full diagram of the entrances and silences is provided in Table 1.

Although the instrumental statements become slightly longer (and the silences shorter) in the latter half, it would be a stretch to portray the piece in a conventional narrative of growth or climax. Instead, its aesthetic remains relatively flat and open, predominantly featuring one instrument playing at a time. Each statement is allowed to reverberate and resonate in the ear for long gaps, until the next emerges. In total, the piece contains more than six-and-a-half minutes of silence, well over a third of the performance. What is the nature of this silence? A purely sonic analysis reveals certain details, although it can only take us so far. The most obvious difference between Smith's piece and Cage's, of course, is that while in *4'33"* silence pervades the entire performance, in *Silence* it is bookended, interrupted, or otherwise ruptured by discrete instrumental statements. To my ear (and I preface this carefully since these interpretations are subjective), this difference carries several ramifications.

First, the piece's constructed dualism between silence and statement calls into question where the boundaries of silence lie. In other words, it asks what actually *counts* as silence, from a listening perspective. This challenge

TABLE 1 Entries of sounds and silences in Wadada Leo Smith's *Silence*

Time	Sound
0:00–0:12	Violin scratching (col legno)
0:12–0:39	(silence)
0:39–1:07	Single saxophone tone (concert B♭)
1:07–1:12	(silence)
1:12–1:13	Drum hits, rim shots and cymbal
1:13–1:25(?)	Cymbal continues to resonate and fade—exact end undetermined (silence?)
1:25–1:31	(silence? Or does the cymbal still reverberate?)
1:31–1:35	Single trumpet tone, muted (concert E)
1:35–2:06	(silence)
2:06–2:14	Single violin tone (pitch bend up to concert D♭)
2:14–3:02	(silence)
3:02–3:03	Single, short saxophone tone (concert A)
3:03–3:49	(silence)
3:49–3:51	Two soft footsteps (silence? music? mistake?)
3:51–4:00	(silence)
4:00	Drum stick click (silence? music? mistake?)
4:00–4:04	(silence)
4:04–4:13	Percussion—one stroke each on triangle, clave, cymbal (or similar idiophones)
4:13–4:14	Single trumpet tone (concert E, buzzing timbre)
4:14–5:58	(silence—very faint click at 5:40, microphone adjustment at 5:46)
5:58–6:09	Tone on very low reed. Roughly an A, with upper overtone ringing three times but no fingering change
6:09	Faint stick click
6:09–6:32	(silence)
6:32–6:35	Violin—predominantly a concert B♭, but with double-stopped notes faintly audible at beginning and end
6:35–6:54	(silence)
6:54–7:00	Trumpet flurry, high D prominent. Very light percussion hits behind
7:00–7:07	(silence)
7:07–7:25	Recorder, with plucked piano strings and light percussion
7:25–7:30	(silence)
7:30–7:32	Clave strokes (might be one or two, second might be artifact of print-through)

7:32–7:45	(silence)
7:45–7:56	Percussion
7:56–8:16	Harmonica
8:16–8:25	(silence)
8:25–8:36	Low trumpet, percussion, single flute note
8:36–8:48	(silence, with some barely audible creaks toward end)
8:48–8:55	Harmonium? (dark chord)
8:57–8:59	Trumpet
8:59–9:09	Key clicks
9:10–9:43	Violin, trumpet, saxophone (violin plays blues inflected melody, trumpet fast blast, saxophone key clicks followed by squeal)
9:43–9:49	(silence)
9:49–10:16	Percussion
10:16–10:21	Recorder
10:21–10:31	Clicks, instruments rustling (silence?)
10:31–10:46	Pizzicato violin and percussion
10:46–10:55	Whistling, percussion fades
10:55–11:04	Saxophone
11:04–11:07	(silence, or is it merely a breath?)
11:07–11:55	Harmonica, followed by long trumpet line, recorder, percussion, ends with percussion hit
11:55–12:07	(silence)
12:07–12:47	Percussion, contrabass clarinet
12:47–12:51	(silence, or is it merely a breath?)
12:51–12:58	Percussion with a high note behind (violin?)
12:58–13:30	Flute, to recorder, light percussion
13:30–13:41	Harmonium
13:41–13:45	(silence, or is it merely a breath?)
13:45–14:29	Percussion
14:29–14:38	(silence, recording fades)

came to bear quite a bit in preparing Table 1. At several moments, close listening reveals faint sounds that can be heard in otherwise ostensibly "silent" moments. Around 3:49, for example, a careful listener might pick up what sounds like two very soft footsteps. Should these be considered part of the music? Are they a "mistake," an unintentional audio artifact of a player switching from one instrument to another? Do they interrupt the silence, or are they a part of it? In Cage's piece such questions have easy answers: since Cage intended any and all sounds to be considered part of the performance, such steps would automatically be valid objects for aesthetic attention. For Smith, in a sound world that is interested in probing the margins between silence and sound (rather than flattening them into the same thing), these questions remain unanswered. Instead of simply declaring silence and sound to be indistinguishable ("there is no such thing as silence"), Smith continually pushes against the boundary between them, building it, disputing it, refuting it, rebuilding it, crafting sounds that can feel as flat as silences and silences that hit us as thickly as sounds.

A corollary to this question could be considered in regard to a unique studio artifact that is audible on the issued recording. When turned up to high volume, many of the instrumental statements are preceded by a faint "pre-echo," in which one can hear the entrances faintly (sometimes two or more times) *before* the "true" entrance occurs. When the instrument ceases to play, a similar echo—now taking the form of an audio delay—can be heard after its exit. These ghostly presences are barely audible and are likely the result of a form of archival decay known as "print-through." Print-through occurs when a tape is left wound and sits unplayed for long periods of time. Eventually musical information (recorded on the tape's surface in magnetic oxide) begins to bleed into other adjacent winds of the tape. As a result, each sound is heard several times in faint echoes that occur both before and after the statement in question. This is especially noticeable in a piece like *Silence*, which features long open spaces punctuated by abrupt entrances. The fact that the recording was made in 1969 but not released until 1974 may have played a role in causing this print-through issue.

Once again, the question emerges of how to listen to this audio "error?" Should it be considered musical material? Does a silence end when the printed-through pre-echo appears? Or should this be listened past, like tape hiss or record pops, or any number of recording artifacts that audio consumers have trained ourselves to ignore? A similar question can be posed about less "accidental" sources of reverberation, such as room echo or instruments with a long decay time like a cymbal. This challenge arises, for example, when charting the decay of the cymbal strike at 1:13, which reverberates for a long period—perhaps all the way until it is interrupted by the trumpet entrance at 1:31. In the logic constructed by the piece, this eighteen-second pause *feels* like a silence, even if an acoustician could detect the cymbal sound resonating throughout. The listener by now expects to encounter such silences (through the episteme constructed by the piece), and it easily feels in line with other silent moments. Once again, rather than being easily explained away through recourse to a silence that never exists, the piece creates a series of questions about what silence might mean, questions that become especially pointed at marginal moments.

Yet another ramification revolves around how a listener might respond to the silences invoked by the two pieces (and again, I speak from my own reactions here). When hearing performances of *4'33"*, my perceptive state usually goes through the following progression. It begins upon the opening of the piece in a state of tension and/or discomfort. As the performance begins, my body and mind react to the wholly unusual experience of sitting quietly in a group of strangers. I appreciate the aesthetic impact of the moment but also become distinctly self-conscious, trying my futile best to remain quiet while also attending to the sounds I hear around me. Over the course of the piece's four minutes, however, I gradually begin to reach a state of greater acceptance. The silence becomes, in a word, predictable. I understand the sonic realm I am inhabiting to be what it is. I note if, and how, my fellow listeners have followed the piece's unspoken entreaty that we remain in silence together, and my body falls into some sort of rhythm. I eventually reach a state of acceptance. Despite knowing that I can never be fully silent, I begin to feel at home within the sound world of the performance and grow confident that at least I'm not going to fall into any coughing paroxysms or otherwise disrupt others' experience. Taken as a whole, then, my overall reception consists of a slow shift from a state of tension toward a state of calm.

In Smith's composition, however, silence never settles into such a predictable pattern. Instead, when an instrument exits and a silent section begins, I have no idea whether it will last a few seconds or several minutes. Likewise, when an instrument returns, I don't know whether I should expect a short burst or a long declamation. The piece is so effective in establishing this uncertain relationship between sound and silence that even in the last four minutes—where there is significantly less silence than in the first half—an expectation of silence continually structures my listening. Every time an instrumentalist pauses between notes, my ear wonders whether they are about to enter an extended silence or continue their musical idea. On some occasions (e.g., at 12:47 and 13:41), short gaps force me to question whether what I just heard counted as another arrival of silence or merely a breath between ideas (was it a silence that speaks, or a silence that screams?).

. . .

A more thorough account of *Silence*, however, should also consider Smith's statements about the piece as well as his musical theories in general. In a recent discussion of the recording, philosopher Eric Lewis juxtaposes excerpts from Smith's classic book *Notes (8 Pieces)* with statements about

Silence made by Smith in a radio interview. In the former, Smith emphasizes how his work as a composer strives to constantly "pay homage to the black, the blackness of my people, and that these creations themselves are for all, and the natural laws that are prevailing under these creations are relative as they are interpreted or perceived by beings of other peoples."[26] Smith also disputes critics that have sought to "[apply] narrow concepts to this improvisational music so that they could easily write about and define it and dictate what is the essence of black music—creative music."[27] In Lewis's analysis these quotes pave the way for Smith's discussion of *Silence* on the radio. As Smith's comments are instructive, I quote them at length here:

> Well, we wanted to look at music that would give us a chance to express exactly who we were. And once you make that particular commitment, you have to find out how you're going to do this. So we decided that . . . we didn't have to accept the history that was given to us before, and we didn't even have to expect some kind of present history or future history. We were able to contemplate the real essence of creative music. . . . "Silence" is a piece that has silence in it, and it came after John Cage's "Silence," but the philosophical connection of silence in this case was to materialize music within the space, and whatever was heard in the environment, whereas in the Cage piece there was absolutely no music in the space, and the gestures were the moments of the environment, you see. So [we were] creating a piece that seemed that it would . . . feel like a piece that came out of Cage's tradition, [but] in fact, we didn't have that problem, because as I say, we are not bound by what came in the past or this particular ensemble's history—you know, like a classical ensemble has a history that's specifically European. We didn't have to worry about that.[28]

Lewis points out the multivalent work being done by the silence of *Silence*. He refers to how Smith, Braxton, and Jenkins are able to "aesthetically thicken" the piece through engagement with multiple genres: the experimental concert tradition and the canon of Black music. Adding further complexity is the fact that both engagements take the form of apparent paradoxes: (1) *Silence* references Cage's earlier work while also explicitly distancing itself from it, and (2) it draws from the Black tradition without allowing that tradition to be circumscribed by "narrow concepts" of what Black music or Blackness could be. This silence exists, to borrow Fred Moten's terminology, in the break between aesthetic and ideological systems.[29] In this way Lewis shows how "the silence Smith employs . . . speaks" by claiming an autonomy that had long been denied to Black people. Rather than being silenced, Smith and his collaborators employ and deploy silence as a part of their own (artistic/aesthetic/political/Black) voices.

Taken in total, Smith's piece and the statements surrounding it express the formation of an alternative conception of silence as an experiential practice, one that avoids both the positivism of scientists and what Yvonne Rainer has called the "goofy naiveté" of Cage's (a)political philosophizing.[30] It does so through transducing silence through a metaphorical shift that conceives of it not as an absence of sound, but a way of imagining *expanses of space*. In another excerpt from *Notes*, Smith describes this as follows:

> each element is autonomous in its relationship in the improvisation. therefore, there is no intent towards time as a period of development. rather, time is employed as an element of space: space that is determined between the distance of two sound-rhythms (here the reference to rhythm is in reference to its absolute-ness: the sum of the elements and the placement of them) and space/silence that is the absence of audible sound-rhythm (just as each sound-rhythm is considered an autonomous element in an improvisation, so, too, must space and space/silence be considered; and when space and space/silence are really-realized, then we will know so well how to perceive and appreciate their uniqueness each time they appear, as easily as we perceive and appreciate the uniqueness of each sound-rhythm): i seek another dimension in music.[31]

Returning to Smith's statements from the radio interview, he describes both his own composition and Cage's in terms of this space: an open expanse to be filled (or not) by sound-producing actors. But whereas 4'33" posits the construction of such space as the end of the composer/performer's contribution, Smith sees it as only the beginning. The broader goal becomes "to materialize music in that space, and whatever was heard in the environment." This is not so much a matter of flattening sound and silence together as it is of thickening and recognizing the subtle distinctions not only between sound and silence but among *individual silences*, which (a) can be as unique as individual sounds, and (b) can be altered or subverted by the sounds that are placed around them. Only through such a model can a listener "perceive and appreciate their uniqueness each time they appear."[32]

Among other repercussions, this model drastically reframes questions of our *responsibility* toward silence, as both composers and listeners. Smith's silence becomes an opportunity for action, a space in which to express one's voice. This is decidedly different from Cage's aleatoricism, which rejects purposeful action as necessarily distorted by ego and taste, and instead implements systems of chance. Cage's stance on the matter can easily be critiqued as a form of what Ruth Frankenberg calls "power evasiveness": by eschewing ego, choice, or action within a world characterized by inequality, one implicitly acts to maintain the power structures that already exist (and that treated white male composers from the European art music tradition differently from Black composers from the African American tradition).[33] Once again, for all that Cage wished to portray his silence as an act of rebellion, it could just as easily be interpreted as a mode of passivity in the face of inequality. This, in effect, is the crux of Cage's goofy naiveté: a belief that if we all simply remain quiet and listen, the universe will make everything turn out all right.

Simultaneously, we recognize all too well here how Cage's modality of silence is one that is only enabled by forms of *silencing*.[34] This refers not only to the silencing of performers (the score's entreaty for the performer[s] of *4'33"* to remain quiet) but also the silencing of other actors in the conceptual space. In his interactions with jazz artists, we see how Cage silenced his would-be collaborators through a refusal to hear them. "Refusal" is, I think, the right word here. It is not merely that Cage didn't know the extensive musical, literary, and cosmological system of Sun Ra; it's that he seems to *insist* upon not knowing it, framing their time together as a meeting rather than a collaboration. Or when Cage works with Jarman's group near the birth of the AACM, he makes no effort to probe, or even acknowledge, their efforts to expand the language of the Black music tradition. Cage presents his silence as a counterweight to what he sees as jazz's reliance on formulae, yet this relation only holds if one ignores the Black artists' own explorations and, indeed, their agency as explorers. He silences these artists by pigeonholing them, then uses his own silence as a form of chastisement.

This view is of course rejected both aesthetically and organizationally by Smith and his AACM compatriots. Quite the contrary: they saw their collective efforts as geared directly toward dismantling structures of inequality, even as they drew artistic inspiration from sources both in and outside of the European canon. In *Silence* this manifests aesthetically through Smith's contention that creating silence/space was not an ending but a beginning. The subsequent step is to see how one could "materialize music" within space and attend to space as an "autonomous element in an improvisation." Silence does not become a static presence, one that is either attainable or unattainable and that can only exist in a certain modality. Rather, it is something that is both malleable and networked. Malleable in the sense that each silence manifests differently, changed by that which comes before and after. The silence that follows an abrupt stop is different from that which follows a slow fade. The silence that follows a laugh is different from that which follows a scream, and so on. And networked in the sense that silence simultaneously carries the potential to change, and to be changed by, the entities that move through it: music, musicians, and listeners alike.

In short, then, silence appears not as an absolute relation, a zeroing out of aural vibration. Rather, it manifests as an affective encounter with absence as confronted by the listener (or, perhaps, a community of players and listeners). It is not so much a function of intention as one of impact—an impact that is *not* lack-of-impact, but a powerful force that speaks volumes. This affective force of silence can be experienced in the echoless confines of an anechoic chamber, in a white-noise filled office, in the reverby artifacts of a printed-through tape, or in the anticipatory gaps between instrumental statements. To be silent, or to hear (through) silence, does not reject ego or the impact of action in deference to a utopian ever-sounding universe. It instead recognizes the importance of sounding voice in molding, shaping, and reformulating a world in constant flux. Not only does silence speak (and scream), but Smith and others speak back.

PAULINE OLIVEROS AND DEEP LISTENING TO SILENCE

A third engagement with the affective impacts of silence can be seen in the work of composer and improvisor Pauline Oliveros. In various forms, silence was a central component of Oliveros's sonic practice known as "Deep Listening," a series of techniques that combined elements of meditation, Zen practice, healing, improvisation, and collective group composition. In her 2005 book *Deep Listening: A Composer's Sound Practice*, Oliveros offers several interconnected definitions:

> Deep coupled with Listening or Deep Listening for me is learning to expand the perception of sounds to include the whole space/time continuum of sound—encountering the vastness and complexities as much as possible.[35]

> **Deep Listening is a form of meditation.** Attention is directed to the interplay of sounds and silences or the sound/silence continuum. . . . The practice is intended to **expand consciousness** to the whole space time continuum of sound/silences. Deep Listening is a process that extends the listener to this continuum as well as to focus instantaneously on a single sound (engagement to target detail) or sequences of sound/silence.[36]

Oliveros taught Deep Listening in a variety of outlets and venues, including workshops, retreats, and in connection with various teaching positions. In

2014 she worked with Tomie Hahn to establish the Center for Deep Listening (CDL) at Rensselaer Polytechnic Institute in Troy, New York.[37] Though Oliveros passed away in 2016, the CDL continues to extend that legacy, offering programming, workshops, and even online teacher certification for Deep Listening practitioners.

I recognize that it may seem counterintuitive to engage with Oliveros's practice within a book purportedly about forms of sonic engagement that lie outside of the realm of "listening" proper. Her project did not purport to search "beyond listening" but rather strived to expand what could be possible via listening: to use listening as a way to connect with oneself, with others, and with the world. In addition, Oliveros didn't present the practice as focusing on silence alone but as embracing all sorts of sonic encounters. Deep Listening engages the soft and the loud, the high and the low, the felt and the imagined. Nevertheless, several resonances can be traced between Oliveros's practice and themes surrounding silence that have been raised in this and the preceding chapter. Maud Jacquin and Elsa Polverel, for instance, write about Deep Listening's focus on "being attuned to—being physically and subjectively in touch with—the as-yet-unheard."[38] This includes not only attuning to sounds that are physically, vibrationally present but also sounds that are remembered or imagined but nevertheless have profound effects on our consciousness. Silence plays a powerful role in exploring and resonating with these effects. We can thus conceive of Oliveros's work developing (among other things) a theory of silence that is in dialogue with Cage and Smith yet also expands in several other directions.

The origins of Deep Listening are often traced to Oliveros's work in the late 1960s. During that time she began crafting listening exercises that she conducted with students. She recounts one such exercise in a 1968 article titled "The Poetics of Environmental Sound":

Listen to the environment for 15 minutes or a longer but predetermined time length.

Use a timer, clock or any adequate method to define this time length.

Describe in detail the sounds you hear (heard) and you feel (felt) about them.

Include internal as well as external sounds.

You are part of the environment.

Explore the limits of audibility:

(highest, lowest, loudest, softest, simplest, most complex, nearest, most distant, longest, shortest sound).[39]

The students were told they could complete this exercise at a time and location of their choosing. At first glance the prompt only obliquely refers to silence (as the "softest" "limit of audibility"). Yet when Oliveros goes on to offer a selection of student responses, silence quickly comes to the foreground. She begins with a series of excerpts that she titles "But Never Silence":

"BUT NEVER SILENCE."

"One thing I noticed right away was the absence of silence. There is always some kind of sound in the air."
"And between the thumps in the silences that grow longer, I am reminded that there is no silence."
"You'd never guess that so much sound could come out of a library which should be so quiet,"
"It was like an orchestra with no rests, no silence anywhere."
"One instance I particularly remember came after a long period of intense silence."
"If it weren't for these breaks in the monotony, this constant sound would become as a silence."
"I desire silence but there is none."[40]

Already we can see points of connection between some of these observations and those of Cage. In particular, the idea of an "impossibility" of silence and ever-presence of sound looms large. This is not surprising, as Oliveros herself credited Cage's impact on her at various points in her career. For example, in an interview from 1987 (conducted for a collection specifically about Cage) she states: "My generation of composers has come to terms with a lot of ideas that come from his work. I believe it is seed work, which has opened the field of sound and has made it possible to do many different things, not as imitators but as ways of growth, development, and change."[41] Oliveros's phrasing here seems quite intentional, acknowledging Cage's influence but framing him less as a pinnacle and more as a figure that inspired others to take his concepts further.[42]

Returning to the curated student responses, we can begin to see divergences from a Cagean model, starting with the very manner in which silence is explored. We could note, for instance, that Cage's way of approaching silence via the anechoic chamber is a decidedly individualistic one. Here a single lofty figure steps into the world's singular, most silent room and comes out with the knowledge that silence can never be attained. He presents himself alone generating this insight (again, minimizing the contributions of the engineer) and offers a definitive statement on the matter. Oliveros's study takes a very different tack. Rather than drawing conclusions based only on her own observations, she offers a compilation of voices, which is made clear in the manner and format of their juxtaposition: separate quotations delineated by line spaces.[43] Silence, like sound, is not presented as an absolute but as a subjective encounter, in which each participant generates their own unique responses. The prevalence of first person pronounces ("I noticed," "I am reminded," "I particularly remember," "I desire") further reinforces silence's role as not an objective, scientistic fact but an individualized affective experience.

Oliveros taught other lessons that more directly undercut the absolutism of Cage's pronouncements. Many years later, in a description of a Deep Listening retreat, Catarina De Re recounts how Oliveros gave her own retelling of Cage's "most-often-told yarn" about the anechoic chamber:

> When John Cage went into this room [an anechoic chamber] he heard a high sound, and a low sound. And the story went that the high sound was the sound of his nervous system and the low sound was the sound of his blood going through the veins. Well—that's the story. However, there is more to that story that is not generally known. John Cage died of a massive stroke just before his 80th birthday. A physician has said that you wouldn't hear blood pressure the way John described it. There was plaque in the arteries building up and that if someone had taken heed of what he had said, they would have known it was building towards a stroke. That was one thing. The other—the nervous system does not make a twang that you can hear like that either—it was also part of the condition that led to John Cage's stroke. So that is another part of the story that hasn't been told.[44]

To my reading, this retelling isn't intended to simply debunk the original account, nor to position sound as a literal medical diagnosis. Rather, the story provides a parable for the way a listener can resist externally imposed meanings of sound/silence and instead refocus on the way sound impacts (vibrationally, affectively, medically, and otherwise) their own body and consciousness at a specific point in space and time. Cage didn't discover a universal feature of silence, nor of the human nervous or circulatory systems. Instead, he was confronted with an experience that was uniquely his own, but he was unable to recognize this or draw benefits from it. As De Re describes, the story emphasizes how an individualized Deep Listening practice can cultivate sound's "power to tune into the very finest elements of our inner and outer environment."[45]

In 1970, Oliveros joined with a group of women at the University of California–San Diego to form the ♀ Ensemble. This group held regular meetings for several years, during which they pursued various forms of sonic meditation, which ultimately became the basis for Deep Listening.

The practice was not conceived as musical performance per se; as Oliveros put it: "Music is a welcome by-product of this activity."[46] Rather, the meetings were designed explicitly as a form of meditation, accessible to all (not merely "trained" performers) that could cultivate their numerous benefits including: "Heightened states of awareness or expanded consciousness, changes in physiology and psychology from known and unknown tensions to relaxations which gradually become permanent. These changes may represent a tuning of mind and body. The group may develop positive energy which can influence others who are less experienced. Members of the Group may achieve greater awareness and sensitivity to each other."[47] In 1974, Oliveros published a collection of meditation prompts from these sessions under the title *Sonic Meditations*, a set that has become a prominent touchstone in the history of text-based scores (despite the aforementioned distance from defining sonic meditation as "music").

Silent elements permeate many of these meditations. Oliveros notes, for instance, that each exercise "is intended to begin with observation of the breath cycle" before any sounding takes place, a grounding device that again emphasizes the sounds and presences of the body. Many of the meditations, including the very first "Teach Yourself to Fly," both begin and end with quietude.[48] Importantly, these quiet/silent moments aren't framed as existing outside of the piece (like the silence that follows the last note of a concert performance) but are an integral part of the meditation itself. Other meditations invoke silence even more explicitly, such as "Native," whose full text is "Take a walk at night. Walk so silently that the bottoms of your feet become ears." In "Have you ever heard the sound of an iceberg melting?" the exercise begins "at the threshold of audibility," swells over several hours through an imperceptibly gradual crescendo of both white noise and increasing light, and then suddenly cuts out both light and sound in an abrupt and extended return to absence: "Darkness and silence should be maintained for ten minutes or more, then illuminate the space with dim blue light for continued meditation in silence and finally exit of the participants." A more oblique form of silence can perhaps be considered in *Sonic Meditations'* repeated explorations of imagined sounds. Several of the meditations use periods of silence to ask participants to imagine (or remember) a particular sound. Although the measurable effect of the exercise (to an external observer) might be silent, each participant would experience this silence differently, reaching into the depths of their own personal sound memories. In each of these examples silence is conceived not as a fact, nor a goal, nor a measurement, but as a form of personal or interpersonal practice that can be utilized according to the needs of each participant and/or the group as a whole.

In foregrounding the role of silence within a framework of embodied meditation, Oliveros again shows crucial divergences from Cage. These divergences dovetail with the two composers' different engagements with Zen Buddhism, a topic that has been studied by scholar Tracy McMullen. McMullen argues that although Cage purported to be a follower of Zen, in many ways his philosophies and techniques were more informed by his Methodist upbringing. Specifically, Cage took Zen ideas out of the context of embodied practice and reframed them solely as efforts to stamp out the influence of the ego and physical body: "If Cage removed anything, it was the body (the sexual, erotic, moved-by-music body), leaving only the 'mind' (in the form of 'externalized law') and the 'self' (in the form of 'the disembodied genius.'"[49] As has been documented, Cage did not regularly practice any form of meditation, including the silent sitting meditation known as zazen. As Cage put it himself (in a sentence that comes off as rather dismissive), "I then decided not to give up the writing of music and discipline my ego by sitting cross-legged but to find a means of writing music as strict with respect to my ego as sitting cross-legged."[50] Instead, chance operations and numerical calculation became his chosen modes of suppressing both ego and body.[51]

While the approach bears a vague resemblance to Zen in terms of overcoming personal desires, this overcoming (like the understanding of silence discussed in chapter 3) takes the form of a numerical/quantitative objectivity rather than through any embodied or mindfulness practice. Oliveros's approach to Zen was decidedly different, as meditation practices were central to both her music and her teaching work. When she began organizing Deep Listening retreats in the 1990s, more than half of the participants' time was spent in silence, which spanned from late every evening until lunchtime of the following day.[52] This schedule not only allowed participants to explore the possibilities of silence itself but also to open the listener up to resonate with other sounds in the environment. As retreat participant Maika Yuri Kusama describes, this process had particular healing effects: "It became obvious to me that the undercurrent of sound—or the sound of silence—can be reinterpreted as the container in which all sound arises and falls back into. Healing happens when this container becomes your body, and all sounds become your home."[53] This notion of silence as container as body constitutes a decidedly different technique for quieting the ego. Kusama describes how sounds that were once irritating, such as lawnmowers, would gradually become accepted as part of the sonic landscape. Here silence becomes not an impossibility but a gift and an essential step toward connecting with an environment and fostering a healing practice.

There is more to say regarding the many ways in which Oliveros approached, utilized, and at times departed from silence over the final decades of her life. Notions of groupwork that explored shared or intersubjective experiences of silence is one possible avenue. The role of silence as a purposeful contribution to a sonic event is another.[54] But for our purposes here, what becomes clear is that over the course of her life, Oliveros undertook a significantly more extended exploration of silence than did Cage, for all of the frequency with which he is cited on the subject. Where Cage developed a relatively brief account of silence in the 1950s that he revisited only with slight alterations, Oliveros approached it repeatedly and from multiple angles. She did not seek to explain silence away as an impossibility but to open it up as a gift—a state and a technique and a tool that could generate diverse affects, in ongoing dialogue with other forms of sonic experience.

CONCLUSION

As the discussion has traveled somewhat far afield, it is useful to pause and take stock. The goal of these past two chapters has been not to put forward a single theory of silence, as much as to examine how silence has emerged as a series of affective and discursive constructs, made to do particular forms of work in particular settings. The military's development of the anechoic chamber represented one such application, acknowledging the impossibility of a fully vibrationless space, but working to build a close approximation in order to facilitate precise measurements and create new machines (initially, machines of war). John Cage encountered these silent spaces and from this encounter proposed his own theory of silence as pivoting around a relationship between listening bodies and omnipresent sound. While he sought to distance himself from the computational associations of engineers, his theory inherits a degree of scientific positivism by declaring silence to be an impossibility. The anechoic chamber then acts as a "technological emblem" for broader philosophies relating to silence, omnipresent sound, Zen, naturalism, and the eschewal of ego.[55]

However, the ingrained universalism of these conclusions leads Cage to deploy these ideals as a sort of "silent cudgel," which he uses to silence would-be interlocutors from other aesthetic traditions, particularly jazz. In contrast, experimental Black artists including Wadada Leo Smith and his compatriots in the AACM developed models that engage with Cage's ideas yet reject the notion that engaging with silence can only be achieved by renouncing the autonomous voice. For them this step would have been antithetical to their organization's broader ideals of musical and social reform, and their goal to develop artworks that sit paradoxically both within, and in excess of, a rich tradition of Black music making. For Smith in particular, silence was not an absolute proposition that could be attained or bypassed, but a metaphorical construction of space that both shaped and was shaped by the activities of actors within it.

Finally, a third model of understanding silence can be found in the compositional and meditative practices of Pauline Oliveros. Unlike Cage's measurement-based rubric, Oliveros approaches silence as part of an embodied sonic meditative practice, necessarily experienced differently by each practitioner. Silence here is not an impossibility, but an essential point of return, a container for other types of sonic experience, and a technique to open up both ear and body to other modes of experience. Despite the individuality of these responses, silence can be particularly potent when shared intersubjectively within a group, as Oliveros did in much of her work spanning from the ♀ Ensemble of the early 1970s, through the Deep Listening retreats of the 1990s, and continuing through the establishment of the Center for Deep Listening near the end of her life (and, via her students, into the present).

By no means are these the only possible conceptions of silence; they represent only a small subset of ideas emanating from the twentieth-century United States. Yet in probing them here, I have sought to both (a) dispute any forms of absolutism or universality in understanding what silence is/isn't, particularly canards about silence as impossible, and the portrayal of Cage as the predominant theorist of silence in contemporary music; and (b) to suggest, following Ana María Ochoa Gautier and others, that silence must be understood within a contextual sphere that recognizes both social and political exigencies (including the silencing of particular communities). Silence can thereby be reconceived as a construct that relates more to a listener's impression of absence or openness, rather than as any externally measurable lack of vibration. It has less to do with whether air pressures do or do not push upon our tympanic membranes and more with the affective impact of encountering something we understand as absence within a moment, whether that absence is real or imagined, routine or profound, healing or discomfiting.

PART II

Textual Interference

4 Projecting Results

Opera Supertitles and the People Who Hated Them

> Religion used to be the topic that well-bred people did not bring up in polite company. Now it is supertitles.
>
> —DONAL HENAHAN, *New York Times*

PROLOGUE

One evening in 1982, Marjorie and Lotfi Mansouri watched a television broadcast of Wagner's *Die Walküre*.[1] At the time, Lotfi was the general director of Toronto's Canadian Opera Company (COC), a position he had held since 1976. The broadcast—filmed in 1980 from Patrice Chéreau's staging at Bayreuth—included translated subtitles of the opera's libretto. This was, of course, a long-standing practice in foreign films but it was Marjorie's first time seeing it applied to televised opera. As Lotfi would later recall in his memoir, the titles had a significant impact on Marjorie's reception of the performance, especially since she was not generally a Wagner fan: "As the subtitles flashed by, Midge said, 'You know Lotfi, this [*Die Walküre*] isn't as dumb as I thought it was.'"[2]

As the two talked further, they began to wonder whether one could approximate the same effect in the opera house itself, projecting live translations during company performances (Lotfi would note that Marjorie "never received the credit she deserves for the idea").[3] He took the suggestion to COC's technical staff, who developed a system to project basic text slideshows on a narrow brownish-gray screen above the stage, sixty-five-feet wide and four-and-a-half-feet high. The system debuted in a production of Richard Strauss's *Elektra* on January 21, 1983, and was greeted with highly positive feedback:

> [W]e projected the heart of the story, the poetry of Sophocles, on whose drama Hugo von Hofmannsthal's libretto is based. The audience response was overwhelming. "At last I could understand everything!" was a typical response. It was an electrifying event and one from which we never retreated. When we presented *Poppea* two months later, our audience now expected—and demanded—to see supertitles.

They caught on fast.[4]

Audiences caught on fast, indeed. The technique, initially dubbed "surtitling" and later "supertitling," quickly spread to other North American opera houses under a variety of names.[5] Beverly Sills of the New York City Opera was another early adopter, and her company debuted their own system that fall.[6] Within a year eleven companies in the United States and Canada had staged performances using titles. Within two years that number jumped to fifty-three.[7] Audience support for the practice was extremely high, with several surveys reporting over 80 percent approval.[8] Supporters and company managers raved about titles' ability to bring in larger and more engaged crowds. In 1990, *Opera News* dedicated a full issue to the subject, noting that titles were then being used by nearly every major company in the country (only four still abstained).[9] When New York's Metropolitan Opera—one of the final holdouts—finally broke down and debuted their unique "Met Titles" system in the fall of 1995 (which projected titles onto seatbacks), the dominance of titling in North American opera houses was essentially complete.

The proliferation of supertitling was swift, comprehensive, and largely celebrated by the opera community. However, the practice also met with fierce opposition from certain corners. Most frequently, the practice's opponents argued that titles were intrusive distractions into the opera house, and they prevented audiences from experiencing the genre in other, presumably more fulfilling ways. The debates sometimes took on a heated tone, as evidenced in the chapter-opening epigraph from *New York Times* columnist Donal Henahan (a strong supporter of titling). The artistic director of New York's Metropolitan Opera took a strong stance *against* titles, declaring: "Over my dead body will they show those things at this house."[10] Perhaps the most hyperbolic writing came from editor Rodney Milnes of the British journal *Opera*, who declared in 1984: "To me [titles] signal the end of civilization as we know it." He went on to liken their proliferation to the spread of cholera as depicted in Britten's *Death In Venice*.[11] Amazingly, these comments came *before* Milnes had even attended a production that used titles.[12] Regardless of one's position on the practice, one thing is clear in reading such statements: something significant was at stake when supertitles entered North American opera houses.

SENSORY NETWORKS, TEXTUAL INCURSIONS

The sonic encounters explored in this chapter center around processes of sensory encroachment. They raise pivotal questions about what happens when a new input enters a performance space and alters existing ecologies of sensation, perception, and attention. But more directly, this chapter is about the impassioned dialogues that sprang up around that encroachment, and what those dialogues might tell us about the affective experience of opera. The highly charged battles over titling in the 1980s and 1990s serve as a point of entry, though it is not my intent to reignite decades-old debates. Rather, I suggest that arguments over titling—tied though they were to a specific historical moment—can provide broader insights into how audiences encounter(ed) and process(ed) the genre's dense multimedia web of linguistic content, narrative storytelling, embodied performance, and musical sound. Furthermore, these contestations reveal details not only about how audiences receive the "stuff" of art (musical, aural, visual, textual, narrative, and otherwise) but also about all of the sticky meanings that are attached to that stuff, meanings laden with overtones of class, ethnicity, labor, personal history, and all sorts of other associations.

In exploring these questions, I build upon recent scholarship on opera and media by such scholars as Gundula Kreuzer, Melina Esse, David Trippett, and many others.[13] In her contribution to a 2010 issue of *Opera Quarterly* on the topic of "Mediating Opera," Esse writes:

> While critics have been debating the merits of filmed and televised opera, the boundaries between mediatized forms and the unsullied "live" have become increasingly blurred. Whether through actual film footage projected on the backdrop, the presence of video screens, turntables, or radios on stage, or more subtle techniques such as rotating stages to imitate tracking shots, opera has been taking account of—even bringing about—its own mediatization for years. Simulcasts of opera in movie theaters and the recent operas filmed in European capitals with a steadicam and broadcast in real time are perhaps the most current manifestations.[14]

Esse's account highlights the ways that opera has remained consistently open to exploring the ramifications of new media. Her piece, as well as several others in the issue, goes on to explore how this tendency has played out in contemporary productions that self-consciously invoke modern media.[15] In another direction, Gundula Kreuzer traces nineteenth-century staging technologies used by Wagner to show how engagements with technology (both technophilic and technophobic engagements) are hardly a recent phenomenon but can be traced throughout opera history and read in dialogue with other intellectual and aesthetic streams.[16] Still other recent work has examined the growth of live simulcasting of opera performance, with the most widely discussed being the Met's *Live in HD* series of performances broadcast in movie theaters.[17]

Supertitles present a very different sort of televisual incursion. They are ubiquitous today not only in experimental productions but even in the most conservative stagings. They do not attempt to translate the experience of live opera into other times, spaces, or media (like a simulcast or videorecording), but they enter the hall itself, inscribing an ever-present televisuality into the space of live performance. In doing so, they provide a particularly pointed example of Philip Auslander's "liveness," that ongoing blurring of the divisions between live and mediatized presence. Like other examples offered by Auslander, titles don't create a video broadcast that attempts to evoke the spirit of a live event; rather, they create a live event that seeks to evoke the spirit of a video broadcast.[18] In referring to titling as a televisual technology, I point not only to their physical presence as projected images. The impact of titles is also closely related to how they approximate an even more canonic televisual technology: the subtitled film. Subtitles in foreign films had been common for decades prior to the development of opera supertitles, and it is difficult to read the latter's arrival outside of that background. Many of the same arguments surrounding titling that I outline in this chapter had been rehearsed earlier in discussions of film.[19]

As in opera, titles appeared in film only after a host of other solutions had been attempted to bridge the language gap, including audio dubbing and the use of intertitles (textual explanations occurring in between shots of the film, as in silent movies). Film scholar Amresh Sinha writes about the curious in-between-ness of subtitles as a textual interloper between vision and sound: "[Subtitles exist] on the borderline between image and voice—an addition, *the third dimension*, to the film itself. The subtitles come from the outside to make sense of the inside, but their own genealogy, in relation to the audio-visual mode, is, if anything, spurious.... They remain pariahs, outsiders, in exile from the imperial territoriality of the visual regime."[20] This observation would seem to place even more at stake in the case of opera, in which the voice acts not merely as a carrier of language but also as the most foregrounded vessel of musical and aesthetic importance.

Yet for all their similarities in appearance and translational logic, opera titles initially seemed to carry very different associations from their filmic counterparts, at least in the 1980s United States. Film historian B. Ruby Rich has argued that due to their association with "art house" cinema in the 1970s, many American moviegoers of the 1980s were strongly resistant to subtitled foreign films. Some production companies even began to produce trailers for foreign films that featured no dialogue, in an explicit effort to hide that a film would be titled.[21] Rich reads this "famous American resistance to subtitles" as rooted in a Reagan-era nativism, connecting it to the ascendency of "English only" and "English first" movements around the same time. She speculates that subtitles—and, one assumes, foreign film more broadly—came to be seen as a rebuke of American monolingualism and thus a somewhat intellectualized and/or pretentious (depending on who you asked) way of consuming media.

In opera, titling initially seems to have carried much the opposite association. In an American opera setting in which foreignness was somewhat unavoidable (at least for the dominant repertory at the time of works in Italian, German, and French), the use of titles was seen as a distinct move toward popularization and democratization. Their association with film—an exponentially more popular media—might have further contributed to this air of populism. Supporters saw the move as a constructive effort to draw in new, more diverse audiences, while detractors saw it as tainting what they perceived to be older and superior modes of experiencing opera. Nevertheless, while subtitled films (in contradistinction to English-language Hollywood cinema) were widely perceived as tending toward elitism and pretentiousness, supertitled operas (in contradistinction to untranslated, non-English opera) were seen as a movement away from those same values. Despite these differences, many of the discussions that emerged about *how* the inclusion of titles impacted reception remained similar between the two genres.

This chapter concentrates primarily on the negative reception of opera titles by critics and practitioners writing around the time of their introduction. I focus on these negative reactions not because I wish to portray the opera community as being largely against titles (it wasn't), nor because I wish to advocate for or against any particular position. Rather, I examine them because I believe the arguments they raise demonstrate how titling fascinatingly forced opera-goers to take stock of their own experience of the genre, to ask themselves impossible questions of what sensory encounters they valued most when the curtain goes up. As such, they provide a window into larger questions surrounding the complexities of viewing an inherently multimedia genre.

I organize my examples into two sections that trace a spectrum of varied but overlapping arguments. These sections are structured loosely around epistemological concerns and ontological ones, or, if you prefer, Hans Ulrich Gumbrecht's distinction between meaning-based and presence-based encounters.[22] The first section focuses on the meaning of titles, primarily considering their role as linguistic signifiers. These meanings interact in complex and sometimes conflicting ways with other language-based components of opera production, including librettos, synopses, and, of course, sung lyrics. The second section examines titles as a performative presence—a new physical agent within the opera house that significantly alters the experience of the audience. I use this distinction between meaning and presence primarily as a rhetorical device, not as the basis of any larger ontological or epistemological claims. To the contrary, such a binary is never cleanly delineated in practice, as the examples throughout this book make clear. Titles act as liminal entities that mediate between meaning and presence, the linguistic and the embodied, *langue* and *parole*, gnostic and drastic.[23] We might say that they mirror the structure of opera itself: a polylogical expressive technology whose effects suffuse multiple levels of sensory input, interpretive understanding, and visceral experience. I merely use the categories of meaning and presence to characterize the many types of rhetorical arguments made against them, some of which focused on concerns over meaning ("they're getting the words wrong!"), while others griped with their very presence in the hall ("get those things out of my face!").

I should also be clear that these distinctions—as well as the specific categories of argument delineated below—are my own and were not drawn by any authors at the time. Quite the contrary, the complaints written in many articles from the period take on something of a searching quality. It is as if the writers know there is something about titles that irks them, but they can't quite put their finger on exactly what it is. Their comments stumble and lurch forward, struggling to verbalize what was an essentially affective (precognitive) response. I believe that these stumblings, however, can be potentially revealing, as they point to difficult-to-articulate aesthetic commitments and values that underlie complex sonic encounters. This is not to say that the published arguments were fully transparent in their accounts of why certain individuals opposed titling. Often lurking just beneath certain critiques (and sometimes bubbling to the surface) is a distinct gatekeeping component—an implication that efforts to "democratize" the genre and appeal to wider populations would bring audiences that didn't fit the mold envisioned by some narrow-minded practitioners. Speakers generally stopped short of declaring just what they thought that mold would be, but it doesn't take much to envision what they had in mind in terms of ethnicity, class, race, and educational background. The statements of titling opponents provide a starting point for the discussion, but I by no means present them as a universal account of listening or viewing practices, either then or now.[24]

UNDERSTANDING AND MISUNDERSTANDING: THE MEANING OF TITLES

> I do not mind what language an opera is sung in so long as it is a language I don't understand.
>
> —SIR EDWARD APPLETON

In considering the significance of the titling debates, it is useful to situate them within a larger historical discussion surrounding European vocal music: the debate over the primacy of music versus that of text.[25] This dichotomy has been discussed extensively among opera scholars and has already come up in the discussion of Michel Poizat in chapter 1. Poizat refers to this split as "a constantly negotiated tension between speech and music," in which composers and performers are forced to strike a balance between the clear enunciation of the text and various forms of purely musical "jouissance."[26] He argues: "It is this constant tension between seeking jouissance and mastering it that in my view again and again gives impetus to what Jacques Bourgeois calls the 'pendular movement' in the history of opera, a swing now to the side of verbal preeminence, that of the text (*prima le parole*), now to the side of musical supremacy (*prima la musica*)."[27] This vacillation has manifested in various ways in different periods of the genre's history.[28] It is palpable not only in discussions regarding compositional, performance, or staging strategies, but also in the histories of subgenres such as *Singspiel* and other forms of "dialogue opera" that alternate between song and spoken dialogue.[29]

When titles first appeared in the mid-1980s, they were sometimes promoted as a solution to this long-standing balancing act.[30] The performer or composer could now feel free to indulge in elaborate musical displays while the audience would still be assured of easily following the narrative. Titles created a way to convey meaning without interfering with the jouissance of the music or the operatic voice. Foreign languages now presented no obstacle, as titles created a way for opera to be staged in two (or more) languages simultaneously (one heard, one or more read). In short, titles were portrayed as a technological solution to a centuries-long debate over music and text. They allowed composers, librettists, producers, and international audiences to eat their cake and have it too.[31]

But opponents of the practice disputed these claims on several grounds. Many argued that the new types of meaning conveyed by titles were not a positive contribution, but ultimately undermined the potency of the operatic experience. Meaning-based criticisms generally clustered around four main arguments, which I refer to as follows:

1. the *translation argument* (that meaning presented via titles is inaccurate),
2. the *effort argument* (that such meaning is inferior or inadequate),
3. the *overcomprehension argument* (that textual meaning itself is inauthentic in an operatic setting), and
4. the *unmeaning argument* (that textual meaning is unnecessary).

To understand the scope of these arguments, it is useful to consider each in greater detail. (A fifth argument, dubbed the *distraction argument*, is examined in the next section).

Of the four, the *translation argument* was the most frequently invoked during the early years of titling. In its simplest form this argument stated that by providing translations of a libretto during a performance, one runs the risk of mistranslating and thereby misleading the audience. This risk is compounded by the fact that titles are not complete translations of the libretto but summaries condensed to fit into a small space. An error or poor choice made by a translator could therefore alter or restrict the possible meanings of a given passage. In the worst cases, such errors led to embarrassing blunders. One oft-told story regarded a dress rehearsal for a 1984 Houston Grand Opera production of *Tosca*, featuring soprano Eva Marton. During a scene where Tosca tells Cavaradossi, "Ma falle gli occhi neri" (meaning, roughly, a request to paint Attavanti's eyes black), the title above the stage read "Give her black eyes." The unintended implication caused the audience to burst into laughter and Marton to furiously exit the stage. She refused to return until the titles were turned off.[32] Not surprisingly, this story was resurrected frequently in articles against supertitling. While such potential for error certainly existed, the *translation argument* ultimately seemed to offer the weakest charge against the practice. Proponents easily countered that problems stemming from bad translations could simply be corrected by commissioning better ones.[33]

A slightly more refined version of the *translation argument* was more difficult to brush aside. Here, critics noted that although major embarrassments may be avoidable, the process of translation always involves choices on the part of the translator that impose subtle but important alterations in meaning. Critic Will Crutchfield voiced this concern in an editorial from 1990: "The bottom line is this: *every* projected title is a double entendre. The performer is meaning one thing at one time; the screen is saying a *related* thing at a *not-too-distant* time; the disparity is inescapable and damaging."[34] Crutchfield was by no means the first writer to point out that translation can never be reduced to simple textual equivalence. Similar arguments have been made by theorists from Horace and Cicero to Walter Benjamin.[35] A common theme among this literature is that the very act of translation calls upon the translator to act as mediator between divergent linguistic and cultural systems. The final translation is always colored by calculated, interpretive, and intrinsically inexact decisions that must be made to bridge this gap. These include, for example, different approaches to the relationship between formal equivalence (a more exact adherence to words and phrase structures) and dynamic equivalence (the alteration of smaller elements in order to make the final text comprehensible).[36] Thus translations can always be accused of being mistranslations in that they must alter the full spectrum of possible meanings. To invoke an Italian adage, "Traduttore traditore"—the translator is a traitor.

Three smaller points are important to note regarding the *translation argument*. First, while it may provide some ammunition against titling, the argument equally impugns other forms of translation upon which nonfluent opera-goers have long relied. Reading a translated synopsis or libretto before a performance—the most frequently suggested alternative—would carry the same dangers of subtly changing the text. The same could be said of reading librettos during the performance or of staging sung translations, each of which has had periods of prominence in various historical eras.[37] Second, while avoiding translations would provide the most exact textual meaning for *some* listeners, it effectively eliminates *all* textual meaning for any who do not understand the sung language. In a foreign context where such listeners would comprise the majority of potential audiences—such as Italian, French, or German opera in the United States—this withholding of meaning can easily be seen as an elitist enterprise.[38] This factor likely played into the frequent characterization of titles as a "democratizing" force capable of attracting larger and more diverse audiences. Lastly, the *translation argument* is unique among the criticisms of titling in that it places supreme importance on absolute fidelity to the text. Translations fail, it claims, because any deviation must inherently compromise an imagined purity of the original libretto. Curiously, some of titling's other opponents would instead argue the exact opposite: that titles are damaging precisely because they foreground textual meaning to an inappropriately high degree.

The second complaint was the *effort argument*, which maligns titling for effectively discouraging audiences from putting productive time and energy toward reading a libretto or synopsis before attending a production. This argument claims that by doing their reading ahead of time, audiences become free to concentrate completely on the performance itself, allowing for "direct, unmediated communication . . . between singer and audience."[39] For Crutchfield this type of reception can be more powerful than textual engagement and can take place even when the audience does not understand the precise words being sung: "If you want opera understood in the general way, then pass out a synopsis of the story, and leave us in direct contact with the singers' *expression* of the words, even if we don't know what each word means. With supertitles, we still won't."[40] In this view opera is best appreciated not through a precise understanding of its dialogue but as a predominantly musical expression of a more generally understood plot. As such, the argument relies on two additional premises: (1) that musical affect, not the declamation of text, is the most important aspect of opera, and (2) that simultaneous interaction with text will inherently interfere with that musical affect.

The first of these premises is examined more thoroughly below in the discussion of supertitles as a form of presence. The second, regarding text interfering with musical content, prompted a somewhat humorous response from Henahan in 1988: "It is puzzling to hear complaints—captious ones, so to speak—about the indignity of having to use ears and eyes at the same time, especially from critics who spend many supposedly fruitful and pleasant hours listening to recorded opera with scores or librettos in hand."[41] Henahan's analogy is well-taken in noting how under certain circumstances, interacting simultaneously on both musical and textual levels is considered a perfectly legitimate way of experiencing the art form.[42] Hence, if there is a problem with titles, it cannot be because textual interaction is inherently faulty. And although Henahan uses the example of recordings (themselves another recent media incursion), for large swaths of opera history it was also quite common for listeners to read their librettos in the hall during live performances, suggesting that textual engagement was not always forbidden.

Others took the *effort argument* to even more problematic extremes, suggesting that titles not only impeded preferred modes of reception but that they could encourage outright laziness. By reducing the work required beforehand, titles constituted—in the words of Metropolitan Opera president Bruce Crawford—a "shortcut," and therefore discouraged listeners from the deeper enjoyment attainable through greater effort.[43] Some even implied that although titles may attract new audiences, these newcomers might be less than ideal and may even do harm to the genre. In the words of Met assistant conductor Joan Dornemann: "Do we want opera to be absolutely accessible to everybody in the world, which is not in the nature of its form? The guy who hasn't put in the time, preparing for the event, is not going to have as good a time as the person who did."[44]

It's hard to imagine a more transparently gatekeeping elitism than implying that the genre should only be accessible to a certain segment of listeners with the means and background to "put in the time." Dornemann's statement is especially egregious in questioning whether accessibility is a good thing, and the resulting implication that opera should only be enjoyed by those with the time, knowledge, and resources to do so. In addition, this sentiment conflicts with the goals of many composers throughout opera's history, whose works were not intended for a small cadre of experts but for mass audiences who understood the language being sung and could therefore follow the plot with relative ease—*without* consulting a libretto beforehand.

Or could they? The notion of comprehension among native speakers was countered by critics employing a third criticism: the *overcomprehension argument*. This line of thinking is forcefully articulated in historian Paul Robinson's essay "Reading Libretti and Misreading Opera." Robinson argues that experiences of opera that overemphasize text are always somewhat spurious in that they do not reflect how operas would have been received in their original context. According to Robinson, text in opera has *always* been mostly unintelligible, even when performed for an audience who speaks the language:

> The intelligibility of an operatic libretto is inhibited, in varying degrees, by the following considerations: (1) opera is in a foreign language; (2) opera is sung, and much that is sung by an operatic voice cannot be understood; (3) opera contains a good deal of ensemble singing—passages where two or more voices sing at the same time, sometimes to identical words, sometimes to different words—and if one operatic voice is often unintelligible, two or more almost always are; (4) operatic singers must compete with a full symphony orchestra—at least from the nineteenth century onward—and, as every opera-goer knows, the sheer volume of that orchestral sound further limits our ability to make out the words.[45]

Thus, to understand an opera primarily through text could overemphasize an aspect of the work that would have been largely inaccessible to an original audience. Titles, therefore, do not merely translate an operatic experience into a new cultural context, they distort that experience by foregrounding text to an inappropriate degree: "Many people seem to be under the illusion that supertitles serve merely to translate opera out of a foreign language. But that is surely erroneous. As with the 'libretto-in-hand reading,' supertitles introduce a textual explicitness quite foreign to what one actually experiences in the theater."[46]

Variants of the *overcomprehension argument* also appeared in the popular press. Crutchfield and others pointed out that in the early twentieth century, American performances of operas were sometimes staged in multiple languages at once, depending on the preferences of individual performers. For example, a single staging might feature a soprano singing Italian, with responses from a tenor in German. This phenomenon led Crutchfield to an interesting conclusion: "The very fact that this could happen on a regular basis . . . confirms what one cannot avoid suspecting anyway: that [such performances were] not playing to an audience expected to understand or care closely about the words."[47] Even though this practice eventually fell out of fashion, Crutchfield uses the anecdote to illustrate that the ideal reception of opera is not about the precise words but again that elusive experience of "unmediated communication" through music.[48]

Although some appealed to the *overcomprehension argument* to promote reading librettos beforehand, it was sometimes also used to recommend another, older approach to staging: the translation of opera into local languages. If a director's goal is to recreate the experience of an original audience—a specific but not altogether unreasonable goal—much can be said for the practice, which was common in American opera houses throughout the nineteenth century (and much longer in Europe). Sung translations allow the audience to follow the libretto without overemphasizing its importance.[49] Unlike titles, sung translations retain three of the obstacles to intelligibility noted by Robinson. If one conceives of ideal reception in terms of maintaining a certain relationship between textual comprehension and musical jouissance (again, specific but not altogether unreasonable), sung translations could perhaps provide the closest approximation to what an original audience might have experienced. Yet at the same time, a model that promotes this approach as providing the most "authentic" audience experience can easily be contested. (Is authenticity even possible or desirable in a genre as continually negotiated as opera? Authentic for whom? For what period? For which audience?) A more conservative view might define authenticity in a more literal recreation of a work, including the retention of the original language.

The fourth—and perhaps most surprising—criticism is what I refer to as the *nonmeaning argument*. This line of reasoning goes further than the *overcomprehension argument* by asserting not only that titles overemphasize textual meaning but that opera is best received when the text is not understood at all. In this view foreignness provides not an impediment but a positive attribute that allows the audience to experience a mode of operatic wonder that transcends language. A particularly poetic formulation can be found in the quote from Sir Edward Appleton that began this chapter. The sentiment is echoed in a 1971 *Opera News* interview with actor and comedian Zero Mostel, who proclaims: "If you hear Boris say [full bass voice] 'I am about to die,' so-so. But if you hear 'Umirayu!' it's wild. It's a mystery, and you don't have to understand it to like it."[50] For a more in-depth (albeit negative) exposition of the idea, I turn again to Crutchfield:

> Some, in fact, feel nothing but gratitude for the language barrier that spares them from having to follow texts they would find stilted or silly. . . . Such listeners have always been on the defensive in the debate (which sometimes takes on a high moralistic tone), because the other side has a way of implying that they belong to a lower species of opera lover. They are mere canary fanciers, escapists, wallowers in soothing, meaningless sound. They do not understand what opera is *really* about; they go for "an exotic and irrational entertainment"—Dr. Johnson's definition not of opera but, as the critic and translator Andrew Porter has so often pointed out, of opera played in Italian for Englishmen.[51]

Crutchfield's description of this phenomenon in terms of exoticism seems somewhat apt, as the idea emphasizes and celebrates the foreignness of opera by recasting language as pure (and perhaps mystical) sound. In an American context, such a listening would most often invoke Europe as an exoticized other, fetishized not only as a cultural model of high art but through an allure that stems from incomprehensibility.

But while the *nonmeaning argument* minimizes the importance of linguistic signification, it generally does not abandon meaning entirely (i.e., treating opera as if it were plotless, instrumental, absolute music). Instead, the argument often overlapped with the *effort argument* in endorsing a pre-performance reading of a libretto. It suggested that listeners could possess a general impression of a scene even if they do not comprehend the exact words on a moment-by-moment basis: a viewer may understand that the words being sung by Don Giovanni are intended to seduce, even if they do not know the meaning of "La ci darem la mano." Robinson refers to this process as "textual anticipation," as listeners use knowledge gleaned from a previous reading to inform the way they hear.[52] In a sense "textual arousal" might be more appropriate, as the prereading not only allows the listener to anticipate what will happen in a narrative sense but also to experience a more visceral affective impact at the moment of encounter. In certain ways the process resembles instrumental program music, as a text read prior to the performance prepares the listener to follow a specific plot. The other layers of operatic presentation (acting, mise-en-scène, etc.) further aid this reception through additional nonlinguistic cues.

However, Robinson also observes that the presence of language constitutes a critical difference from instrumental forms, even when its meaning is not understood. For him, language itself acts as a fundamental signifier of humanity, profoundly altering the way an audience relates to a performance: "Even when they are unintelligible, [the] presence [of words] identifies the singer as a human actor with specific feelings, giving voice to specific thoughts. This explains, at least in part, why we would not tolerate pure vocalise even in place of words we cannot hear.... I am inclined to suggest, therefore, that the words in opera are emblems of human volition. As such, they are part of our experience of opera even, as it were, when they are not."[53] This explanation differs in a crucial way from the *overcomprehension argument*, which implies that the words are largely (but not entirely) unimportant. Here, the *presence* of words is critical; their *meaning* is not. Their impact lies in their recognizability as meaningful signs that are knowable but not known, a sort of trans-semiotic or semi-semiotic acknowledgment.

The premise of a voice without meaning returns us again to the theorizations of the Lacanian object voice. Mladen Dolar writes extensively about the object voice as those elements of vocal expression that sit outside of the sphere of linguistic signification. Though he, like Poizat, argues that the object voice is lost after infancy (when the use of language develops), the act of singing can temporarily resurrect it by stressing nonlinguistic aspects of vocal production. The musical voice disrupts our usual association of the utterance as a bearer of language and thereby highlights the rift that always exists between voice as ontological object and voice as semiotic transmission:

> Music evokes the object voice and obfuscates it; it fetishizes it, but also opens the gap that cannot be filled.... Bringing the voice from the background to the forefront entails a reversal, or a structural illusion: the voice appears to be the locus of true expression, the place where what cannot be said can nevertheless be conveyed. The voice is endowed with profundity: by not meaning anything, it appears to mean more than mere words, it becomes the bearer of some unfathomable originary meaning which, supposedly, got lost with language.[54]

Though Dolar is not discussing opera, it is striking how closely his point mirrors the *nonmeaning argument*. Notions such as Crutchfield's call for "direct unmediated communication ... between singer and audience" can be fruitfully understood alongside Dolar's notion of the voice as "the locus of true expression, the place where what cannot be said can nevertheless be conveyed."[55] Indeed, it seems difficult to frame singing as "unmediated" without such an underlying premise (a more conventional view might suggest that the singing voice is constantly mediated—not only through language but also through the semiotic cues embedded in musical syntax).

I suggest that a variation of Poizat/Dolar/Lacan's theorizations of the cry (and the object voice) could be read as underlying the *nonmeaning argument*, as well as certain versions of the *effort argument*. In this light the experience of not understanding (at least in a rudimentary linguistic sense) becomes compelling precisely because it detaches the singing voice from the realm of linguistic signification. The operatic voice becomes, in a sense, a single prolonged cry—a continuous, intensely powerful striving toward an unattainable prelinguistic object voice. Although this experience of striving might still be possible for an audience that speaks the language being sung through the effects of musical jouissance, imposing a language barrier heightens the effect by cutting off the very possibility of linguistic understanding. This mode of reception casts aside any notion of authenticity and instead argues that the removal of the opera from its native sphere into a foreign one may actually imbue it with *more* potency than it would otherwise possess.

Titles undoubtedly change this relationship in several ways. On the one hand, their presence challenges efforts to imagine a voice without meaning, since that meaning is projected for all to see. But on the other hand, paradoxically, titles also do just the opposite. By literally demarcating a separate space for the communication of textual meaning outside of the voice, titles may perhaps be seen as *freeing* the voice, allowing it to explore the full spectrum of nonlinguistic jouissance without the burden of textual communication. Such a stance returns to the notion of titles as a kind of "solution" for the genre. Here, titles do not merely mediate between music and text but act as both a bridge and a barrier between linguistic and nonlinguistic realms. Titles allow song to strive unfettered toward the unattainable, nonlinguistic object voice, while preserving (in a separate space) the textual meanings of the libretto.

THE WRITING ON THE WALL: THE PRESENCE OF TITLES

An analysis of titles as a form of presence requires us to consider how they relate to opera's many other performative materials. In his book *Unsettling Opera*, David Levin calls for analytic methods that foreground the genre's deeply heterogeneous nature. He states that by overemphasizing the importance of the score, musicologists have tended to ignore many powerful elements that contribute to an opera-goer's total experience. To correct this, Levin champions an approach based on an idea of "polylogism."[56] Considering opera's multimedia nature, he argues that scholars should not begin their analyses by favoring a single location of aesthetic primacy (such as the idea that the music is primary and other elements are ancillary). Even a position that creates a binary of aesthetic poles (i.e., *prima la musica* versus *prima le parole*) constitutes a severe reduction of the genre's full expressive potential. Instead, opera must be approached through a polylogical framework that considers all aspects contributing to the total performance. This would certainly include the score and libretto but also set design, mise-en-scène, dramaturgy, instrumentation, stage direction, singers qua singers, singers qua actors, singers qua communicators of text, and so on. These elements are not isolated but constantly interact, reinforce, and rub against one another (as well as against the social context of the performance, the audience, etc.) in constructing the illusion of a seamlessly unified work.

Levin does not suggest that all of these factors must carry equal weight, but nor does he imply that their relative importance is preordained by the genre itself. Rather, the significance of each factor is constantly subject to negotiations between the artists involved (both on and off stage), the work being performed, and the historical and cultural contexts surrounding a production. This constant jostling between experiential levels leads Levin to characterize opera as fundamentally "unsettled." In bringing these elements back into the sphere of analysis, his aim is to unmoor scholarship from its misleading overemphasis on the score and toward the embodied, affective impact of the total performance at the moment of reception. The presence of titles can be constructively considered through Levin's polylogical framework. Like every component of opera, titles create effects that emerge in constant dialogue with other aspects of a production.

For this reason, many titlists prefer to work closely with designers and dramaturgs when creating a script. Titlist Francis Rizzo, for example, notes that a diligent titlist may need to prepare different title scripts for different productions of the same opera:

> When I did *Wozzeck* for Los Angeles, I prepared an entire draft and sent it to David Alden, the stage director. Then I realized the way he was taking the opera for L.A., as opposed to the Met, made it much more contemporary. So when the Captain referred to "our regimental chaplain," I put up "our good padre," and Wozzeck spoke of his child as "the poor kid" rather than the "poor little tyke." . . . You also have to

consider the tempo of the performance. I did *Figaro* for Washington Opera, and we used the same slides at Wolf Trap last summer. Well, Daniel Barenboim did an expansive reading of *Figaro,* but Antonio Pappano at Wolf Trap took it at quite a clip. The combination of a much faster tempo and the fact that the screen at Wolf Trap was farther away—it's a much bigger theater—meant I had to throw out almost every other slide.[57]

Rizzo's comments exhibit a deep awareness of the way that his titles relate not only to the libretto but to multiple components of a production. His scripts are not simply a static translation but are informed by their relationship with other features of each unique staging. Along the same lines, a *New York Times* article about the New York City Opera notes how the title operator views a video feed of the conductor (rather than the stage) to time precisely when to project, change, and remove slides.[58] The act of following the conductor, much like an instrumentalist, provides a poignant example of titles' interaction with musical sound. Not only do they operate rhythmically in a kind of textual dance in time with music, titles can literally alter the affective impact of the music for listeners, while at the same time the music alters the affective power of the title text. Titles change the way we listen, the way we see, the way we encounter and bear witness to an operatic production.

In a few cases titles have also been used to provide intentional counterpoint with other elements of a production. During a 1988 staging of *Tannhäuser* at the Lyric Opera of Chicago, for instance, director Peter Sellars envisioned a distinctly dramaturgical use of titles that aimed to create new forms of aesthetic contrast. Although Sellars ultimately had to curtail his plans due to technical limitations, his initial concept was to include three separate sets of titles. The first (projected in white above the proscenium) fulfilled the traditional role of offering translations for the sung text. The second (blue along the back wall), offered sacred thoughts of love running (mostly) through the mind of Tannhäuser. The third (red, in various areas of the stage) conveyed the character's more carnal sexual urges.[59] Here we find titles being used in a way that goes far beyond simple translation. Instead, the dramaturg foregrounds the performativity of the projections themselves, using them to generate additional layers of audience experience—alternative affective translations, perhaps.[60]

While such displays could certainly influence textual or hermeneutic interpretations, they also carry the potential to change the affective impact within the moment of performance. Knowing Tannhäuser's secret sexual urges, for example, could fundamentally shift the visceral response of an audience member upon seeing the character enter the stage. The effect resembles Ludwig Wittgenstein's concept of seeing an aspect of an image: "I contemplate a face, and then suddenly notice its likeness to another. I *see* that it has not changed; and yet I see it differently."[61] In other words, knowledge from outside an encounter brings the potential to not only shift one's understanding of the encounter but also the experience of it; one *sees differently*. Titles, with their ability to summon affective energies from outside the moment, have the potential to evoke similar effects—not only altering what we know but also how we see and hear.

That the presence of titles fundamentally influences the polylogical negotiations of opera seems inevitable. What is debatable is whether these new relationships are beneficial or detrimental. Perhaps the single most widespread criticism of titling dealt with their very presence in the concert hall. This objection, which I call the *distraction argument*, asserted that not only do titles seduce novices into an inferior mode of enjoying opera, but their presence precludes the very possibility of experiencing the genre in other older ways. Even for opera-goers who dislike titles, their visual prominence above the stage creates an insistent demand for attention, a control over the audience's sensory apparatus that is impossible to ignore. As such, opponents argued that titles not only enabled an alternative way of experiencing opera, they imposed it. This argument was central, for example, in the Metropolitan Opera's decision to develop their unique "Met Titles" system in 1995, in which titles are not projected onto the stage but onto screens in the back of each seat. Since the individual screens could be turned off, the system allows viewers to view the titles or not, depending on their individual preference.[62]

Two corollaries to the *distraction argument* emerged as well. The first, and more frequent, was the complaint that titles distracted from the primacy of music, which some argued should be at the center of any performance. Hugh Southern of the Metropolitan Opera expressed the point boldly: "Enjoying opera is not consistently grounded in a close understanding, line by line, of the libretto. Many plots, and much dialogue, are not distinguished—sometimes they are nonsensical. It seems to us that translating them might be unhelpful and irritating. . . . [I]sn't there something to be said for tradition, which accords pride of place to music in the operatic aesthetic?"[63] Some other versions of this argument suggested not a single point of primacy but an ideal ratio of importance between multiple elements: "Music and dramaturgy are 75 to 80 percent of the opera experience, and the text *per se*, word for word, is really a pretext. It's just the armature on which the composer erected the musical structure. Titles reverse the ratio, so that the 20 percent experience becomes the 80 percent experience, with the music receding into the background, like a kind of accompaniment. Who can think that's good?"[64]

This variant provides slightly more nuance by recognizing (albeit minimally) the polylogism embedded in the genre. But in asserting a fixed relationship between elements, it still fails to acknowledge Levin's second point: opera's unsettledness. Quite to the contrary, the suggestion of an ideal ratio that places music first among equals problematically suggests that opera has been firmly settled into a distinct hierarchy. Such a view cannot account for the many shifts and negotiations that have taken place throughout the genre's history. It cannot, for instance, explain the pendular swings between music and text, nor can it clarify adoptions or rejections of various performance practices, listening strategies, or stage technologies.[65] And again, the idea that opera ought to be experienced in the absence of text is hardly a transhistorical given (in light of the aforementioned practice of reading librettos during performances) but a distinctly post-Wagnerian perspective.[66] Thus, asserting an inviolable primacy of music (free from text) does not only constrain an art form that has long been unsettled; it does so in favor of a particular historical and cultural moment.

A second form of the *distraction argument* relates more closely to the interplay between the affective impact of performance and the hermeneutic process of engaging with or interpreting a given text, or, what Carolyn Abbate has called "drastic" and "gnostic" modes of music reception.[67] This form of the *distraction argument* asks whether the imposition of linguistic semiotics that is built into titling imposes a gnostic reception and, consequently, distracts from a more powerful drastic one. In their close link to the libretto, titles emphasize one of gnosticism's primary avatars of a work-based understanding of music. Like the score, the libretto generally sits on the gnostic side of Abbate's model—an autonomous, abstract text that is realized through performance. In this light, titles seem to represent a forced entry of the textual/gnostic into the realm of performance, diluting the potential for drastic affective experience. But one could counter such a claim by noting that titling fundamentally changes the nature of text as well, potentially thrusting it into the realm of the drastic by *injecting it directly into the realm of performance*. In the hall, the libretto is no longer an abstract ideal informing a myriad of adaptations but a physical presence that participates directly in the performance itself. Titling *drasticizes* text by presenting it as a form of sensory input to be encountered alongside and in close relation to other sensory inputs. It becomes part of the unsettled sensory assemblage that is the performance itself.

And this is not merely my argument. Supportive commentators at the time of titling's rise similarly argued that the incorporation of titles could noticeably enhance the drastic impact of a performance. This sentiment can be observed, for example, in statements by a number of performers and composers who spoke out in favor of titling, endorsements that deserve mention. Contrary to the occasional claims by opponents that singers disliked titles, a 1990 issue of *Opera News* included numerous quotes from singers and composers who praised the practice (and, interestingly, very few who opposed it).[68] Often these statements referenced titles' ability to enhance the very thing detractors said they undermine: direct communication between performer and audience. For example, composer Dominick Argento, who had previously opposed titles, said of one titled production: "Virtually every line provided an audience reaction that the characters onstage immediately sensed, and to which they responded. The audience's fuller involvement heartened the singers and strengthened their performance. The phenomenon is one that actors in the straight theater are familiar with: audience reaction actually fuels the performance."[69] Argento's suggestion that titles can afford a more intimate and direct connection stands in stark contrast to Crutchfield's objections noted earlier. It seems to point to a distinctly affective mode of opera reception and a strengthened connection between performer and audience that can be augmented through titling. Even if it is through the conveyance of gnostic meaning that titles encourage such connection (by allowing the audience to follow the plot), this heightening of audience receptivity creates a notable change in their engagement with the actual performance.

For the most adamant opponents to titling, this observation may not have been enough to dispel the argument that a semiotic/meaning-based encounter might weaken the potential for affective engagement. But while projected text offers a new medium of transmission, we must also remember that it is not titles alone that instill semiotics into the opera experience. Language, after all, has been present all along. Any listener who *does* understand the language of a performance has always been occupied with some form of semiotic decoding, experienced in tandem with musical absorption (which, of course, carries its own semiotic systems). In a more general sense, the very recognition of a narrative plot requires ongoing acts of contextual interpretation. Even if one does not understand the words, following a plot requires reading body language, the dramatic implications of staging, associations invoked by musical signifiers and tropes, and perhaps textual arousal from preshow preparation. In short, the very recognition of opera as a narrative genre requires the audience to make use of interpretive faculties in order to follow the story from one point to the next. Only the use of projected text as a vessel for this meaning is new.

CONCLUSION

Since the Metropolitan Opera installed its titling system in 1995, much of vitriol of the early titling debates has reduced to a simmer. While the current tranquility may appear to make the preceding something of a historical exercise, the dominance of titles remains a central and largely uninterrogated aspect of twenty-first-century opera production. Their existence has changed the way that opera is produced, viewed, and heard. Though we may today be inclined to cast a critical eye on the hyperbole employed by early opponents, it is equally possible to remain skeptical toward the notion that titling is transparent or unobtrusive. Something remains at stake in opera titles; exploring the continued resonance of these debates can provide insight into how the genre continues to be staged, interpreted, and encountered.

In a broader sense, the debates over titling provide a particularly clear window into the sensory networks that underlie any listening experience. As an example of a new, mediatized incursion into a (always already mediatized) live performance space, they provide a strong example of Auslander's theories of performative liveness in an increasingly televisual world. Above all, the titling debates remind us how the presences in the room, as well as the meanings they carry, constantly rub against one another in any act of sonic encounter, transferring affective and hermeneutic energies across layers of experience. The arrival of these "performing texts" speaks less to a separation between presence versus meaning, or affect versus understanding, than it does to their constantly being folded together.

5 Diaries and Postcards
Archival Privilege, Empathy, and Intimacy

PROLOGUE

The death certificate always catches me by surprise. It's nestled into a folder labeled "Correspondence: 1970–1976," accompanied by a letter from her parents and a bit of correspondence with the police. It gives only a glimpse, but here's what we can glean.

The young woman—she went by a nickname, so let's call her Glow—went for a hike by herself one day in early June. While she was out, she fell from a high precipice and died. Her body was found the next day. Only a few possessions that were with her are listed in the police report: a torn pair of Levi's and a brown T-shirt, a ring with blue-green stones, a single tennis shoe (what happened to the other one?). The cause of death is listed as "skull fracture due to trauma," after a fall from a mountain cliff. At the time of the accident, she was twenty-six years old.[1] The stoic formality of the certificate does little to temper the feelings it evokes when I encounter it; it is a talisman of loss couched in the driest procedural terms.

The body was identified by her partner, a young composer with whom she lived. I'll just refer to him as the Composer. The scattering of documents about her come from the Composer's personal archive, which today is housed at a prestigious university where he briefly taught several decades later. The couple had known each other since childhood. Elsewhere I peruse their high school yearbook, where she was two years behind him and was active in numerous activities. She earned a place in the National Honor Society, served on the class council, wrote for the school newspaper, and was a member of the International Relations Club, French Club, and swim team.[2] The Composer left their hometown for college in the late 1960s, but the two remained in touch, and references to Glow can be found here and there in documents saved from his studies. A few years after graduation, the two were living together in a house on the West Coast. They were never legally married, but in many ways they acted as if they were; mail was occasionally addressed to her using his last name, and she even accompanied him on an extended grant-funded research trip to Europe. Further testimony to the couple's closeness is reflected in a letter from her parents sent a month after the accident. They thanked the Composer for his support and sent a detailed account of the family's grief and how they were coping. The letter signs off with "We think of you always and love you."[3] At the age of twenty-seven, the Composer was a widow.

If we continue leafing through the correspondence, we find that the Composer will soon love again. Within a few years he lives with a new partner. And by the early 1980s he meets his eventual wife—a brilliant instrumentalist with whom he remains until the end of his life. But none of this knowledge ever seems to dull the impact of coming across the certificate, tucked amid jokey letters and dry professional memos. On the several occasions when I have stumbled across it, I never feel ready. All of the sudden, amid the mind-numbing repetitiveness of the paper archive, I find myself moved against my will.

I want to know more about Glow. About her work and dreams and desires and aspirations. What would her archive have held, had she lived long enough to fill it? I want to know why she decided to walk alone that day, and why the Composer didn't go with her. I even want to know how she got her nickname. But as Brent Hayes Edwards reminds us so succinctly: "Finding something in an archive poignant in this way does not necessarily mean there is anything to say about it," and the "dead end may be the most common kind of archival experience."[4] No institution houses an archive for Glow. Aside from those who knew her, Glow's short life and sudden death survive only as memories in fleeting, unexpected scraps, tucked away in a loved one's papers.

SHOWERS OF SEEDS: ARCHIVAL EMPATHY AND PREPARATION FOR LISTENING

Historian Arlette Farge writes stunningly about the experience of doing archival research. In one of many vignettes from her book *The Allure of the Archive*, Farge relates pouring through dusty judicial collections from eighteenth-century France when she happens across an unusual artifact:

> I come across a slightly swollen file, open it delicately, and find a small pouch of coarse fabric pinned to the top of a page, bulging with the outlines of objects that I cannot immediately identify. A letter from a

> country doctor accompanies the pouch. He is writing to the Royal Society of Medicine to report that he knows a young girl, sincere and virtuous, whose breasts discharge handfuls of seeds each month. The attached bag is the proof.
>
> I face the decision of whether or not to open something that has not seen the light of day in two centuries. I open it delicately, withdrawing the thick pin from the two large holes it has poked in the slightly rust-stained twill. This way I will be able to close the pouch neatly by fitting the pin back into the holes, just as it was before. A few seeds escape and rain down on the yellowed document, as golden as they were on their first day, a brief burst of sunshine. What if these really came from the woman in the bloom of youth whom the doctor so trusted? Puns aside, this feeling reflects the surprising power of these seeds, still intact, as real as they are immaterial, meant to be both the fruit of a body and a scientific explanation for menstruation.[5]

One of the things that resonates so strongly about Farge's anecdotes is that for all of their unexpectedness, something like this experience has a subtle familiarity for anyone who is invested in archival research. Work in the archive can be rote, endlessly poring through reams of irrelevant materials to answer a small set of meticulously crafted questions. At its best the process can be meditative; at worst, tedious. But most frequently it is filled with repetition and a sense of endlessness. Yet even in the most staid archives, unexpected showers of seeds can happen at any moment. In that next folder something might appear that is completely unexpected—perhaps miscategorized, perhaps uncategorizable—that wrenches us from our torpor.

What Farge captures so effectively is not merely the novelty of such encounters but their disorientingly affective impact. In the blink of an eye, the seeker suddenly feels more connected to the people and presences of the archive. Not merely interested in an abstractly conceived "object of study" but connected to actual living entities—to human beings and fleshy bodies and palpable events and tangible things that pop with renewed vibrancy. These figures balance on the precipice of being forgotten but cling to remembrance through tenuous paper lifelines. For Farge this connection is not the end of the encounter but its beginning. It provides an opportunity to pose new types of questions: "The sun-colored seeds ... are at the same time everything and nothing. ... Their story takes shape only when you ask a specific type of question of them."[6] Such encounters simultaneously enfold (a) an affective impact in the moment of discovery (the seeds as "golden as they were on their first day, a brief burst of sunshine") as well as (b) the opening of channels for new discursive insights into the past (the seeds as "both the fruit of a body and a scientific explanation for menstruation"). It is this duality, this tactile intimacy juxtaposed with the possibilities and pitfalls of interpretive potential, that lies at the heart of this chapter.

· · ·

> [W]e might say that it is easier, or that it seems more scholarly, to talk about pitch, rhythm, form, historical context and debates, and meaning than it is to describe, for example, the feeling and effect of being transformed.
>
> —NINA SUN EIDSHEIM

The story I allude to in this chapter traces my own process of grappling with archival intimacies within a particular set of sonic encounters. I say "allude to" rather than simply "tell" because I have made a conscious decision not to tell certain parts of the story—at least not here.[7] The archive in question is housed in a university repository where I worked as a processing archivist after my graduate studies. The collection was the personal papers of the above referenced Composer, which had been donated to the institution some years after his death. My path to engage with this individual wasn't a deliberate choice—in fact, I had neither heard of him nor heard a note of his music prior to taking the job. It was, rather, a day gig to make ends meet while I floundered on the academic job market. My background working in private musicians' archives led to the invitation from the library, which didn't have enough full-time staff to process the collection. I was brought in as a part-timer, a luxury that many smaller archives don't enjoy. In addition to professional papers, recordings, and scores, the archive contained many items of a more personal nature: correspondence, postcards, yearbooks, and other such objects. It also included a smaller but not insignificant amount of material from the Composer's spouse in the final decades of his life, an incredible instrumentalist whom I'll call the Virtuoso (discussed in detail elsewhere in this chapter).

Much of the material preserved in the collection is what one might call superfluous, at least if the archive is supposed to simply trace the Composer's professional career. But this chapter is, in part, about that superfluity, about its porous boundaries, and about what it might do (or more specifically, what it has done to me) in relation to the process of listening to an individual's work.

ARCHIVAL PRIVILEGE AND ANONYMITY AS METHOD

By now you have undoubtedly realized that I have chosen to omit the individual's name who sits at the center of this chapter. I have made this decision for several reasons but central among them is a desire to consider how operations of privilege (particularly white, male, cis-hetero privilege) can be reproduced in an archival context. The Composer, without question, was a tremendous beneficiary of myriad forms of privilege, as am I in my position as a scholar. A brief (and necessarily vague) bio can begin to trace the story.

The Composer is by no means a well-known figure. He was born around the mid-twentieth century and studied music from a young age, including piano and conducting lessons. He moved east to study at an elite university (joining his brother, who was already a student there) and majored in music, working with several well-known academic modernist composers. He became involved in a vibrant scene of somewhat irreverent, new music-oriented comrades in the area. The group spent their time experimenting with a heady combination of high-modernist composition, psychedelic counterculture, drug use, and performance art. Perhaps the cheekiest example of this confluence came when he and his brother founded a "Fan Club" for a certain serialist luminary, an organization that imitated—with palpable irony—the models of pop music fan clubs of the time (members even received a signed 8 × 10 glossy photo of the luminary himself).[8] After completing his bachelor's degree, the Composer followed his adviser to pursue graduate studies at another institution on the West Coast (the adviser had also just moved to take a position there). There the Composer received a master's degree, after which he was immediately(!) invited to join the faculty.

The Composer remained at this institution for the rest of his life, teaching composition and conducting ensembles. Over that stretch he received several awards and commissions from various organizations and also developed a strong reputation as a conductor of contemporary works. In his teaching career he seemed to be deeply devoted to (and beloved by) many of his students and colleagues, who knew him as a quirky but meticulous intellectual with a wide range of diverse interests (tarot reading, mycology, etc.). The Composer maintained a relatively quiet life in a small town near the school, where he lived for several decades until his death. In his later years he suffered from bouts of depression and alcoholism, and he passed away in the mid-2000s. Sometime after his passing, the Composer's personal papers were donated to the institution where I worked, where he had taught for one year as a visiting faculty member in the early 1990s.

Even in this thumbnail bio, it should be clear that throughout his life this individual enjoyed myriad personal and professional advantages. While little material in the archive outlines his family's economic background, they seem to have been well-off; his aunt, in fact, made a fortune as the creator of an internationally famous product in the 1950s that remains popular today. He attended one of the nation's foremost universities (as a legacy sibling, no less), where he had the freedom to experiment widely (musically, chemically, and otherwise), while simultaneously developing a network of professional connections that secured his employment for the rest of his life. His musical proclivities helped as well; at a time when university music departments were dominated by the European canon and compositional extensions of serialism and aleatoricism, the Composer's work emerged directly out of these dominant traditions. This left him well situated for both teaching opportunities and commissions. His privilege is further evident in his career path, particularly his ability to land what would turn out to be a lifelong, permanent faculty position at his MA-granting institution *immediately after completing his degree* (and scarcely three years after finishing his undergraduate studies). Although he was almost entirely unknown to the general public, the Composer maintained a level of professional stability that was practically unheard for practitioners of other musical traditions (non-Western traditions, pop music, Black music, etc.), as well as being exceedingly rare for minorities and women in music departments of the time.

And perhaps there is no greater testament to the Composer's privilege than the archive itself, which is now preserved in perpetuity. The collection landed at the institution where I worked not because he was a figure of particular prominence (it was not actively sought out by the library; there was no bidding war), but because of the Composer's brief stint as a visiting professor and the library's general policy of accepting collections donated by faculty. Yet preserving a collection from a brief 1990s visiting faculty member is hardly politically neutral, just as the hiring of new faculty members (then as now) is not politically neutral.[9] In this case, his hire came at a time when this music department—particularly in composition—remained predominantly steeped in white European and American traditions. Thus the seemingly natural, seemingly neutral choice to preserve the archives of former faculty must also be recognized as a choice to devote ongoing resources to preserving a period of predominantly Eurocentric practice in the institution's history—a curious sort of "legacy admissions" in the archival realm.

The recognition of these forms of privilege certainly impacted me in my relationship with the Composer and his archive, particularly in regard to responses that I discuss below as "archival empathy" and "archival intimacy." At times I certainly found aspects of the Composer's background vexing, particularly when I compared his breezy path through life with the loft jazz artists I was collaborating with in my other work (and which I was still in the process of completing).[10] At the same time, I couldn't ignore the reflections of my own privilege in the Composer's story. If I lacked some of the family resources that he came from, I have certainly benefited from the structural privileges of being a white cisgender male working in the academy.[11] I too had followed an older sibling (my sister) to an elite undergraduate institution and then attended another for grad school. And I, too, was working (albeit in a temporary, part-time position) in a job that I had received through the support and contacts from my time in those schools. Even my other research interests on the music of politically revolutionary Black experimentalist artists suddenly became tenuous, as my position in the archive seemingly pulled me away from that work as well. If the archive threw into relief the distinction between the Composer and my other research endeavors, it simultaneously cast light on the connections between us, and on how I too had benefited from many forms of privilege within music academe.

For all of this recognition, it remained and remains difficult—within my process of working with the archive—to see the Composer only as an empty product of privilege. And I don't believe this is only because of the similarities that exist between us (although this is a factor I must continually keep in mind). It is difficult not because the Composer didn't benefit from unjust systems (he certainly did), but because of the sense of intimacy I developed in the process of working with his personal effects. This is a process, as I implied previously, that's easy to get swept up in while working in any collection. It is the same type of empathy referenced by Marika Cifor, who writes about the ways that archives can reproduce systems of power, even on the individual researcher level: "The (re)production of power through appraisal decisions means that too often users are provided only with the opportunities to empathize with the records and therefore the affects of those in positions of power."[12]

My experience resonates—from a somewhat different direction—with Cifor's observations about the closeness that archival engagement can allow and conversely that archival exclusion can forestall. The collection certainly puts some of the Composer's flaws on display but also his moments of kindness and caring. His obliviousness but also his care for students and his community. His moments of fragility but also his moments of perseverance and strength. His predominantly Euro-American compositional influences but also his wide-ranging listening habits and interactions with colleagues of color. I read how the Composer's students described him as a tirelessly devoted teacher, who would let private lessons spill over their allotted time into several hours, and how friends and colleagues enjoyed warm and supportive dinners in the couple's cluttered home. In time, I even developed an appreciation for the Composer's music, particularly as I unpacked the curious collection of allusions, motivations, and structural systems that it was based on (and which, I contend, are often not evident through listening alone). The process made him, in short, a richly textured presence with whom I developed a certain connection—warts and all—through the long story that unfolded in the margins of his papers. In the end I didn't end up loving the Composer or hating him, but I did end up feeling a degree of fascination, admiration, and ambivalent affinity.

Where Cifor's critique hits home is in regard to the stakes of that affinity, and in turn the stakes of archiving itself. For if I was able to develop a sense of connection with the Composer, it was *solely, entirely because of the archive*. Echoing Cifor, I refer to this connection through the term "archival empathy," to describe to the feeling of connection to an individual or institution through the process of close engagement with their archive. Again, the stakes of such empathy lie in the way that the presence (and at times promotion) of particular archives can impact what histories *are allowed* to resonate. I empathized because I was put in a position to empathize, because *these* materials were preserved and placed before me where so many others were not. In many cases, the systemic reproduction of archival presence can reproduce itself further once the archive begins attracting users: an archive exists; a researcher engages, empathizes, and eventually writes about it; others read the work and empathize as well; perhaps these others visit the collection themselves; this leads to further scholarship and perhaps the identification of new archives; and the cycle continues. Archival privilege begets further archival privilege.

Cifor is not alone in exploring the manifestations of power and privilege within archival practice. A wave of writers in recent decades have explored issues surrounding the creation and maintenance of archives. Some of this work has taken place from within the field of archival studies itself.[13] Other writing has emerged from branches of the humanities that employ archival methodologies.[14] As Achille Mbembe writes: "It seems clear that the archive is primarily the product of a judgment, the result of the exercise of a specific power and authority, which involves placing certain documents in an archive at the same time as others are discarded.... [This] in the end results in the granting of a privileged status to certain written documents, and the refusal of that same status to others, thereby judged 'unarchivable.' The archive is, therefore, not a piece of data, but a status."[15]

While Mbembe and others write in regard to the archive of powerful states and institutions—in particular, seeking methods to decolonize hegemonic archival practices—others write about the potential for alternative and/or community-based archives to disrupt such systems.[16] A recent manifestation of this impulse can be seen in the emergence of the #ArchivesForBlackLives movement, which grew in connection with the community-centered initiative known as "A People's Archive of Police Violence in Cleveland." Jarrett Drake, one of the founders of that movement, writes: "The unbearable whiteness and patriarchy of traditional archives demand that new archives for black lives emerge and sustain themselves as spaces and sites for trauma, transcendence, and transformation. The state memorializes violence against black bodies through the making of archives, but communities, organizers, scholars, librarians, and archivists can partner as equals to resist this second layer of violence and provide spaces for people to be held to account and for communities to heal."[17] Such communal archives seek to reclaim the potential for historical cultivation, taking it out of the hands of centralized institutions and returning it to local communities. My own previous work on lofts emerged from these types of collections, particularly Juma Sultan's private archive of loft jazz.[18] More recently, digital archiving technologies create even more powerful potentials for both preservation and access, as work like Drake's makes clear.

The Composer's archive lacks such a social or political underpinning. Instead, it is a relatively unheralded personal and professional collection that has been gifted the privilege of being housed in perpetuity at a major research institution. It is an archive that no one seemed particularly keen to acquire, yet it was accepted because it was supposed to be accepted; the precedents of structural power required that it must be accepted. This is, I argue, another manifestation of the sorts of selection processes critiqued by Mbembe, Cifor, and others. Although it does not overtly exemplify violence toward marginalized communities, it is a collection that has been preserved where others have not. And through that preservation, it is placed in front of readers who might reproduce the narratives that it enfolds. At least, this is how it was placed in front of me, without my purposefully seeking it out, but due to a professional role that was necessary for my own financial stability. My role as archivist was in many ways to be a cog in the machine by which systems of archival power and privilege reproduce themselves. I was a white man who had been selected to empathize with another white man, who had been selected to have his life preserved "at the same time as others are discarded."[19]

It is for all of these reasons that I have chosen to redact the names of both the Composer and the Virtuoso from this chapter. As much as I may feel my own sense of empathy and connection with the Composer through the processes of our archival touch, as much as I learned from the process of learning about him, I see no reason why my writing should elevate his legacy above that of others whose archives have been undervalued. Omitting the Composer's name will also, I believe, free me to speak candidly about his flaws and failings, about the structures of the archive, and also about our moments of connection.

I recognize that in omitting names, I run the risk of erasing aspects of privilege that are embedded in archival practice. Tonia Sutherland has critiqued certain types of curatorial omissions as "archival amnesty," arguing that many archives have purposefully avoided curating collections that document systemic violence (such as records of lynching) and other abuses against marginalized groups, which "has real and lasting implications for restorative and transitional justice."[20] Perhaps by redacting his name, I'm letting the Composer off the hook for the operations of his privilege? Perhaps I'm protecting him, succumbing to the tendency to sympathize with men in privileged positions that Kate Manne has called "himpathy."[21] I recognize these as risks I run and cannot claim innocence. But ultimately I have chosen anonymity because I believe there is more to lose by inadvertently canonizing the Composer (and thereby reproducing cycles of privilege) than there is to gain by calling him out. His collection is, like so many others, a single example of ever-present structures of inequality that continue to inflect archival practice as well as academia more broadly.

. . .

The four sections that follow trace my responses to two particular sets of (nonmusical) objects in the collection and how my relationship with those objects has altered the way I encounter the sounds of the Composer's and the Virtuoso's music. I intend this work to emerge in dialogue with other studies of affect in the archive as well as with work that considers processes of pre-listening preparation and how it can impact the reception of musical sound.[22] My engagement with the archive functioned as something like an extended program note: it provided contextual and biographical details about the artists and compositions that altered my proclivities to hear their music in certain ways. It is this latter aspect that connects most directly to the themes of this book: by considering how these scraps of text once again interfere—perhaps productively, perhaps not—with the way musical sound is encountered. The first and third sections are ruminations on particular sets of superfluous artifacts that resonated strongly with me during my time in the collection: a set of postcards and diaries, respectively. The second and fourth chronicle my responses to musical performances captured on recordings of the Composer and the Virtuoso, read through the lens of these seemingly superfluous objects.

CASE STUDY #1: POSTCARD ABSURDISM

When I search for words to describe my impression of the Composer, one that comes to mind is "playful." Over and over throughout his life, he seemed to pursue new interests with a delighted enthusiasm—from music, to cooking, to the study of mushrooms, to the prophetic arts of the tarot and *I Ching*. Systems of organization and connections between realms (sonic and otherwise) consistently seemed to captivate him; he relished opportunities to cross genres, styles, ideas. This became a hallmark of his conducting as well, and his ensembles often programmed concerts that were quite eclectic in style and scope. He was always willing to dive into a new piece with absolute seriousness but never hemmed too closely to a single musical school of thought. This constant proclivity for irreverence and play was enabled, of course, by the Composer's level of personal and professional security noted earlier. Nevertheless, it provided one of the more compelling throughlines connecting his music and his life more broadly.

One of the more obscure corners of the collection is a shoebox-sized container of postcards. For the most part these cards were not sent *by* the Composer but *to* him from various friends and associates. Their presence nevertheless speaks to a long-standing postcarding practice that operated in both directions; the Composer received postcards because he sent postcards, which becomes clear in the content of what survives. Two of the his most frequent postcard interlocutors were a couple made up of a fellow composer he had known in college and that composer's partner, a visual artist. Let's call them Norman and Ted. The Composer and Norman had collaborated numerous times during their college years to organize concerts of their compositions alongside other works. Even these early concerts were noticeably eclectic. Material could range from Baroque violin sonatas, to works by contemporary experimentalists like John Cage and Morton Feldman, to radio hits by the Shangri-Las or the Mamas & the Papas. After graduation the Composer's path with Norman diverged, but the two kept in touch via postcards and letters. Unlike the Composer, Norman never managed to parlay his musical studies into a long-term academic position, and he would eventually drift away from composing altogether. Norman lived with Ted for many years in a coastal city in the southern United States, where he made ends meet playing instrumental parts in local ensembles and working various odd jobs. Ted, however, did achieve a degree of success in his visual art, which sometimes made appearances in the postcards as well.

The correspondence from Norman and Ted can be grouped into two main types. Those written by Ted tend to be more overtly jokey, often sent on kitschy photo cards from campy tourist destinations. Many feature whimsically cryptic language, laden with wordplay and inside jokes, which were often only partially decipherable to me. One, for example, features a drawing of a tightrope walker holding an umbrella and beach ball surrounded by all-caps implorements: "FOLD YOUR NAPKIN! DANCE MYSTERIOUSLY! ACT CHARMINGLY! THINK OCCULTLY!" Some speak in a more deliberate code, such as one stating: "I should like to re-glaze my greenhouse, & my red one, & the yellow one. Please ship panes, lots." This seems to be a reference to sending marijuana seeds, which the Composer cultivated at his home in the late 1970s. Other notes seem less coded and more purely absurd or surrealist. And still others simply show a layering of juxtaposed images (some from the original card, some hand-drawn by Ted, some via stickers) with no words at all.

The cards written by Norman tend to be a bit more discursive. They provide longer stories and updates on the couple's life, although they too are sprinkled with wordplay and absurdist flourishes. One letter (not a postcard but a full letter in this case) begins:

> Dirst Spiral Priest, Carefully grab yer antlerhorns & plan to dig-in for the evening. We, who use capitals in lieu of type (assuredly more legible than handwritten scrawls), observe certain lunar eclipses in your daunted hopes in there—we send our finest spirits for late night visitation. No, this doesn't mean we send Blastoff & Kikoo [Norman and Ted's cats] but that *is a problem!*"[23]

Other correspondence from Norman is more straightforward, often relaying frustrations in his musical life. Norman's musical activities included playing in pit orchestras in local entertainment contexts (he mentions a Beatles-themed show as well as a production of *Annie*), but little time to work on his own compositions. We find asides like "I envy your creative endeavors. Mine alas are minimal to non-existent."[24] Or "I get very sad because I've not written a note for 1½ years & don't know if I should trust my instincts."[25] In one letter, Norman troublingly attributes his failures to the success of Black composers in obtaining grants, a disturbing flash of casual racism that occasionally crops up in the almost exclusively white correspondence maintained within the Composer's archive.[26]

A shadow that creeps through much of this correspondence is the figure of the pair's other close college friend, whom we'll call Neville. Neville was also a composer, and his work reveled even more thoroughly in absurd, impossible juxtapositions that mixed allusions between classical, rock, and pop art traditions. During college, Neville and the Composer co-led a rock/performance art band known whose name was a direct tribute to a serialist composer. In an alumni magazine published during the pair's senior year, Neville is pictured brooding in the manner of a rock star in a dark unidentified room, next to a prominently placed sign that reads "[The Composer]'s Icky Garden" (perhaps another marijuana reference). On an adjacent page the Composer stands in a leather jacket and sunglasses, an outfit more in tune with rock counterculture than the staid image of university music departments. The accompanying text echoes this, noting that he "likes to appear intensely hostile when performing, dressed in black boots, sunglasses, and black leather jacket, chomping savagely on a cigar."[27] Neville's profile includes a quote from a review that frames him as "a very odd young man, a sort of half grown-up child who likes to have his fantasies acted out, a sort of orchestrator of chaotic noises and actions.... When it works—and to predict when it will work is obviously impossible—it is both funny and frightening."[28]

Despite their closeness in college, Neville was not as frequent a mail correspondent as Norman and Ted. What contact survives, however, shows an even higher density of jokes, wordplay, and coded messaging. If Norman and Ted's correspondence dabbled in camp absurdism, Neville's luxuriated in it. The longest example is an extended letter from 1977 that begins as follows (all spelling and formatting maintained from the original):

Mein lieber schwann! what

wonderfilled news that Charlie Watts is gonna run down your "[composition]" i never thought he had the taste but i *do* know he has the disciplie and o.c. you are more than welcome at my herse. there's nothing like a good perf. and they are rare, as well we all no. your missive arrived in the middle of a very

black

period of surrealism. for reasons too elaborate and strange to recount (what do you mean, "misfit"?!) i was not turning on the lights. now that [Neville's sister] is in agadir (don't jump to flash conclusions!) i am here waiting for shalom to arrive and give me $8.50. so you can imagine how excited i was to hear of your immanent i no arrival. please –end details b.c. g. and i are very frond rov rapports. and love to drink coffe while you're charter to entebbe, keep yer head down, is all i can say, when the strafing be (don't jlump on flasshy confusions) gins.

gins, what an idea![29]

Like Norman, Neville was unable to find full-time work as a composer. Several correspondences focus more on the men he was dating rather than any artistic pursuits. One letter laments that he had not composed anything for more than five years. Neville died prematurely in the early 1980s, when all three friends were in their thirties. Like the loss of Glow, the moment was a painful one. In one of the collection's few cards written by the Composer himself, we find an uncharacteristically solemn note sent in the wake of Neville's passing:

> Dear [Ted] & [Norman],
>
> [Neville] died last Wednesday ... of cancer of the liver in
>
> New York Hospital.
>
> I tried to call, but I don't have your unlisted number.
>
> He was in the hospital for several weeks trying with all his will & energy to survive; he very much wanted to survive. There was nothing that could have been done.
>
> There's nothing more to say now.
>
> Love,
>
> [The Composer][30]

As I read this letter, I can't help but feeling that the Composer wrote it in a great deal of pain. Its somber tone clashes so starkly with the few other examples we have of his lighthearted postcards. The others show the Composer deploying a writing practice very much in line with those of Neville and Norman. Again, jokes, wordplay, and codes weave through discussions of various topics:

> Dear X-turtles,
>
> Summer senza mia greetings. Now I'm sittin' 'round learning to print because I'm copying my new chorus stuck: [gives title of piece] while growing "trick cigarette stuffing" (still no seeds have blessed my mail box from riot land).
>
> With respect to reproduction of prass barts: I have heard tell from several sources that Xerox now comes in any size—LA is suppose to have several machines so Cubida Land must too—you might call around—this would be best by far.. Alpheus used to reproduce from opaque → transparency but a) it's very expensive b) it's not very good (dirty) ...[31]

Again, we find a particular sense of humor overlaying details of professional advice and life updates, all laced with small hints of countercultural transgression. The correspondence also contains elements of a camp sensibility in the sense identified in this same period by Susan Sontag. We may read, for instance, the writing's "love of the exaggerated, the 'off,' of things-being-what-they-are-not," its "glorification of character ... understood as a state of incandescence—a person being one, very intense thing," and its "sensibility of failed seriousness, of the theatricalization of experience."[32]

It should be noted that these lighthearted postcards are not the only types of letters present in the Composer's correspondence. Especially after the 1980s, the Composer saved a wide range of formal and professional letters as well, particularly related to his work as a conductor. He would sometimes reach out to composers whose work he was performing to solicit feedback about how to approach their pieces. For all of his countercultural flair among friends, the Composer was clearly adept at codeswitching to navigate the professional world of music and academia. Heterosexual privilege undoubtedly aided in this navigation as well. Despite the three composers exhibiting quite similar musical approaches in their college output, it is notable that the Composer alone (the only hetero individual among the three) managed to secure and maintain a long-term position in the academy, despite the other two receiving similar (if not greater) accolades and awards for their early compositions. Nevertheless, the closeness of the friends remains palpable, and infectious, and their continual repartee stuck with me strongly from the cataloguing process. My question, then, is: How might my awareness of this playful, seemingly meaningless hobby inflect the way I encounter the Composer's musical output?

COMPOSING THE ABSURD

The Composer's compositional practice was deeply process-based. Most of his scores in the archive are accompanied by dozens of pages of notes, planning documents, and diagrams outlining everything from macro-level forms to individual pitches, rhythms, and timbres. Notes for several of his compositions include pages of horizontal hash marks called hexagrams, which are derived from throwing yarrow sticks as part of *I Ching* divination practices (a technique in which he was likely influenced by John Cage).[33] Others feature "magic squares"—grids of numbers in which each row and column add up to the same total. These materials were used to generate tone rows and other compositional material, which were then manipulated via serialist techniques. As alluded earlier, these quasi-randomized yet systematically ordered processes placed the Composer's work squarely within the two major traditions of twentieth-century academic high modernism:

serialism and aleatoricism. They foreground values such as numerical rigor, the creation and/or dissolution of new systems of order, the embrace of chance operations, and the elevation of systematic discipline over romantic or emotional inspiration as the basis for composition.

Negative criticisms of the Composer's music often referenced the somewhat impersonal qualities that these processes could evoke. In a particularly scathing example, a cellist who had been commissioned to perform a solo cello piece took the time to write him a savagely scornful letter:

> I wish I could tell you that someone felt benefitted by having heard this piece but I can't. The most common remark was "paper music." But then I think there is great resistance to music which has or seems to have no aurally redeeming factors. I hated working on this piece every moment that was necessary. But nonetheless, my performance was significantly more accurate than the performance on the tape you sent me, which you seemed to think was good.[34]

This accusation of "paper music" implies a perception that the music reflected cold intellectuality over emotionality, system over affect. The Composer received positive reviews as well, but when criticism came, it tended to come from this direction. Yet as I got to know the more personal details of the composer's life, I found it increasingly difficult to hear his music in this way. This was not because it is necessarily incorrect (such interpretations clearly don't have anything like a verifiable truth value), but because something had changed in *me* through my extended engagement with his archive. In particular, it became difficult for me to hear his music except through the lens of his ridiculous postcards.

The composition I examine is an early work, by far the most ambitious composition of the Composer's college years—I'll refer to it as *Pebble Beach*. The piece was premiered by a group of classmates in a concert they organized in a university dining hall.[35] It was not created by the Composer alone but was a collaborative undertaking of himself, Neville, and (initially) a third friend. A detailed program note describes the bizarre origins of the project, and it too is littered with the sorts of jokey allusions that foreshadow his postcarding practice. The note was handwritten in all lowercase (à la Neville) and Xeroxed on colored paper:

> [the composer], [neville], and [third friend] were all at [university] in 19[XX], fulfilling various obligations. although the three of them were good friends, they found they really knew very little about each others' music. at first they decided to discuss musical matters at cocktail parties, but somehow they never got around to it. and studying each others' scores wasn't much help. so they finally decided to compose a piece

together. clustered precariously on a . . . fire escape one night, they planned a piece that each one of them would then compose. getting a little carried away, they made up over one hundred formal specifications that each piece would have to fulfill. specifications like:

> the piece must be in 40 sections, no two of which are of the same duration
>
> one section must contain 300 triplet eighth notes and be entitled "specialty."
>
> 0':05" into the piece is a chord describing [neville.]
>
> 4':10"   "   "   "   "   "   [third friend].
>
> 6':20"   "   "   "   "   "   [the composer].
>
> one section must be wonderful, but devoid of information about social misery. include reference to your favorite animal, not all aged. Titillate . . .
>
> each piece must end with a piano arpeggio.
>
> U.S.W.

[the composer] and [neville] finished their scores in time to celebrate new years, 19[XX]. after wandering around one night in great confusion on the pebble beach golf course, the felt their effort might be called ["Pebble Beach."] these are all premiere performances.[36]

As the note describes, the piece had its origins in a kind of elaborate game, and the full list of "over one hundred" rules is preserved in the archive. Some of the rules are strictly formal, such as those that dictate specific tone rows or motivic material. Each page of the (predominantly unmetered) scores was required to last twelve seconds, and the two versions therefore had identical requirements for both overall time and the length of each individual section. This architecture was designed so that the two pieces could be played either separately or simultaneously, with some elements syncing and others radically diverging.

Some of the rules offer more general musical suggestions, such as one that specifies that a section be marked "fugue-like," one that requires including an "impossible unison line." Others are more process-oriented, focusing on how the composers were to work. One specifies that "section 25 must be composed after section 13, which must be composed after section 17." And still others were theatrical or metamusical, such as requiring that one section be titled "Tribute to the MIGHTY OAK" and another be about a disease of each composer's choosing. The scores that were eventually produced also included details that would seem (at least at first glance) to have no impact whatsoever on the actual music produced. These included instructions about what the players were supposed to think about at certain moments of the performance, without making any sound on their instruments.[37]

It was, by any measure, a ridiculous list. And more to the point, it is quite clear that both composers *knew* it was a ridiculous list; it was designed explicitly to be ridiculous. Nowhere is this more apparent than in addendums that each sent to the other while the piece was being composed. These addendums gave instructions to *change* certain parts of the composition, even after it was already being written (oh, yes, did I mention that certain rules specified that they could change the rules?). The Composer's alteration to Neville read as followed:

Dear [Neville] (radar technitian [*sic*]),

1) Discard any plans you may have for 6'20"-6'30" in the piece.
2) Take the money (enclosed) and buy a cheap quart of bourbon.
3) Sometime on October 27th (Theo. Roosevelt's Birthday):
   a. Spend two hours "partying" (with aforementioned bottle and whatever);
   b. Then sit down and have a *great deal* of fun (laughing, swearing, spitting, etc.) writing whatever you like to fill in the 10" mentioned way above.

[-Composer][38]

Neville's countergambit, sent a month later, was even more detailed, instructing the Composer to ask his girlfriend (the aforementioned Glow, five years before her death) to mail him a random comic book. The Composer was instructed to cut out three panels (on pages specified by Neville) and to subject these to a series of processes designed to generate new pitch material.

The final scores retain all of the absurdity one would expect from such a process. In the Composer's version, for example, the opening performance instructions specify that the alto saxophone part is to be played by an amateur "Grade 2" level saxophonist, who is instructed to begin the performance by eating prune whip yogurt on stage before the piece begins. Neville's version includes a several-page-long text in the middle about a funeral for an "African chieftain," which is never conveyed to the audience but is merely supposed to influence the instrumentalists' interpretation. At one point the Composer specifies that a player is supposed to chew a piece of gum and stick the gum onto the music stand. This instruction leaves a particularly tangible legacy in the archive, as two pages of the performer's copy of the score (also in the archive) are partially inaccessible as they remain stuck together with gum. Yet for all of this absurdity, the scores are also remarkably meticulous—and, dare I say, beautiful—documents. Every notation is sharp and clear, every graphic component placed painstakingly on the page, every accent and instruction exact and evocative, every element precisely thought out. While the pair may have seemed on the outside to take nothing seriously, they clearly approached the overall task with a deep dedication that comes across in the final version.

The premiere of the piece was recorded on a reel-to-reel tape, which is also housed within the collection. As I listen to this artifact, several details stand out. From the first moments the audience is particularly audible. The room appears to be filled with exuberant college students, and their attitude toward the performance catches my ear—particularly their ongoing chatter and occasional laughter. It is not uproarious laughter, not derisive laughter, but laughter at the bare preposterousness of the spectacle unfolding before them—at the knowledge that their classmates had given themselves an impossible set of tasks, seen them through with absolute devotion, and placed the outcome on stage for all to see. This should not, I feel, be mistaken for mockery or a lack of seriousness. For all of its irreverence, the dense score is *incredibly* difficult to realize, and the performers are quite well-rehearsed. To my ear, the laughter—both of the creators and of the audience—comes across as a laughter of wonder (with perhaps a degree of uncertainty or nervousness). They laugh knowing that an absurd sonic world has been built out of thin air, and they have come together to observe the repercussions of this preposterous exercise in world-building. It is, in a word, joyous, and joyous in a way that is often lacking in concert hall presentations of contemporary new music (both then and now).

Is it too much to extrapolate something deeper from this moment of dining hall joie de vivre? Can we read a similar sense of exuberance at other moments in the Composer's career? Or should *Pebble Beach* simply be bracketed aside as mere youthful indiscretion—the bourbon-fueled romps of younger days before the Composer grew into a "mature" artist? For me as an outsider, encountering the Composer's work through the smudged lens of archive, it is at such moments that the postcards return to color my thoughts. I'm struck by the pair's continual sense of ridiculous wonder, of joy at building complex, impossible machines and witnessing the sound worlds they churn out, of an aesthetic of play rooted not in a sense that one *should* but in a sense that one *could*. This sort of disconnect from the world—its breezily anarchic "nothing matters" sensibility—is itself born of privilege, for it takes a secure position to soak so long in the lakes of the absurd. Again, I feel my responses imbued with a rich combination of admiration and antipathy, spurred by the beautiful and the pointless.

It is this sense of absurdity that I see reflected in the Composer's postcarding practice over the decades that follow. He never quite outgrows his quirky, jokey sense of exploration, even if at times he sets it aside for the sake of professional decorum. What happens if we carry the affect of this moment forward to performances of the Composer's later pieces? To the aforementioned cello piece, for instance, written off as so much "paper music?" What if his continued musical approach was rooted in a similarly disciplined rigor applied to processes with no inherent meaning? Or perhaps a belief in the confluence of meaning and meaninglessness, maybe as the basis for a certain brand of spirituality? What if he retained a desire to tease out the infinite possibility and the unavoidable absurdity of this thing we do, even as grown adults, called playing music? Not to glorify computation (as the cellist assumes) but to simultaneously engage and lampoon the very possibilities of complexity? What if we greet the Composer's high-modernism not with solemn-faced reverence but with the laughter and wonder with which we would greet a grade 2 saxophonist eating prune whip yogurt on a makeshift dining hall stage?

CASE STUDY #2: THE VIRTUOSO'S DIARIES

It was fairly late in the cataloguing process when I came across the Virtuoso's diaries. They weren't immediately recognizable as important objects—simply four unmarked books with lightly decorative covers. As the Virtuoso outlived the Composer by several years, it is unclear if he ever saw them or knew they existed. It's possible that they simply got lumped in with other materials when family members prepared the collection to be sent to the archive.

To this day, I have some reservations about their presence in the collection. On the one hand, the contents feel undeniably private. They inscribe deeply personal aspirations, goals, triumphs, and disappointments from throughout the Virtuoso's life and career. Yet on the other hand, it isn't unusual to include diaries in historical archives, as they record aspects of history that can be lost in administrative papers alone. Increasingly since the 1980s, diaries have been employed as source material in a wide range of historical studies. They have provided particularly invaluable sources for engaging with the lives of women during various historical periods, whose lives and writings have too often been excluded from other types of public repositories.[39] Nevertheless, the entries being so recent makes looking at them feel fraught and voyeuristic. I continue to struggle with how to process them, or whether they should be there at all.

I make the choice to include them in this discussion, however, based in part off their very first entry, which already seems to speak to the presence of an unnamed future reader. Penned at the age of sixteen, it is an auspicious opening, declaring nothing less than a philosophy of life and art with the lofty self-assuredness of a teenaged artist. Following several opening quotes from the poet Conrad Aiken, the Virtuoso's prose begins as follows:

> A fitting way to begin? I suppose that is my philosophy—my purpose, if there is such a thing—to love beauty. I opened deliberately today a door of my mind—to show the vastness and extent of what I consider meaningful. I only hope the effect was what I intended. It hurt me, and it also hurt the receiver. But it had to be done.

At the conclusion of the entry, she pauses to ruminate on who might read these words.

> Reading back, I often think how stupid this might sound to someone, which brings me to the point of why I am writing it. For someone else, for me? I don't know. Another question with no answer? Maybe it's just 'cause I have all this things roiling in my mind & I can't really tell anybody, but if I write something, *anything*, down, I have the vague feeling that someone will someday read it & maybe can feel in some small way the way I feel.[40]

There are sometimes moments when the archive seems to speak back to you. Where it feels like it is reaching toward you as much as you are reaching toward it.[41] Here the Virtuoso speaks to a future reader in an unknown time. Of course in her teenage years she could have had no idea that reader would be a complete stranger—a white male musicologist in the 2010s, reading her words in a library hundreds of miles away. I hesitate. Do I have a right to continue? Can I be the one who "feel[s] in some small way the way [she] feels?" Will anyone else? Or if I do not, will these texts simply languish unread, the feelings she desires to share left untapped? And complicating matters further, would the Virtuoso at the end of her life feel the same way about having these thoughts read as she did as a teenager? To whom am I ethically answerable? Her at sixteen? Her before her death several decades later? Both?

In the end, I cautiously proceed. She says she has a story to tell, thoughts to share, even if I am not the ideal narrator. I can only do my best to convey them in a way that honors her. Perhaps others will follow (I hope so). But leaving them unexamined seems like a more egregious erasure.

. . .

The majority of the diary entries are written when the Virtuoso is between the ages of sixteen and twenty-five. They follow her through her teenage training as an instrumentalist, through her undergraduate years at a conservatory, and through her graduate studies at the institution where she meets the Composer. From the outset the entries portray a dedicated, self-critical, and sensitive individual. The diaries are clearly used for therapeutic value, and the Virtuoso tends to write most during periods of disappointment and depression (she even notes this herself in an early entry).[42] This observation points to how the diaries give only a partial view of the Virtuoso's full life experience: her successes and times of joy often tend to be bypassed, and must be inferred between the lines (as we will see further below).

Music plays a central role in her both her scholastic and emotional life, and an intense dedication to her craft is evident from the outset. In the midst of many entries detailing the pains of young love, she describes how music provides a consistent point of stability and comfort:

> I guess music is the only stable thing I can hold on to. I'm afraid of people. They hurt too much, too often. I'm never sure of their truth. They lie too much. Say things I don't believe, don't want to hear. They are fickle and base. The music sometimes hurts, but that's only because it's so beautiful and I don't mind that.[43]

She practices intensely, but rarely writes about that. More often, the entries focus on her social life and romantic relationships, which repeatedly cause her pain when they fail to live up to expectations.

Music provides her anchor, and the Virtuoso places so much faith and hope in her art that it becomes the source of both her greatest joys and greatest disappointments. The latter comes to the fore when she auditions for conservatories near the end of high school, an occasion for which she practices at a grueling pace. Exhausted and emotionally drained, the news that she does not get into Juilliard leaves her reeling for months:

> 17 years old and I'm totally disillusioned by life, love, and now my last bastion, my last defense knocked out from under me. If I don't even make [my fallback conservatory]—that's it—totally, completely.... It's the last imaginary thing I staked my life on, and it's gone. There's nothing, nothing more to live for. And if Plato is right, then I am ready to die.

Although she would ultimately be accepted into another well-known institution, the wound from the Juilliard rejection would sting for some time

("Not that I'm not grateful [for the acceptance to the other school] but [the Juilliard rejection] quite deflates the ego"). The entries of her college years are marked by a continual love-hate relationship with music, accompanied by periods of isolation in practice rooms, fraught love affairs, and a deepening depression. Auditions continue to bring out her most depressive tendencies, and the cutthroat nature of the program causes additional stress. She continually pushes herself to improve and practice harder, while bemoaning classmates whom she sees as lacking a real dedication to beauty, but who succeed only because of social connections:

> I will show them—show them all—what a joke play along and laugh, laugh, fools—they are the fools, not me. They can't see, I can see through them, around them, above them! To the depths and heights—from delirium to despair! To the end—to the bottom of the world—filled with black. And the hysterical laughter filled with tears consumes me.

At times, she practices eight to nine hours a day, seeing practically no one except her cat and plants.

By her early twenties, in her final undergraduate years, her depression reaches its most intense period. It is compounded by professional pressures that mount as she approaches graduation (including applications to graduate school). These entries are some of the hardest to read, as she makes repeated attempts at suicide. At her nadir a full page is simply scrawled in capital letters with the repeated phrase "I DON'T WANT TO LIVE." Eventually she is accepted into a master's program at a different school in another part of the country, which eases the pressure somewhat and marks the beginning of a new chapter in her still young life. She doesn't like the school at first, finding it less rigorous than her pervious institution. But she gradually comes around by the spring semester, appreciating it less for its arts training but more for its sense of community: "Between [various friends and teachers], it's kind of given me a new outlook of myself—and I feel good about myself and confident about myself in a way I've never felt before."

It is during her master's studies that the Virtuoso first meets the Composer. And I pause to provide a content warning here that the following sections detail a romantic affair between a male instructor and female student—a deeply troubling context, to say the least. He is already a teacher at the school, being eleven years her senior. The Virtuoso is actively composing at this time, and she takes private composition lessons with him for several semesters. One of the diary's most momentous entries is an account of one such lesson, during which he teaches her about the *I Ching* (a practice that she continued exploring long after). She writes about both the lesson and the Composer in glowing prose:

> I will never forget the tone of his voice, the windowless room, only lit by a fluorescent desk light—holding the yarrow sticks. It was somehow very mystical and spiritual. But what amazes me even more that this man only sees me 2 or 3 times a week [but H]e is so goddamn perceptive!! What other person, in the capacity of a teacher, who sees countless other people as much [as] me could be that intuitive.

The entry goes on to state that the Composer had become a more important influence on her than anyone else during her time at the school, and she expresses a desire to get to know him more: "[He] represents a spirit and an essence, a philosophy, a way of being to me—and not only to me but to many. I wish I knew the real person, his feelings, behind all that. I wonder what the thoughts and feelings of the real person are."

You may already feel uncomfortable reading about this emerging relationship between a teacher and a significantly younger student (I know that I do). Up to this point there had been no romantic contact between the two. But the floodgates open a month and half later: "My mind is totally blown out of the universe—I feel like I'm in hyperspace—[The Composer] is madly in love with me!!!!! God, my life has turned 180°—I'm totally devastated everytime I think about it!!!" At a lesson the previous day the Composer confided to her that "I've had the biggest crush on you for the last two years," and claimed that she had made him feel a way he hadn't felt for years. The entry spins out the romantic tale in blissful tones:

> I felt like jello inside—I told him I felt so much the same for him and we held each other and kissed. Then we went for a walk in the fields across from school . . . and held each other like we never wanted to let go . . .
>
> Nothing has ever been more right—God I want [this to] work so badly I'm afraid it won't . . . God I want this, oh please God—it's too wonderful—it will never happen again—we can't let this go.

Numerous uncomfortable complications had to be overcome for the relationship to proceed. In addition to being her teacher, the Composer was also living with another partner at the time. Yet the blossoming of the relationship is portrayed in the diary as being so mutual and so intense, that both sides would work to make it come to pass.

The Virtuoso's ardor remains strong in the weeks that follow. Unlike her other (already infrequent) moments of bliss in the diaries—which were always short-lived and bookended by bouts of depression—her relationship with the Composer spawns an extended period of happiness. Fascinatingly, it also provides the archive's most textured window into the Composer's personality—which are only hinted at in his own materials:

> I see more and more sides of him emerging—fascinating because for so long I saw only the one side—there's the man that too was defeated by life—the man that's too sensitive of the world—too honest—I hope I can help him out of that—not the honesty—I mean finding ways of dealing with it better. . . . He functions fine within the world but yet he doesn't accept I don't think what I have been able to—well, I guess, how could he?—seeing his circumstances. Maybe he is even much more sensitive than I am. That part of him scares me some—only because I know what I've gone through and the enormous struggle I went through to deal with it . . .
>
> Then there's the side of him that's totally brilliant but doesn't know how to change his oil filter or fix a flat tire on a bicycle. There's the side of him I never saw—the old . . . hippie—long hair and a beard—taking huge quantities of whatever—having the energy of six people on speed, writing crazy music with [Neville]. There's the boy in him that's still shy all of a sudden, who looks at me with dog eyes. And there's the lover—strong, passionate, sensitive, romantic, who swears by candlelight that he loves me—and I love him.

It's hard not to read these descriptions of the Composer against the other material I had encountered in the archive. The manic activity of his college years and personal stagnation of the early 1980s are hinted elsewhere, but the Virtuoso outlines them in full color. As the Composer himself seems to have kept no diaries or similarly confessional materials, her accounts give a singular window into his interior life.

Reading the diary's account, I remain deeply disturbed by the couple's early relationship. They would later claim that they got together only after the conclusion of her studies.[44] The diary contradicts this, however, showing the relationship beginning in February of her final semester. At the very least, the power dynamic was starkly uneven, with him a faculty member in the program where she was a student. For myself, a jazz scholar reading from the late 2010s, it's hard to not read these actions against a recent wave of news stories about sexual harassment and the disgusting exploitation of power differentials in jazz studies programs and among musical colleagues.[45] As such, the episode raises troubling specters of abuse and predation.

With the benefit of the archive's hindsight, I know that their relationship will eventually grow into a healthy, long-lived, and mutually respectful one. In fact, I knew of their devoted life together well before I had encountered the diary's troubling account of their initial meeting. The two would marry seven years later and remain together until the Composer's death. They collaborated on numerous musical projects and their home became a welcoming place of retreat for colleagues and visiting artists. Yet coming across these entries on their own, as a moment in time arising without knowledge of the future, with a teacher declaring his desire for a student (during a lesson, no less!)—a student who has long battled layers of depression, fragility, vulnerability, and failed love affairs—the encounter continually presents me with a distinct discomfort. Even as I write this, it sits like a stone in the pit of my stomach.

I still sit with this discomfort. I don't know what to do with it. On the one hand, framing their relationship purely as exploitative would seem to undermine the Virtuoso's agency as an autonomous figure and diarist, who perceived (correctly, as it would turn out) that the relationship could provide an escape from a long cycle of abusive partnerships. But on the other hand, papering over these worrying details in service to a "happy ending" seems to endorse the idea of such starkly unequal affairs in a way that I remain deeply troubled by. I make no effort to resolve this dilemma, and instead I sit with the discomfort it produces: glad for the Virtuoso's happiness in the outcome but still disturbed by the broader implications.

Perhaps the most oblique testimony of the Virtuoso's love for the Composer comes not in the diary's entries but in its absences. As noted, she tended to write most consistently during bouts of sadness and depression. And almost as soon as their relationship begins, the diary's entries immediately become more sporadic. The few entries from this period speak predominantly to how happy she was with the Composer. Whereas previous periods found her writing almost every week, soon a year goes by with only two entries. Then three years with none at all. Notably, these years also saw many of the Virtuoso's highest professional accomplishments. She wins awards as a composer and cofounds an ensemble that would create some of her most celebrated work. Yet none of these triumphs appear in the diary. Even the couple's wedding is bypassed entirely. In these years the diary becomes a space to check in only occasionally, rather than a place of respite amid a difficult existence.

This is not to say that she did not undergo professional frustrations, and several of these appear as well. A number of entries express frustration at her inability to secure a full-time faculty job at the school, despite the enormous success of her ensemble. Whereas she witnesses male colleagues talk themselves into jobs by "shooting their mouths off" (a phrase echoing her earlier criticism of her college classmates), she writes about feeling typecast as being merely the Composer's partner, rather than an artist of equal stature. She eventually finds work on the school's instrumental faculty for several years, only to be disrespectfully dismissed after a debacle in which she was made to reaudition for her own job (which was then not renewed).

Amplifying this frustration is an awareness that despite the couple's frequent collaborations, she observes how as the Composer grows older (as a white male composer/conductor), he receives an *increasing* stream of job offers, while as she grows older (as a female composer/instrumentalist), she is too frequently dismissed as being past her prime.[46] This double standard galls her, as does his occasional inability to see it, leading to some of the very few entries in which she expresses frustration with the Composer. In one episode she describes a dinner with him and several other male faculty members. Over the course of the meal she grows disgusted at their chummy insider banter, so caught up in their own internal politics that they can barely be bothered to acknowledge her presence. It's a stark tableau of male privilege recorded in the diary's pages. As she calls out this privilege, however, her writing suddenly becomes laced with anti-Semitism (the only example of it in the diary), which pulls me up short: "I guess it's because they're all Jewish (and I swore I'd never have a relationship with a Jewish man again—too insecure and neurotic)." Any moment I begin to empathize with the archive, such moments of failure pull me back (who are these people whose stories I've grown invested in)? But despite the Virtuoso's disappointment in the Composer in this and other moments, despite her ability to recognize his flaws, the vast majority of her descriptions of him remain consistently loving, reverent, and grateful, even within the most private confines of her diaries.

The Virtuoso fills three diaries over a period of twenty-one years. And then, for nearly a decade: nothing. She returns to them only after the Composer's death, with a series of heart-wrenching entries. Her depression returns in full force, and her journaling practice returns with it. A handful of entries:

> [H]ere I am—as Moses said. Well, what's [it] like to be a widow at the age of [XX]? That's the question on most people's minds. I would guess a lot of people go through a divorce or some such around now—but death—eyh—signing death certificates—naming beneficiaries and such.
>
> [Composer]—I want to go to Alaska by owl. Will you take me? I want to know where my starship captain has gone. Where are you [Composer]? Yours fondly, [Virtuoso].
>
> Where are you [Composer]? We need you. We are all trying so hard to be here. I don't know if I can continue. This is not my handwriting. I don't know if can continue.

Perhaps the most grieving examples come in a series of entries that are simply written in enormous letters, filling up entire pages in anguished cries:

"Where are you [Composer]?"

"I will go out of my mind."

"I will blow my head off with a shotgun."

It is unclear how long these undated entries of the fourth diary continue; unlike the earlier diaries they contain no dates. The Virtuoso herself would pass away just a few years later. In an obituary a friend would write that the Virtuoso never really recovered from the Composer's premature death.[47] These final entries provide a window into the depths of her mourning.

. . .

I have taken far longer than I intended in writing this section on the Virtuoso's diaries. Admittedly, I could think of no other way to relate the affective force of the materials or their impact on me as a reader. I cannot claim to truly know the Virtuoso (especially while many of her friends and family remain living), but I have nonetheless become invested in her story, her successes and failures, her joy and pain. The writer of these diaries comes through as a complex figure who steadfastly believed in the power of music to transcend a world that constantly disappointed her. She approached her music as not a diversion but as a path to salvation. It was the only way she knew to work past the challenges of a life filled with love, loss, despair, sexism, triumph, and disappointment. While the diaries undoubtedly give a skewed account (ignoring, as they do, many moments of happiness and foregrounding periods of despair), they present a powerfully expressive account of her existence.

GRAVITY, EXPRESSIVITY, AND THE SOLO

The diaries are by far the most detailed artifacts related to the Virtuoso that are preserved in the Composer's collection. And while they provide the richest personal texts on both figures, they speak relatively little about her musical practice. Unlike the Composer's detailed scores, notes, and documents surrounding his own pieces, no comparable material exists for the Virtuoso in the collection. The diaries' singular presence thus already runs a distinct risk of archivally reinforcing gendered associations: his memory persists in scores, planning documents, professional correspondence; hers in the private, personal, and emotional space of a diary. This creates a potential to skew the stories we are capable of telling from within the walls of the archive; it is another dead end.

With these limitations in mind, my engagement with the diaries did again alter the way I encountered the Virtuoso's music. Specifically they suggested to me a contrast between the Virtuoso's musical practice and that which I outlined earlier for the Composer, despite their numerous collaborations. Her writings convey a comparatively greater sense of gravity surrounding musical endeavors. I mean this not in the sense of rigor or dedication (which he certainly possessed as well) but an impression that during times of difficulty, music was the only thing that kept the Virtuoso tethered to the world. She strives for perfection, beats herself up when she falls short, pours every ounce of her being into her craft. Whereas with the Composer it sometimes feels as though if music hadn't worked out, he might have simply drifted to other interests—gardening, or mysticism, or playing in pit orchestras with Norman—the Virtuoso's world possessed no other options; she devoted herself to music with her entire being. If his approach to music was rooted in a sense of irreverence and play, hers expressed a much more direct need for art to be metaphysical and transcendent.

Music was the Virtuoso's respite, her point of stability in a world that deserved no trust. But it also created the constant possibility of failure. Every audition, every performance was a matter of life and death, not an opportunity to chuckle or listen in wonder at whatever sounds happened to emerge. It's one of the factors that initially made her uncomfortable at the school of her master's program: the Composer and his colleagues' sense of carefree exploration seemed to her to reflect a loosening of standards, an abandonment of the pursuit of perfection. Even as she adjusted and grew comfortable in the new milieu, her position there was never stable. She remained in that category of faculty off-handedly referred to as "contingent," always one administrator's decision away from having her professional life pulled out from under her. Once again, we see here how the Composer's relative comfort—the comfort to joke, to laugh, to try things out without concern for consequences—derives in large part from the privilege of his position in an artistic and professional world. This makes the Virtuoso's comparative precarity all the more enraging.

This is not to make either figure one-dimensional. The composer certainly saw his share of tragedy, including the early deaths of both Glow and Neville. And as the diaries attest, he had deeply vulnerable, sensitive, and brooding sides. He battled depression and alcoholism as well, but left no diaries to chronicle his pain. It is only hinted at in the archives. And likewise, the Virtuoso could be deeply funny and jovial, even within (again!) a small handful of postcards that she sent back home to the Composer during her travels.[48] The two loved to entertain at their home and enjoyed many years of happiness together. But they seemed to arrive to this point via different routes. Even their divergent handling of loss is notable: three years after the Composer lost Glow, he had moved on and was living with a new lover. Three years after the Virtuoso lost the Composer. she too was dead, following the struggles imprinted in her final diary.

. . .

The Virtuoso's most prominent recording was an album recorded in the 1990s under her own name. The album takes its title from a solo composition for her instrument written by a prominent serialist. The piece was written specifically for the Virtuoso and makes up the album's first track. It is fiercely difficult, overfilled with challenging registral and dynamic jumps that create an impression of dense counterpoint. Single notes often require manipulations in timbre and loudness that can turn on a dime, shifting from raspy, overtone-laden groans to bel canto declamations. As a whole, it is a piece that requires absolute focus and concentration to achieve both accuracy and expressivity. When I listen to the Virtuoso's performance—unavoidably tinted by my reading of her archive—I hear something quite different from the supposed impersonality of an egoless serialism. There is nothing like paper music here. Folded within her staggering technique, the performance feels distinctly emotional—each note saturated with humanity, desire, pain. She takes the piece at a slower clip than later recordings, wrenching every nuance from every note. Despite the overabundance of material that must be kept under control, her performance doesn't feel harried or compulsive about fitting everything in. Each moment is savored, turned over, and excavated, even as it makes way for the next flurry that comes just behind.

If the Composer's musical process pivoted around play with chance operations and working with whatever happened to come out, the Virtuoso's required approaching whatever was present (whether tonal or atonal, mimetic or abstract) with all of her technical and expressive resources, drawing out potential reservoirs of meaning and import. Other selections on the album show similar tendencies, though via other routes. Her approach toward two pieces written by the Composer strike me as slightly more dispassionate. The performances here convey something more like an aleatoric flatness—letting each note and phrase sit and rest on its own presence rather than culling it for expressive potential (in the liner notes the Composer refers to the works as striving to be both directionless and timeless). A slightly different sort of reservedness permeates her interpretation of an aleatoric piece by another composer, which sways along curves of woozy impressionism without building anything resembling an arc or climax. By contrast, her take on an electro-acoustic composition presents an incredible study in tension and release, building to shattering heights and declamations in a series of powerful episodes. The contrast in her approaches not only conveys the full scope of the Virtuoso's instrumental command but her devotion to crafting a unique aesthetic appropriate to each piece.

In total, though—like my listening to *Pebble Beach*—I can't help but listen to the music in dialogue with the archive's traces. My journey with the Virtuoso through years of struggle, disappointment, and unflinching belief in music's power to lift her up underlie every act of my audition. A note or phrase that might have passed without comment becomes elevated in my ear into a moment of all-consuming meaning and expression. The album is more powerful to me as a result, certainly more than it would have been to me before my experiences in the archive. Is this a distortion, or an enhancement? Am I an unreliable narrator? I'm not sure. But unquestionably my affective encounters in the archive have left me changed.

CONCLUSION: ARCHIVES AND AFFECTS, PUSHES AND PULLS

Taken in total, my experience working through the collections of the Composer and the Virtuoso remind me repeatedly about the blurry lines separating the realms of affect (sonic/musical, material, empathetic) and discourse (textual, factual, narrative) in the archive. I entered into the process with practically no connection to the pair in either capacity. I neither knew anything nor had any particular feelings about them. But over the course of cataloguing their materials, I gradually found myself enmeshed in both. I learned more about them and I grew connected enough to feel both moments of admiration and moments of disgust and disappointment. There were times when the archive pulled me toward them and times when it pushed me away. And often I couldn't foresee or control when these movements would occur. Like thumbing across Glow's death certificate in a stack of boring letters, like spilling an envelope of golden seeds, I found myself stumbling into feelings at unexpected moments.

You could argue that my situation was a unique one. A researcher doesn't typically enter into an archival engagement with as much of a blank slate as I had, knowing so little about the subject. Yet like Farge, Cifor, and others have suggested, this affective potential of the archive to move us never really goes away either, no matter how much knowledge we accrue. Even a seasoned expert can come across artifacts that compel them admire their subjects in new ways, or that force them to confront an uglier side of their stories. In the case of artists and musicians, how can we not encounter their artistic output differently after the terms of our connection have shifted? Silent stacks of paper though they are, I can't unhear the Virtuoso's diaries, the Composer's postcards. What we can do is to try to remain aware of these pushes and pulls as we listen, think, and write about them. And more specifically, we can try to think about how these affective pushes and pulls weigh upon the disciplines, institutions, and power structures in which we conduct our work.

As I have proceeded through this chapter, it dawns on me that much of what I have written might be read as akin to outdated (and sometimes problematic) approaches to musical biography. The process of interpreting musical works against a backdrop of biographical details is as old as musicology itself. But there are several important divergences as well. First, I make no claims to truth in any of my interpretations. To the contrary, the more I outline them, the less certain I am. In hearing the Composer's work alongside the absurdism of his postcards, I don't suggest that this is how they "should" be heard. Rather, I claim only that my own listening bears traces of the archive's affective residue. This might have very little to do with any sort of objective reality. Archives are fickle, incomplete things, always skewed by their materialities, organizational paradigms, and curatorial choices.

Perhaps those who knew the Composer or the Virtuoso would hear things differently, as they carry a different set of memories and intimacies. Perhaps a different set of artifacts would yield a different response. Perhaps there were other lost letters or destroyed diaries that could tell a different story. Perhaps all of this speaks more about my own proclivities to bask in lighthearted postcards rather than deciphering dense numerical diagrams or systems of divination. I claim only that these particular materials moved me, they shifted my ears in new directions and provoked me to hear differently. Such observations lie not in the realm of facts, but in the affects passed between objects and their observers. This again speaks to the importance of cultivating broader, activist-archiving practices as outlined earlier, allowing for a broader range of stories and engagements.

Second, I am not separate from the archive's biases. Like all readers, I am equally conditioned by the social structures that come with my positionality. As such, it is important to continually ask how my own position impacts the relationships I developed with both figures. Because archival affects are not inevitable. Two readers might respond very differently, just as two listeners might respond differently to the same piece of music. But the stakes of those responses remain crucial. Am I too quick to see the Composer and the Virtuoso as relatable because of the background I share with them as a white person of privilege? By relying too heavily on an archive that cements gender, race, and other hierarchies, am I merely reproducing systems of power that persist at the material level just as they do at the social one? Is my choice to omit their names an appropriate intervention to disrupt systems of canonization, or a cowardly one to limit culpability for people I now feel connected to? These are ongoing concerns that undoubtedly color my interpretation. I can only have failed.

In the end I can recognize only that my encounters in the archive have left me changed, exiting with different capacities than I entered with. Different ways of hearing and different ways of writing. Those changes rub against other affective movements put into motion by the music itself. The archive provides an endlessly unfolding program note to the sounds I encounter, leaving me unable to hear them with fresh ears that never existed.

PART III

Death and Deadness

6 Deploying Deadness in Louis Armstrong's House

PROLOGUE: A WALK FROM THE TRAIN

Let me be your guide, as we soundwalk a house of the dead.

The year is 2005. You decided to travel by subway, getting off at 103rd Street–Corona Plaza. The bustle of businesses and pedestrian traffic beneath the elevated train resounds with a buzz familiar to anyone who has spent time in Brooklyn or Queens (Manhattan's is a little different, of course). The train rattles into the distance as you descend the stairs and turn north, away from bodegas and other small business, into the more residential neighborhoods. It's amazing how quickly the scene changes. A block in and you see houses—not apartment buildings but actual single-family structures. Soon it's almost entirely homes and families. Cacophony fades and the soundscape breathes, punctuated by kids coming home from school, friends and family greeting each other (in both Spanish and English; the neighborhood is home to a vibrant Dominican community), even the occasional bird call. It's the sort of outer borough soundscape that doesn't get shown in media depictions of New York but provides a crucial community for millions of residents.

In about ten minutes you reach your destination. It's a modest two-story house, similar in most respects to many others that you've passed. Its most unique element is its brick façade, a contrast to the clapboard that covers most of the neighboring homes (it once covered this one, too). The lot next door has no building, but instead it encloses a small Japanese-inspired garden of crisp wandering lines and a small koi pond. You meander over to the front door but find it locked. So you go to the only other entrance you see, in what appears to have once been the garage. Now, however, it's a fully enclosed glass storefront, through which you enter a small, one-room gift

FIGURE 6. Louis Armstrong House Museum, exterior. Courtesy of the Louis Armstrong House Museum.

shop. A docent looks up from the desk and smiles: welcome to the Louis Armstrong House Museum (Figure 6).

. . .

Open to the public since 2003, the museum is located inside Armstrong's residence from the final three decades of his life, practically the only home he ever owned. It's a modest house by any measure, but especially when you consider Armstrong's stature as perhaps the single most influential musician of the twentieth century. It was purchased in 1943 by Armstrong's wife, Lucille, who arranged the sale while Louis was away on tour. Prior to that, the trumpeter had spent so much of his time touring that he generally rented his residences (though he had briefly co-owned a house in Chicago).[1] It was Lucille who finally convinced him that a permanent home was worth the investment. She envisioned it as a temporary space—a "starter home" in real estate parlance—to live in until they were ready to upgrade to something more lavish. Louis, however, was so profoundly moved by the gesture and fell so deeply in love with the neighborhood that he never wanted to leave. In lieu of moving, Lucille instead made incremental upgrades in the

Deploying Deadness in Armstrong's House / 143

FIGURE 7. Louis Armstrong on his front steps with neighborhood children. Photo by Chris Barham, courtesy of the Louis Armstrong House Museum.

decades that followed (the brick façade and the garden are the two most prominent). The couple lived in the home for the remainder of their lives, with Louis passing in 1971 and Lucille twelve years later in 1983 (Figure 7).[2]

Standing inside the gift shop, light streams in through floor-to-ceiling windows where the garage door once stood. The neighborhood outside remains visible; the street is so close you can almost touch it. It's a cozy space (get used to it, most of the house will be), but it's neatly organized with shelves of CDs, books, T-shirts, and the sort of merchandise one might find in any museum gift shop. A few select images of Armstrong are displayed as well, including a blown-up photo of the trumpeter performing in Ghana in the mid-1950s. The docent amiably tells you that the concert was purported to have drawn a staggering five hundred thousand fans.

The soundscape of the shop marks an immediate change from the world outside. The street's white noise gives way to the strains of Armstrong's famous recordings, which welcome you in with their familiarity. Not too loud, of course—they mustn't drown out conversation or impede transactions. But loud enough for Armstrong's iconic voice and golden trumpet to shine through. There's no chance to get lost in the sound, though, since the docent has continued to engage you in small talk: "Where are you visiting from today? Did you find us okay? How was the walk from the subway?" Sometimes two or three employees are present, rarely more, but today it's just one. Eventually they go over the museum details and admission prices: eight dollars for a forty-minute guided tour. Upon paying the fee, you are invited into an adjacent room to browse an exhibit area inside of what was once the home's basement. You're welcome to wait here until the tour is ready to begin. Or you could also choose to stroll through the garden if you'd prefer. The weather is nice, so you choose the latter.

WHAT ARE WE DOING HERE?

The employee who is helping you, I should probably mention, is me. Or at least it was. From 2005 to 2006, I worked part-time at the Armstrong Museum, giving tours, helping to manage the shop, and opening and closing the space several days a week. My official title was "museum assistant," and I worked closely with program officer Deslyn Downes Dyer, and executive director Michael Cogswell. Over that period I gave approximately one hundred tours of the home to groups ranging from a single person to large tour and school groups. Visitors included knowledgeable jazz afficionados, interested neighborhood residents, and uninitiated tourists who were learning Armstrong's story for the very first time. The arc of the tour followed a standardized script written by Cogswell, which was laid out in a small booklet I received on my first day: "Interpretive Program for the Louis Armstrong House: A Handbook for Docents, Volunteers, and Other Staff of the Louis Armstrong House."[3]

Each guide was encouraged to put their own personal spin on the material, focusing on details of particular interest to them. As museum assistant, I worked with about seven or eight guides, each of whom had their own particular flavor (some are described below). You see, when I offered myself as your guide, I do bring certain relevant credentials. More to the point, though, you're probably wondering why I've chosen to return to this space now, here, in the midst of a book about sonic encounter. The answer hinges upon the unique role that sound plays within the museum's mission of reanimating Armstrong as a palpable, almost ghostly presence. Cogswell even liked to say that he set up the house so it would feel as though the Armstrongs had just stepped out for a moment and could return any second.

The most powerful examples of Armstrong's ghostly presence come through a particular form of sonic encounter that occurs several times during the tour. As a guide, I repeatedly witnessed these encounters evoking intense affective responses from visitors (I'll say more on the nature of the encounters shortly—I don't want to ruin the surprise). Current guides in 2020 have assured me that this use of sound remains a central part of the museum experience.[4] Yet although it is a deployment of sound that triggers these responses, I argue that the effect stems from something deeper than the simple presence of sound alone. Nor does sound act only as a secondary supplement—mere window dressing to a predominantly ocularcentric museum experience. Rather, the power of these sonic encounters emerges from an intentional, curatorial *suturing of sound and space* that is central to the museum's logic. Sounds confront us differently because of the spaces in which they are heard, just as the spaces confront us differently because of the sounds we hear within them. This may appear as something of a truism, but the particular impact, the specific brand of overlaying sensory pasts and presents during the tour allows these audio-spatial relationships to echo and feedback in resonant ways. Sound and space are not the only factors in play either. The tour prompts additional imbrications between aspects of memory (individual, cultural, and neighborhood), emotion, musical affect, quasi-religious reverence, and domestic intimacy, giving rise to powerful cross-wirings of sensory and affective circuits. It is this overloading of our perceptual circuitry, I argue, that fuels the overwhelming responses that I witnessed so frequently.

Two conceptual frameworks are central to the descriptions I offer. The first is that of the soundwalk, a device that I use to structure the following account. The practice of soundwalking has a long and well-known tradition within sound studies. In its simplest form, soundwalking simply refers to any act of walking while attending closely to the sounds that one encounters. Hildegard Westerkamp, a pioneer in the practice, introduces it this way: "A soundwalk is any excursion whose main purpose is listening to the environment.... The intention of soundwalking is listening. Soundwalks can take place in the mall, at the doctor's office, down a neighbourhood street or at the bus stop. The focus on listening can make this a meditative activity, sometimes shared in silence with others."[5]

As Andra McCartney observes, despite Westerkamp's statement that a soundwalk can occur in any location, the early history of the practice was most often associated with ecological projects spearheaded by figures like Jean Francois Augoyard, R. Murray Schafer, Westerkamp herself, and other researchers associated with the World Soundscape Project in Vancouver, Canada, in the 1970s. This work emphasized the way that sound—particularly (though not exclusively) the sounds of nature—provided a way of becoming oriented in the world. Sound, they argued, was an integral mode in which we understand the environment around us. As such, the project advocated that characteristic soundscapes should be protected, just as we protect essential landmarks or cultural artifacts.[6] Later artists would take the practice in other directions, including soundwalks in urban settings, soundwalks incorporating added and/or musical supplements, and soundwalks conducted in conjunction with various forms of recording.

The choice to structure this chapter as a soundwalk through the Armstrong House is not intended merely as a literary device. It draws from soundwalking's long tradition of engaging with the ties between sound and space. But instead of focusing primarily on the way that sounds orient us in our environment, I am equally interested in the way that our environment orients us within sounds. Namely, I ask how encountering particular sounds in the context of particular spaces can work to change their impacts. Space prompts us to hear sounds differently, generating different affects from what we would experience in, say, an anechoic chamber or a scholarly archive. Though one could argue that the museum (as a registered National Historic Landmark) does preserve certain elements of the home's sonic environment, I am especially interested in ways that the museum's administrators and tour guides construct the tour to function as a particular type of sonic experience. In a nod to the museum context I use the terms "curation" and "curational" to refer to this type of sonic composing. Though the intent of this process is primarily educational/pedagogical/honorific, this does not preclude the possibility of generating powerful affective responses.[7]

While I narrate what follows in the first person, I grant that my interpretation is merely one reading of this tour process, and that others undoubtedly experience it in very different ways.[8] My perspective was one of a white cis male student of jazz history but an outsider to the neighborhood (though I did get to know numerous residents over the year that I worked at the Armstrong House). Despite my limited positionality, I argue that the museum's curational process functioned (for better and for worse) by attempting to place sounds into a carefully tailored narrative, which I attempt to retell from my position as a tour guide.

In addition to considering sonic orientations in space, I am also interested in orientations in time. Like other historic house museums, one major purpose of the Armstrong House is to evoke a sense of pastness. It creates an imagined world in which visitors can place themselves alongside Armstrong, musing over what it would be like to cohabit the space with him. This necessarily becomes something of an exercise in temporal crosswiring: we *know* we are in the present, but we *imagine* ourselves in the past. The museum is deeply complicit in this process and designs sensory inputs to facilitate the illusion. We envision ourselves seeing what Armstrong saw, touching what he touched, walking where he walked. And, of course, sounds play a pivotal role.

The second conceptual framework for this chapter is that of "deadness," a term coined by Jason Stanyek and Benjamin Piekut. In their article on the subject, deadness refers to the continued resonance, labor, and profitability of dead artists and individuals. It is not an absence but a continued collaboration *between* the living and the dead through various media, which the authors refer to as "intermundane." Extending models of distributed agency drawn from Karen Barad and Bruno Latour, the theory suggests that the dead continue to generate effects in the present through their various traces, mediated and otherwise. And just as the dead continue to act as agents in the present, the archival media that preserve their traces are similarly agential. Indeed, the "dead" in Stanyek and Piekut's deadness refers not only to the deceased themselves but to any labor or capital that can be abstracted from human bodies (and sometimes extended beyond their life), whether through technology or other means. In their words: "Our investigation into the intermundane suggests an extension of this important point—that not only living human workers, but also the ostensibly 'dead' labor of technology and discipline, and even the 'dead labor' of the human dead—contains within it the seeds of unpredictable futures that can and do retrace worlds."[9]

Although Stanyek and Piekut note that the concept of deadness can be applied in multiple realms (not only auditory ones), the origins of their investigation are sonic. Their central case studies center around "posthumous duets" that feature deceased artists performing alongside living ones. A particularly prominent example in the article is the 1991 collaboration between Natalie and Nat "King" Cole on the song "Unforgettable." Such duets are possible because of several features of recording technology, including that of *revertability* ("a temporal process of undoing a work of recording in some way, whereby presumptive wholes can be disarticulated and taken back to a prior stage in a process of assemblage"), *recombinatoriality* ("the capacity toward articulating what are taken to be discrete, nonidentical parts into new arrangements"), and *corpaurality* ("the imbrication of sounds with fleshy bodies . . . [which are not merely] the relation between sounds and individual bodies—what might be called 'sonic bodies'—but also the ways that these corpauralities infuse with and cling to others").[10] In a broader sense, then, all sound recordings (whether the creators are dead or not) can be considered artifacts of deadness, in that they use media to extend the labor of the past (the recording session, for example) into effective applications in the present (the moment of playback).[11]

In that this chapter also considers the affective potentials that adhere to sound recordings of the dead, in some ways I take up a rather literal extension of the authors' original topic. At the same time, however, considering the role of the house itself as another (physical, haptic) artifact of deadness takes up, in a modest way, their invitation to extend their vocabulary into other sensory realms. In other words, where "Unforgettable" combines recordings of the "past" with recordings of the "present" to create a new type of intermundane sonic artifact, the house museum combines multiple forms of sensorial deadness—some sonic, some not—to resurrect the dead within a multimodal network of sensory inputs and textual scripts. This is hardly a unique phenomenon (others are considered below), but it is central to the way any historical or memorial construction takes place, whether physical, textual, sonic, or otherwise mediated.

Up to this point I have been quite vague about exactly what sounds and recordings I'll discuss in this chapter. This vagueness is by design; in the progression of any soundwalk it's important that you encounter sounds at the proper moment and in the proper location. Revealing my cards too early—though it might make this introduction more transparent—could ruin the effect. And with that, our tour is set to begin. Please join me in the exhibit area to watch a short introductory video that provides some background on the museum and Armstrong's life in the house.[12] Once that is finished, we will assemble outside at the front steps.

STOOP AND VESTIBULE, FRONT HALLWAY: NEIGHBORHOOD CONNECTIONS, LIMINALITY, AND THE ENTRANCE TO A SHRINE

The tour begins with a set of opening remarks from the guide. The tone is friendly, and in small groups the visitors often introduce themselves as well. During my time working at the museum, I noticed that various docents took different approaches to these introductory remarks. One, a musician himself, insisted on giving a detailed blow-by-blow biography of Armstrong's entire life and career, a chronicle that could take upwards of twenty minutes (of a forty-minute tour!). Another—a lifelong resident of the area—focused more on Armstrong's love for the community of Corona and his interaction with local residents. A third docent—a neighborhood high-schooler named Patricio Canela (who today serves on the Museum's Advisory Board)—focused on facts and lessons he had learned about Armstrong by working in the house, and how it had become a point of pride for himself and the community. Cogswell encouraged this diversity of approaches, seeing it as a way for guides to give their own spin on the home and for visitors to feel a sense personal connection. All of the guides eventually turn the discussion back to the history of the house, recounting the story of Lucille's purchase and the emotional impact of Louis's first arrival (he is said to have burst into tears). Armstrong's relationship with the neighborhood is stressed here in the interpretive guide as well, including charming details like Armstrong getting his hair cut at Joe's Artistic Barbershop on 106th Street or eating ice cream and watching TV westerns with local kids.[13]

Since this portion of the tour takes place on the front steps (weather permitting), the soundscape returns you to the space that you encountered during the walk from the train (Figure 8). Yet already the docent's descriptions cause you to hear the space differently. Rather than hearing the abstract white noise of what is (for nonresidents) an unfamiliar neighborhood—plodding forward while looking for a destination, eyes darting from a map in your hand to the street signs above—what you hear now is the soundscape of *Armstrong's* neighborhood. Or, to an extent, it begins to sound like *your* neighborhood, as you strain to hear the world through Armstrong's ears. The passersby aren't the anonymous strangers that New Yorkers are habituated to walk past with disinterest but potential friends and neighbors. In fact, it is not only you who perceives the neighbors differently; they may treat you differently as well. Many neighbors would smile or say hello as they pass by tour groups, recognizing them as visitors to the neighborhood.[14] This new encounter of the same soundscape—vibrationally identical to what you heard before—generates new affects as you begin to allow yourself to slip inside of the tour's imagined past.

In the early 2000s the most conspicuous neighborly presence was the incomparable Selma Heraldo (b. 1923), the Armstrongs' close friend who lived next door in the very house in which she was born. Hardly a day went by during my tenure at the museum that Ms. Selma (that's what everyone called her) didn't stop by to say hello, talk with the staff, and introduce herself to visitors. She had her own collection of stories that she would retell about Lucille and Louis, and about the couple's stature in the neighborhood. As a lifelong resident, she knew every family, every kid on the block, and would greet them as they passed. Her presence was a powerful, living linkage between the space's past and its present, and her boundless hospitality and charm supplemented the tour's efforts to make visitors feel like welcome guests. Ms. Selma passed away in 2011 and remains tremendously missed by the museum's staff and the community as a whole. In her will she generously gifted her house next door to the Armstrong Museum,

FIGURE 8. Louis Armstrong at his front steps. Photo by Jack Bradley, courtesy of the Louis Armstrong House Museum.

where it now houses administrative offices, providing yet another visceral link between the work of the museum and the surrounding community.

. . .

When the opening remarks conclude, I invite you to follow me up the steps and into the house itself. You walk in first while I remain behind to ring the front doorbell, ceremonially announcing our entrance and inviting you to experience the home sonically. The doorbell, I should note, is not original, as it had to be repaired when the museum was renovated prior to opening. Yet Cogswell insisted on having it function to mark the entrance to the space: an intentionally designed, sonic ritual of domestic arrival. The ringing of the doorbell is specifically required in the tour script and is part of the training for all new guides.

As the front door closes behind us, you experience perhaps the most profound sonic shift of the entire tour; over fifteen years since I have worked there, this moment of sonic encounter still looms large in my memory. As the noise outside is abruptly shut out, the sound is suddenly sucked out of the room, and the space instantly becomes *extremely* quiet. The floors in the front hallway are covered in wall-to-wall carpet and the walls are shrouded in a textured, clothlike wallpaper that I tell you is made of seagrass. The effect of the textured cloth surfaces is a space that is sonically bone dry. Recalling chapter 2, the moment is somewhat reminiscent of shutting yourself into an anechoic chamber. Here, however, the silence does not so much register as technological mastery but as a combination of the domestic and the pious. This is not the silence of a lab but the silence of a shrine. Though you're just feet away from the sounds of the community on the front steps and the echoes of Armstrong's horn in the gift shop, the profundity of the silence prepares you for another mode of engagement. We turn the corner and enter into the first room.

LIVING ROOM: RELICS AND DEVOTIONALIA

The introductory room of the tour is Armstrong's living room (Figures 9 and 10), and the silence still clings as we walk inside. The room is laid out as though it is still lived in. Fabric upholstered furniture dominates the space. Sunlight trickles in through partially closed curtains to supplement the light from a chandelier and matching wall sconces. A tasteful assortment of knickknacks lines the shelves and cabinetry. It almost has the feel of a model home for real estate showings, if not for two prominent images of the home's owner. One is subtle—a small statue of Armstrong placed atop the piano. The other is more imposing—a large painted portrait that looks down from the far wall and provides the room's most conspicuous decoration. The carpet and seagrass wallpaper flow in from the hallway, meaning the soundscape remains imposingly quiet. We have to quickly adjust the volume of our voices to compensate for this change from the outside, a physical shift in comportment that is demanded by the sacred space.

FIGURES 9 AND 10. The Armstrongs' living room. Courtesy of the Louis Armstrong House Museum.

This seems an appropriate moment to consider the Armstrong House within a larger tradition of house museums for musical icons. Such spaces are not a new phenomenon, yet nor are they a practice from time immemorial. In the Western art music tradition, musicologist Abigail Fine examines the emergence of so-called "composer houses" in nineteenth-century Europe, placing their emergence at the intersection of a burgeoning museum culture and a long tradition of religious reliquary (particularly Catholic traditions that preserved relics connected to saints). By the early nineteenth century, it wasn't uncommon for private upper-class individuals to possess and preserve objects connected to celebrated artists such as Beethoven, especially those that inspired quasi-religious cults of followers. Fine argues that such objects functioned as both memoria (objects of memory) and devotionalia (relics/objects of devotion). Locks of hair were especially common, and Beethoven himself was even known to give away locks as mementos during his lifetime (a practice that today might appear somewhat ghoulish). As Fine writes: "Hair offers a powerful example of why celebrity 'relics' have such value: it functions almost as a synecdoche of the absent body, a part that stands in for the whole."[15]

With the growth of public museum culture during the nineteenth century, ownership of these relics gradually shifted from private collections of fetish objects exchanged as gifts among the upper classes (selling them was frowned upon, although it did occur) and toward publicly accessible museums and archives. These museums functioned as both sites of display and sites of preservation, with many accepting more materials than they could showcase at a given time. Thus they become "sanctuar[ies] for forsaken memorabilia."[16] House museums also became important pilgrimage sites and tourist-oriented hubs that informed the identities of the cities where they were located. Salzburg and Bonn billed themselves as "Mozart-Stadt Salzburg" (Mozart-City, Salzburg) and "Beethoven-Stadt Bonn." This cemented their cultural (as well as financial) capital while simultaneously burnishing the legacy of the composers as not only heroic but indeed saintly figures. At the same time that composer houses framed the composers as monumental figures, they simultaneously worked to foreground their smaller, domestic existence by "[transferring] the intimacy of the home into a public space. They sought to give visitors the same tangible encounter with composers that had once been limited to musical initiates."[17] As such, the logic of the house museum sits—as Fine argues—somewhere between a metaphysical historiography and a materialist one. It is a location where artists are portrayed both at their most saintly (as figures worthy of devotion, casting their domiciles as holy ground) and also at their most human (as mortal, fleshy bodies who ate and drank, relieved themselves in toilets, rested in chairs when they lost their breath).

This European model is, of course, not the world's only tradition for preserving relics related to iconic musicians. A contrasting example, for instance, could be found in the preservation of the "Sosso Bala"—a sacred instrument of the Mande people of West Africa, which is preserved in the village of Niagassola in northern Guinea. Believed to date from the thirteenth century, the Sosso Bala plays an integral part in the Mande epic of Sundiata Keita, the legendary founder of the Malian empire. It was won by Keita in his military victory over the King Sumanguru (who invented and built the instrument) and played by Keita's praise singer, Bala Faseke Kouyate.[18] Since then, the instrument has been passed down through more than twelve generations of the Kouyate family, moving from village to village before reaching its current home in Niagassola. It is protected as a UNESCO object of intangible heritage and today is preserved "with other sacred and historical objects" from the Sundiata era.[19] Strict customs govern the care and treatment of the Sosso Bala, and it can only be played by a single member of the Kouyate family for specified ritual purposes.[20]

Returning to where we stand in Armstrong's living room, your eyes fall upon a small spinet piano that sits near the entrance. Like the Sosso Bala, visitors aren't allowed to touch it, but the instrument does occasionally get played, under specially approved circumstances when the home is visited by prominent pianists. Under even more stringent restrictions are Armstrong's trumpets, of which the museum possesses five. Again, strict rules dictate who may handle these most sacred objects. But under the right circumstances, in the hands of specially appointed masters, the instruments are made to sound again.

Other aspects of the room hew closer to the European model described by Fine, preserving and presenting even the most banal aspects of Armstrong's material life. If the composer museums of Europe balance on the fulcrum between metaphysical and materialist visions, much of the Armstrong tour script leans toward the latter. Instead of dwelling on the saintly, the tour stresses Armstrong's image as an approachable, neighborly presence who loved to play with kids, joke around with friends, enjoy a good meal. There are relatively few stories in the script about his musical triumphs (which Cogswell felt many visitors would already know) and more about his everyday hobbies, the food he liked to eat, and his relationship with Lucille. Armstrong's saintly powers are conveyed less through the text of the tour script and more from the ritualistic (and, of course, preservational) regulations surrounding visitors as we traverse the staid silence of the shrine: don't touch the walls, don't play the piano, don't step off the specially designated carpet runners, don't sit on the couches. These might seem obvious, but the home's inviting domesticity prompts a surprising number of visitors to attempt all of these things on a regular basis. One of my jobs as tour guide (and de facto keeper of the shrine) is to ensure that they don't happen, maintaining the purity of the relics and their unvarnished connection to the body of Armstrong.

DEADNESS'S FIRST FINALE

Before leaving the living room, there is one last thing we must do. If you're a keen observer, you might have noticed one tiny detail that looks out of place. Near the light switch on the wall, there is a small, modestly decorated button that looks something like a doorbell. I inconspicuously stroll over and press it. Immediately, a familiar gravelly voice breaks the room's stark silence:

> LOUIS: At home in Corona, Long Island, New York. February 26, 1956.
> LUCILLE: [*correcting him*] February 6th.
> LOUIS: Correction. February 6th, 1926. I'm sitting up here with Lucille and she's—
> LUCILLE: [*correcting him again*] 1956!
> LOUIS: [*both break into laughter*] O pardon me!

It's difficult to convey in writing the effect that encountering Armstrong's voice often has on visitors. During my time as a tour guide I witnessed multiple people begin to cry unexpectedly upon hearing the recordings. Others lit up with smiles and gazed upward or spilled into fits of laughter (sometimes joyous, other times a bit awkward). Still others appeared deeply uncomfortable at the somewhat ghostly presence. On one occasion a guest immediately looked terrified, blurted out that he had to leave, and walked off into the adjacent hallway toward the front door. When I followed him, he apologized profusely, saying he didn't know what came over him, but that he suddenly felt overwhelmed and had to get out of there as fast as possible.

I'm sure you can guess how the system works—most visitors figure it out fairly quickly. The button triggers a sound system (located in the museum's basement) that plays an Mp3 clip of Armstrong's voice. This clip—the first of several we hear during the tour—comes not from commercial records or film appearances but from the trumpeter's sizable collection of

FIGURE 11. Louis Armstrong with reel-to-reel tape recorder. Courtesy of the Louis Armstrong House Museum.

private tapes. When he wasn't on stage, Armstrong was an avid amateur recordist who delighted in capturing all manner of private conversations and events (Figure 11). The museum has preserved 650 of these tapes, each offering a unique glimpse into Armstrong's offstage life. When played during the tour, these intimate, private moments re/sound within the already intimate, private, and sacred spaces of the Armstrong home. They provide an audio corollary to the tour's logic of taking a look behind the curtain at the private life of an icon. And perhaps most powerful of all, many of the clips are played back in the very same rooms where they were originally recorded.

The deployment of the clips provides an especially potent example of Stanyek and Piekut's notion of sonic deadness. The aural presence of the dead Armstrong—embalmed in magnetic oxide—is resurrected to generate affective responses in the present, responses that are reflected in the powerful, palpable reactions of visitors. The moment takes the form of a haunting—an unexpected, impossible encounter with the dead in the space of the present. Yet unlike the examples considered by Stanyek and Piekut, this haunting is not only a function of sound media's ability to preserve and resurrect dead labor. Rather, it is enacted through a series of crucial priming mechanisms that set the stage for these moments of ghostly clairaudience.

As anthropologists have long noted, experiences of ritualized liminality do not emerge out of thin air.[21] The contexts and practices surrounding the liminal moment must be carefully crafted. Armstrong's private recordings, for instance, don't have nearly the same effect when played back in another location. Their effect in the house is heightened by the fact that Armstrong speaks both *from* and *to* the place where you are standing. I suggest that one of the powerful aspects of the "At home in Corona" clip is the impression that Armstrong is speaking (impossibly) directly to our very tour group, in a future he could not have known. Deadness, then, is not a quality embedded in the sound of Armstrong's recorded voice alone, although the voice provides a pivotal trigger. It is, instead, an affective response to a multitiered process of resurrecting the dead through multiple sensorial means. To use Stanyek and Piekut's terminology, the processes of revertability and recombinatoriality are not limited to the audio realm. Instead, these clips of Armstrong's voice are selected, isolated, reverted to a fragmentary state, and *recombined with space,* room sound, and script text, to create a more deeply immersive encounter of haunting. The sound is the trigger, but all aspects are integrally sutured together to create the overall impression.

Every sonic detail about the tour's progression to this point further heightens the effect of this deadness. Following the opening remarks on the front steps (loud white noise, the tour script's establishment of Armstrong's saintly status), visitors are plunged into the penitent silence of the entryway and living room (disorientingly quiet, sacred), before being confronted, unexpectedly and impossibly, with the vibrational presence of the saint himself. Different tour guides would set up the clip in different ways. Some gave detailed background about the tapes beforehand (which prepared the visitors, though somewhat dulled the effect). Some would give no preparation at all and simply press the button inconspicuously during a lull in the conversation. The docent Patricio Canela sometimes presented it in an endearing and almost cartoonishly ghostly fashion, saying nothing about the tapes but telling his groups, "They say if you're very quiet, you can still sometimes hear the voices of the Armstrongs roaming through the house" (this was a big hit with school groups). If they hadn't already, guides would then describe the nature of Armstrong's recording hobby after the clips were played.

In assessing the type of encounter triggered by the clips, it is useful to consider them in relation to two terms that often come up in sound studies scholarship. The first is the notion of "acousmatic" sound, a term that refers to a sound that is separated (most often visually) from its source. The word can be traced to Pythagoras, but it came into particular vogue in the twentieth century through the work of electronic composer Pierre Schaeffer, a pioneer in the tradition known as *musique concrète*. Schaeffer used the notion of the acousmatic as a positive attribute that aided in the development of what he saw as purer approaches to listening (so-called "reduced listening," in which the sound alone is perceived, not the musicians or other visual distractions). Yet Brian Kane has pointed to how this separation of sound and source—the splitting of sonic effects from sonic sources—has at other times been associated with feelings of anxiety, uncertainty, or panic.[22] This undoubtedly plays into the intensity of visitor reactions.

The clips have a very different relationship with another term often considered alongside acousmatics. In 1969, R. Murray Schafer famously coined the related term "schizophonia" to describe the splitting of a *recorded* sound from its original source, which creates a sense of dislocation between what is seen and what is heard. The term's similarity to "schizophrenia" was intentional, as Schafer coined it as part of a larger activist project to preserve natural soundscapes.[23] Many authors writing about the topics tend to conflate and/or confuse the terms "acousmatic" and "schizophonic," as both deal with the notion of severability between sounds and sources. But as Kane points out, acousmatics differs from schizophonia in that the former requires no notion of a copy and an original; prior to sound recording, other technologies such as hidden orchestra pits, screens, or veils could be used to create acousmatic effects. Thus, while a schizophonic (recorded) separation of a sonic copy from an original source *can* constitute a form of acousmatics, it is by no means the only form.[24]

The visitors' reaction to the uncanniness of hearing Armstrong's voice within the house represents a peculiar corollary to schizophonia. In some ways the effect is something like schizophonia's opposite, a sort of antischizophonia. Rather than wrenching a sound away from its source, the museum's deployment of deadness operates by *suturing the sonic copy back* into its original source. Or at least one of its sources. Louis and Lucille are gone, of course, but what remains is the room itself. The space from which Louis Armstrong speaks in the clip—including its "room sound," that elusive sonic baseline implicit in all recordings—is the very room in which visitors stand. If Schafer and others have pointed to the disorienting nature of recording as enabling an unnatural separation of a sound source from its recorded copy, this act of antischizophonic reattachment can prove equally unsettling.[25]

What we have, then, is an unusual circumstance in which sound is *acousmatic but not schizophonic*. The notion that the sound must have a hidden source (acousmatic) was specifically important to Cogswell, who took care to hide the speakers inside the walls so that no playback device would be visible. The only visible clues are the small, inconspicuous buttons that trigger the recordings. And even these are adorned with brass decorative touches, made to look more like an antique doorbell than a controller for a digital audio system. This concealment creates an impression that the recordings emanate *from the room itself*, again a reversal of schizophonic splitting. As such, not only do the recordings seem to lay bare the distinction between acousmatics and schizophonics, but the two processes are placed in direct opposition with one another: it is the acousmatic nature of the playback device that reverses the schizophonic split of the recordings themselves. There is more to say on the clips, deadness, and acousmatic sound in subsequent rooms. But for now let us continue on our tour.

FIRST-FLOOR BATHROOM: REFLECTIONS UPON REFLECTIONS

The next stop is perhaps the smallest room in the house but also one of the most memorable. It is a cramped bathroom nestled between the living room and the dining room (Figure 12). To make up for the small space, the Armstrongs had all four walls and the ceiling covered in mirrors, and adorned it in gold and marble fixtures. The effect is both dazzling and disorienting, as every image continues toward infinity. The space is hard to convey in pictures, which tend to make it seem enormous. In person the effect is more of a paradox; it feels simultaneously cramped and endless. The room is too small for groups to enter, so it is roped off, and we peek in briefly as we pass by. In a postcard available in the gift shop, we can see an image of Armstrong standing in the room, reflected from all angles in a blue bathrobe.

The notion of infinite, slightly askance refractions is an attractive metaphor for thinking about how Armstrong himself is continuously recreated through variously mediated forms of history. These not only include his own recordings, interviews, film and television appearances, articles, books, and so on but also preservation projects including the house itself and the

FIGURE 12. Louis Armstrong in his first-floor mirrored bathroom. Courtesy of the Louis Armstrong House Museum.

audio clips deployed within it. In what appears to be a perfectly transparent entity—a time capsule preserved intact from the artist's own time—countless curatorial choices undergird the museum that appears to us today. Three curators—at the time, one living and two deceased—were most central in organizing the way that Armstrong's voice and image is re/presented in the space of the museum. Let me introduce two of them here, reserving the last for later in our tour.

CURATOR #1: MICHAEL COGSWELL, MUSEUM EXECUTIVE DIRECTOR, 1994–2018

The first curator is someone I've mentioned several times already: the museum's first director (retired in 2018, deceased in 2020), Michael Cogswell. An archivist with a background in musicology and jazz performance, Cogswell was hired in 1991 by Queens College to oversee the processing and creation of the Louis Armstrong Archive in the college's Benjamin S. Rosenthal Library. Located a few miles from the house, the archive preserves various personal effects of Armstrong that don't fit in the museum. It is a space geared more toward academic researchers, with the museum serving as the operation's public face. As of 2021, nearly all of the archive's holdings (including the audio of all 650 private tapes) can be accessed online by registered researchers. When Cogswell was appointed to oversee the construction of the house museum later in the 1990s, incorporating excerpts from the tapes struck him as a natural addition. The plan for the audio system was even incorporated into the renovations of the building itself, during which Cogswell installed the speakers hidden inside the walls.

In 2011, I interviewed Cogswell and program officer Deslyn Downes Dyer about their work in the house, including the incorporation of Armstrong's private tapes. For many years, Dyer oversaw the day-to-day operation of the museum, so she was well acquainted with the progression of the tour and guest responses. Both shared my impression of witnessing deeply emotional reactions from visitors upon hearing the sound of Armstrong's voice during the tour. Cogswell spoke specifically about how such reactions differed when hearing the audio in the house versus hearing it in the more institutional environment of the archive:

> Human beings interact with the physical world through five senses. When you're in the historic house, you have more sensory input. You're actually standing in that physical, emotional space. You have the sights of the furniture and the paintings. [Earlier] Deslyn mentioned smells, that's true! We have people that walk in, "Oh! This reminds me of my grandmother's house! It smells the same way!" Then you have the audio, which is a very powerful sense.
>
> All those things work together. That's part of why I think you have people burst into tears here in the historic house. It has happened in the archives too, but [it's less common there. At] the archives you go into the reading room, you fill out a form, you register, you sit in the reading room, we bring out a CD, you put on a pair of headphones. It's not the same sensory experience.[26]

Cogswell's observations confirm the notion that the primed, multisensory progression of the house tour alters how the recordings are encountered. In the more antiseptic setting of the archive, their technological mediation is all too clear.

Cogswell is by no means alone among museum administrators in working to combine sensory modalities through multimedia exhibits. Such efforts have been increasingly common in museum curatorship for several decades, and it has become a profitable industry. One of the largest companies involved in museum audio curation is Antenna International, an organization that as of 2020 maintains eleven offices and has created audio tours and sound environments in fifty-two countries.[27] Often this work involves re-creations of sonic pasts—newly recorded sounds that are designed to invoke an earlier era. The Armstrong House is unique in that the existence of private tapes somewhat eliminates the need for such recreations. Instead, the sounds one hears have their origins directly in the times and spaces being evoked.

Cogswell strived to enhance these connections through the choice of clips played in each room. When I worked in the museum in 2005, the clips generally fell into one of four main categories (with a great deal of overlap between them). The first type, perhaps the most infrequent, are what we might call "direct address" clips. Here the audio seems to portray Armstrong as speaking directly to the visitor in the second person. The aforementioned clip from the living room, with Louis and Lucille fumbling through the date, takes such an approach, creating the bizarre impression of the departed Armstrong narrating his own tour.

The second category we might call the voyeuristic. By this, I refer to clips that give the impression of being a fly-on-the-wall observing the Armstrongs' life at home. Another clip from the living room clip provides an example, in which Armstrong playfully jokes around with one of the neighborhood kids. Others of this type were featured in the den, with Armstrong joking and telling stories while relaxing with friends. Showcasing such moments of down-to-earth domesticity is a staple of the tour. For Dyer these encounters enable visitors to construct a more complex, personal relationship with Armstrong: "Louis is REAL in the house. Some things he couldn't say on stage or on radio, he's saying on the clips. Or things you didn't think about because you saw him on TV or in an interview, he's able to talk about. What is it like to listen to Louis at dinner? He's listening to music. He's got his dogs. He's having a good time. . . . He's been removed from this pedestal and I think you can connect with him as a real person."[28] Dyer's notions of creating connections with the Armstrong family and making the trumpeter "real" came up frequently during our conversation, and they speak to the heart of the museum's goal of fostering an impression of co-presence. The tour is less about presenting Armstrong the grand historical figure, and more about—as Cogswell frequently reminded us—portraying the family's life at home.

A third category we might call "place referential" clips, in which Armstrong makes direct references to objects in the room or to the house itself. Again, this gives the impression of Armstrong almost narrating the tour, as he vocally points out features that the visitor can then observe with new eyes. In the den, for example, one hears Armstrong describe the significance of having a room to pursue his personal hobbies:

> *Armstrong:* Lucille fixed something I never had in my life before. She gave me a room and made a den out of it. . . . That really knocked me out because we couldn't afford no den in them early days. We'd better sleep in that room! [Laughs] Now I got a den! I can look at all my tapes around the walls and just pick out what I want to hear!

Or, in another, Armstrong discusses a portrait of himself that is mounted on the wall:

> ARMSTRONG: [There's a] picture of Tony and I standing by this [painting] . . .
> INTERLOCUTOR: Did he sign the picture?
> ARMSTRONG: Yeah, well he signed his real name. Benetto or something.
> INTERLOCUTOR: Benetto. Benedito.
> ARMSTRONG: That's it, Tony Bennedito! [both laugh].

In the context of the tour, such clips can reinforce (or preface, depending on the approach of the guide) explanations that are offered in the tour script. The guide, for instance, is responsible for filling in the gap by telling the visitor that "Antony Benedetto" (the name signed on the canvas) was not merely a painter but was the birth name of the singer Tony Bennett. The relationship between the clips and the tour guide is therefore complimentary, as both contribute to totality of the experience.

The last category of clips are musical excerpts of Armstrong singing and playing his trumpet—a type that, perhaps surprisingly, are somewhat infrequent. But I'll return to these later in our tour.

CURATOR #2: LOUIS ARMSTRONG

The second pivotal curator is, of course, Armstrong himself, who created the audio recordings used throughout the tour. The collection of 650 tapes, recorded between 1950 and 1971, totals more than a thousand hours of audio. In addition to private conversations and get-togethers, some tapes feature Armstrong acting as a DJ, providing spoken introductions to recordings by himself or others. This vast wealth of material has been culled by Cogswell for the collection of ten or so clips (the exact number changes)

FIGURE 13. Louis Armstrong holding a tape box covered in his collage art. Courtesy of the Louis Armstrong House Museum.

that are used within the museum. Cogswell speculated that a good deal of Armstrong's motivation stemmed from his fascination with recording technology and the tape machines themselves. Yet it would be a mistake to think of the tapes as the product of technophilia alone. They also relate closely to another cherished hobby of Armstrong: the composition of collages. The link between them is more than just conceptual. After recording each audio tape, Armstrong would adorn the tape box with such collages, often featuring photographs and newspaper clippings of himself, along with friends, other unrelated magazine clippings, decorative images, and so on (Figure 13). As Armstrong once described it, the collages gave him an opportunity to "pick out different things during what I read and piece them together and make a little story of my own."[29]

Armstrong's collage work is discussed extensively in an essay by Jorge Daniel Veneciano, who argues that it can be thought of in relation to the figure of the "bricoleur," the "handyman" who works predominantly through juxtaposition of materials at hand. He goes on to suggest that a similar "bricolage aesthetic praxis" can be heard in Armstrong's musical work as well: "Under Armstrong's arrangement the collages permit another perspective from which to access aesthetic sensibilities that suffuse a spectrum of creative endeavors. They do so in evidencing a visual correlative to an already developed musical sense of swing aesthetic."[30] Veneciano points out how as preserved objects the collages sit between notions of the impermanence of scotch tape and the long-term fixity of the archive, a liminal position that echoes that of improvisational music itself: "The conflicted prospect of rendering permanence to a music based on impermanence is the challenge of the bricoleur's aesthetic practice—putting the provisional to work."[31]

While Veneciano's article draws perceptive connections between Armstrong's collage work and his musical career, the link between the two hobbies of collage and private tape recording is, in many ways, even more direct. Both activities, after all, demonstrate fascination with mediated processes of reproduction, selection, and recombination conducted within the space of the home, primarily for private consumption. Both practices involve bricoleur-esque, handmade, DIY re/negotiation of materials whose origins lie in the *highly* mediated world of the commercial entertainment industry. This is the case whether Armstrong was DJing and redubbing commercial records on reel-to-reel tapes or rearranging images clipped from glossy magazines. This continual process of self-remediation is one of the things that makes the hobbies so intriguing. Armstrong—already among the most documented figures in the history of music—spent a significant portion of his free time crafting yet further constructions of his own visual and sonic presences. In Veneciano's phrasing: "Armstrong's photo-collages allowed him to intervene in the construction of his public media representation."[32] Or, in Armstrong's: they allowed him "to make a little story of my own."

The logics of both activities also sit somewhere between curatorial, archival, and aesthetic impulses. They bear comparison to other collections such as that of early twentieth-century Harlem socialite Alexander Gumby. Operating out of a Harlem studio that functioned as "a salon, an art gallery, a workroom, and a performance space," Gumby collected rare books and a range of ephemera, personal photos, and newspaper clippings.[33] All of these were arranged into a series of more than 150 handmade scrapbooks that he described as representing "The History of the Negro from 1850 to 1960."[34] Yet the scrapbooks were not simply passive repositories. Rather, as argued by Kristin Gilger, the act of scrapbooking foregrounded elements of choice, emphasis, and juxtaposition, allowing Gumby a voice in curating the narratives he affixed upon the page. Like Gumby's work, Armstrong's activity of creating tapes (both their audio and their visual collage accompaniments) can itself be seen as an act of creative composition and nonpositivist archiving.

Cogswell similarly speculated that one of Armstrong's motivations for creating the tapes was to supplement his own historical legacy and continue communicating with fans after his death. As he put it in our interview: "I think somehow he knew—not in an egotistical way—that these tapes would survive him. Did he imagine that his house would be a national landmark and there would be a hidden audio system in his den? No. But would he approve? Yeah!"[35] For a figure like Armstrong, whose actions were endlessly interpreted, analyzed, and/or distorted by critics and commentators, the hobby may have given him an opportunity to reclaim a degree of input into his own afterlife. In this light, when Cogswell began curating materials for the museum in the 1990s, he was—in a very real way—curating material that had already been curated, remediating remediations of clips and fragments. He did this not in the absence of Armstrong but in collaboration with him across time and space. Armstrong, like Cogswell, was not merely a curator in the archival sense but also in the older religious sense of the word: to curate, from *curare*, a priest entrusted with the care of souls.

DINING ROOM AND KITCHEN: NARRATIVES OF GENDER IN THE HOUSE TOUR

Past the bathroom we enter the Armstrongs' dining room. A rectangular table fills most of the space, with place settings positioned at each head. We pause briefly so I can tell you about Armstrong's love for food, including his personal recipe for red beans and rice. Another button on the wall completes the effect by offering perhaps the most transparently voyeuristic audio clip of the tour. Soft orchestral music fades in as we hear the Armstrongs enjoying a casual meal. Forks clink, a dog barks, Armstrong jokes about the Brussels sprouts, which he playfully calls "miniature cabbages." Unlike the other rooms featuring sound, only a single clip is programmed here.[36] In some ways this clip is the tour's most seamlessly "on the nose." It fits the décor of the dining room so well that it almost sounds like what an audio re-creation company would make if they wanted to

FIGURE 14. The Armstrongs' kitchen. Courtesy of the Louis Armstrong House Museum.

make a simulated clip to provide ambiance. We move through it fairly quickly, toward a gleaming space just ahead.

The entrance to the kitchen marks a striking shift in atmosphere (Figure 14). After several rooms of the same beige, seagrass wallpaper, we are suddenly thrust into an electric blue-and-white wonderland of metal and plastic. Every cabinet, shelf, and appliance in the kitchen was ordered in these colors, including the custom-built refrigerator, which is built flush into the cabinetry (a top-of-the-line Sub Zero model, the guide informs you). The six-burner, double-oven stove is also customized and includes a plaque reading "Custom made by Crown for Mr. And Mrs. Louis Armstrong."[37] Blinding fluorescent lights have replaced the soft sconces featured up until this point. The sound of the room seems to open up as well, as the shift from fabric and carpet to metal and linoleum creates a brighter, less dampened space. In total, the area has a feel of representing the future, as imagined by the past of the late 1960s.

CURATOR #3: LUCILLE ARMSTRONG

In the tour script the kitchen revisits a theme that has already come up several times: in many ways the home is not Louis's space, but Lucille's. She not only purchased the house itself, she also selected most of the objects inside, including this custom kitchen. Collaborating with an interior designer named Morris Grossberg, Lucille selected practically every wallpaper, every window dressing, every piece of furniture. Strikingly, then, the very objects that devotees come to worship (with the exception of the audio clips, of course) were mostly not curated by Louis, but by Lucille. If we're being precise (and some guides are more precise than others), we might note that many aspects of the home's current state do not actually reflect how the home appeared at the end of Louis's life, but at the end of Lucille's, since she continued living there for another twelve years after the trumpeter's death. What is embalmed is not Louis's home from the early 1970s, but Lucille's from the early 1980s (with a few exceptions, noted below).[38]

Several of the tour guides I worked with expressed feeling as much of a connection to Lucille as they did to Louis. In 2009, Dyer even curated a special exhibit about Lucille in the downstairs exhibition area. The script provides substantial background on Lucille's own career as a dancer at the Cotton Club, where she and Louis met around 1938. It further notes her trailblazing role as "the first dark-skinned dancer in the Cotton Club review."[39] Lucille's importance to Armstrong's career was not unique. In an article from the *New York Times*, Robin D.G. Kelley discusses the long tradition in jazz of male musicians' wives acting as crucial business partners, managers, and supporters, despite often receiving neither recognition nor respect for their contributions. He writes: "Women like Nellie Monk and Lorraine Gillespie were not simply muses who inspired their husbands' creative passions or housewives relegated to the background of their spouses' public lives. Rather, they became a significant social and economic force in the jazz world and thus were ahead of their time."[40]

While Cogswell's interpretive program is deeply respectful of Lucille's role as a partner and collaborator, I nevertheless recall certain tour guides whose descriptions of Lucille fell into problematically gendered tropes. One troubling story told often by one guide stemmed from an article written by Louis in 1954, in which the trumpeter said: "I always made it plain to all my wives that that trumpet must come first before anybody or anything. That horn is my real boss because it's my life."[41] Importantly, Lucille fiercely pushed back against this idea in one of the more infamous private tapes in the archive—a tape featuring an extended fight between the couple.[42] Yet the story still circulates, generally framed as a demonstration of Louis's single-minded devotion to his art. The underlying implications are painfully clear: that the role of the (male) artist's wife is to stay in the background, in a support role without getting in the way. As Lucille was Louis's fourth wife (and by far the longest-lasting, with their marriage spanning from 1942 until Louis's death in 1971), a further implication suggests that she was the one who most thoroughly accepted this circumscribed role, in contrast to the "bad wives" that came before—including piano pioneer Lil Hardin.

This insidious framing—which, again, circulated despite not being recommended in the official tour script—is illustrative of the heavily limited role allowed to women, and especially Black women, within jazz's patriarchy. Tammy Kernodle discusses this issue in the aftermath of World War II, and her description is worth quoting at length:

> Musicians, critics, and fans created a spectrum of readings that defined the woman's role in [jazz] culture. The use of the term "woman" was a reference to females who inhabited this space as wives, girlfriends, patrons, or groupies. All of these roles positioned women as being diametrically "outside" of the culture, on the periphery, but comprising central networks that supported the creative activities of men. Most importantly, these "women" did not disrupt the *work* or camaraderie of the men, but enabled it. They were essentially participating in a manner that maintained their status as "women" or as female bodies who acknowledged and exercised in appropriately gendered spaces. The counter to the "woman" was the "b——." In this case "b——" became the reading of the female body that disrupted male-defined spaces. The b—— did not support the creative efforts of the male artist; she took away from his art by taking his place on the bandstand and devaluing what he does. The b—— also creates conflicts between him and other men by challenging the power structure of jazz in an attempt to manage the business affairs or correct perceived injustices against her lover or husband. The lack of any real historicizing of jazz wives has allowed for the proliferation of negative readings of their engagement with public jazz culture.[43]

Kernodle's account connects closely to issues surrounding how Lucille is framed. In circulating the problematic story of Lucille as a figure whose needs must always come after the trumpet, she is presented as an archetype who could offer support without disrupting the overarching fantasy that jazz "work" must occur within a homosocial male space.

Such an account of course does nothing to dismantle patriarchal structures but instead reinforces them by maintaining their essential binary: Lucille is the good wife who stayed in the background, while Hardin and others were the bad ones who "disrupted male-defined spaces." It echoes other galling depictions of Armstrong's marriages that crop up in other jazz historical sources. Sherrie Tucker, for instance, describes how they are portrayed in director Ken Burns's documentary *Jazz:*

> The audience is instructed to cheer as he loses pushy Lil ("his wife who often played piano"—there is no place in this story for her own career). We are to cheer again as he is miraculously liberated from Alpha (a subsequent wife—pictured with a vampish leer, wearing a fur-coat—who, in full knowledge of Armstrong's love for Lucille, stubbornly refuses to divorce him because she wants to devour his paychecks). And finally, we are prompted to coo and say "aww" when he finally settles down with his prize, Lucille, who is depicted as an uncomplaining, cookie baking "former dancer" (kind of like Laura Petry on the old *Dick Van Dyke* Show). Lucille is portrayed as the ultimate object of desire for anyone who has ever yearned for a domestic partner who has no needs or ambitions of her own, doesn't mind whether her husband comes home or stays away for months at a time, and yet still manages to create the home life he has always wanted.[44]

Other narratives from the tour script might be seen as reinforcing a similarly regressive framing: Lucille would often stay behind and tend to the house while Louis went on tour, Louis taught Lucille how to cook his favorite meal of red beans and rice (no mention, of course, of what foods Lucille enjoyed), Lucille's role was decorative (again, a lot of discussion of wallpaper) while Louis's was artistic, and so on.

In other ways, however, the tour simultaneously draws attention to Lucille's stature as a powerful and savvy figure, especially though her role as the pivotal manager of Armstrong's legacy in the wake of his death. Such work requires a sharp combination of business tactics, estate management, commercial promotion, and historiography. After Louis's passing, it was Lucille who laid the groundwork for the entire preservational apparatus that maintains the home today. She worked tirelessly to build the Louis Armstrong Educational Foundation, a nonprofit the couple founded together whose "mission includes supporting musicians, Jazz education, performances and programming."[45] Lucille was integral in the decision to will the house to the New York City Department of Cultural Affairs after her passing for preservation as a historic landmark.[46] During the years between Louis's death and her own, then, the home therefore occupied two key roles: it was both Lucille's everyday home and it was a time capsule that had been earmarked (by Lucille herself) as a repository and historic site, an archive and an artifact. The tour provides several details about Lucille's work in this capacity, but at times its focus on the couple's domestic life could obscure just how monumental Lucille's accomplishments were.

One of the fascinating—and still evolving—aspects of how Lucille's story is presented can be seen by considering the sensory modalities through which each member of the couple appears within the tour. And here, I must step away somewhat from the year 2005, to consider changes that have taken place in the intervening fifteen years. During my time working at the house, *visually* it was the influence of Lucille that dominated the mise-en-scène. Louis was presented not as the one who selected or curated the physical materials in the home but more as a legendary presence who moved through it. His visual presence only appeared a few times—primarily in the portraits hanging in the living room and the den. In the *audio* realm, however, it was Louis who predominated, through the repeated reinsertion of his ghostly voice. At the time, every audio clip prominently featured Louis's voice, while Lucille was heard only occasionally (and usually in the background). Like the portraits, the recordings give affective weight to the space by resurrecting Armstrong as a sensory presence—a vibrational manifestation of haunting. The spaces in the home that were primarily associated with Lucille—the kitchen, bedrooms, and dressing room, for example—had no audio component. Happily, these curatorial choices have been revised in the intervening years. As the clips are continually refreshed, several recordings of Lucille's voice are now represented in the tour. In the most recent iteration in 2020, Lucille is heard prominently in clips in the living room and den, granting her a direct vocal presence in telling the story.[47] This choice to not segregate the couple by sense—Lucille as visual decorator, but Louis as voice—is a positive development in representing Lucille's powerful agency.

Returning to our tour, let us proceed next to the second floor of the house. As a gesture of respect to our host, please acknowledge Lucille's portrait as we pass it on the staircase.

BEDROOM: THE DEATH CHAMBER

If the first floor focuses on happier times in the Armstrongs' lives, our ascent to the second floor begins to reckon with narratives of death. It begins at the staircase, where we see the stairlift that was installed during the final weeks of Louis's life, as he suffered from congestive heart failure. We pass by it and proceed up, en route to the bedroom (Figure 15). The bedroom serves a dual purpose within the tour. It is, first off, the tour's most intimate space—our entry into the couple's private quarters after the more public entertaining spaces of the ground floor.[48] Yet somehow there isn't quite enough present to make this element compelling. The

FIGURE 15. The Armstrongs' bedroom. Courtesy of the Louis Armstrong House Museum.

room is minimally decorated and has only a few objects to look at: a bed, some furniture, a chandelier, a few knickknacks. While the home itself had been preserved since the Lucille's passing, many of the items inside were auctioned off to raise funds for the educational foundation. This included most of the couple's clothes as well as their blue Cadillac. The bedroom is a space on the tour where this loss is keenly felt. Somehow it feels less lived in, less present than the downstairs areas. If the living room maintains the impression that the Armstrongs have just stepped out, the bedroom (initially) feels more like something out of a furniture showroom.

The room's more poignant purpose is its function as the artist's death chamber. It is here that I relate to you the story of Louis's final days. While convalescing at home amid his final illness in July of 1971, Louis celebrated his birthday with a party outside in the garden. They ate cake, invited a few friends over, and listened to Armstrong's music on a twenty-four-hour radio tribute on WKCR (an annual tradition that the station maintains to this day). Two days later, on July 6, Armstrong passed away peacefully in his sleep, in the very room where we now stand (unless you ask, I won't mention that it's not actually the same bed—Lucille purchased a new one sometime later). I pause to let a pregnant absence permeate the room, allowing us to ruminate on the passing of the saint. There are no audio clips here, only another powerful silence, this time a silence of mourning.

Accounts of death often play a prominent role in the commemoration of canonized artists. Abigail Fine examines the phenomenon in regard to Beethoven, whose Vienna home in which he died was preserved for seventy-five years after his passing.[49] Other material traces of Beethoven's death were equally revered, including objects from within the death chamber such as his shaving razor. The morning after Beethoven passed, a Viennese artist visited the room to cast a death mask of his face, and by the end of the nineteenth century, reproductions of Beethoven's masks had become fashionable items to decorate bourgeois music rooms in Germany and Austria. And although the best-selling of these masks was actually a casting taken from earlier in the composer's life, Fine describes how this was often *mislabeled* as his death mask, speaking to a (somewhat counterfeit) desire to relive and commemorate the moment of passing.[50] Our quiet moment in Armstrong's chamber here plays a similar commemorative role, drawing a direct material connection between the space where we stand and the moment when the artist's flame was extinguished.

There's one more major stop on the tour, but before we leave the bedroom suite, feel free to take a brief walk through the adjoining bathroom and dressing room. Then rejoin me in the hallway, as we prepare to bring the tour to its culmination.

DEN: PANELS OF SAINTHOOD, WALLS OF ASSEMBLAGE

Step with me now into the final room of our tour: Armstrong's second-floor den (Figure 16). It's a brusque wood-paneled space, an atmosphere in stark contrast to the delicate decor in the rest of the home. The tour script describes the den as "the most significant room in the House. Louis's room."[51] This is the artist's sanctuary, a personal space to pursue his hobbies of writing letters, collaging, and, of course, recording himself on tape. If the rest of the house presents Armstrong the "regular guy," the den reinscribes a narrative of genius. It is a space for the great figure alone, the private refuge of a giant. Here Armstrong would work, play, and entertain friends. The objects on display maintain the illusion: his shelves of tapes, a pair of glasses, a page of a handwritten catalog he was preparing. The room overcomes the narratives of death, resanctifying Armstrong as an ascended presence.

Of course, Armstrong's voice makes an appearance here as well. This room, in fact, contains the most clips of all, to be cycled through at the tour

FIGURE 16. The Armstrongs' den. Courtesy of the Louis Armstrong House Museum.

guide's discretion. It is the only room in fact that features clips of Armstrong playing music, including unaccompanied renditions of "Beale Street Blues" and "Somewhere Over the Rainbow." There's even one of him playing trumpet along with a recording, a striking behind-the-curtain look at his musical process. Other clips return to voyeuristic models, finding Armstrong in conversation with visiting friends or describing aspects of the space. The clips are uniformly joyous, and the room provides the emotional climax of the forty-minute narrative. In my time at the house this room tended to evoke the most powerful responses from visitors, including many occasions where visitors shed tears at the sound of Armstrong's presence.

Ironically, from a preservation perspective, the den is the least authentic space in the entire museum. After Louis's death, Lucille had redecorated the room entirely, covering it with wallpaper in a style more akin to other areas of the home. While renovating the museum, Cogswell and his team chose to restore the room to a state in which Armstrong himself would have known it. Thus, while the rest of the home was preserved largely intact, the den is a from-scratch re-creation based off of photographs: a reproduction of reproductions.

To make things even more challenging, the room had been redecorated several times while Armstrong was still living, forcing Cogswell to make a

FIGURE 17. Lucille and Louis Armstrong in the den, circa 1970. Courtesy of the Louis Armstrong House Museum.

choice about which period to re-create. The wood-paneled version you see here is based on photos taken near the end of Armstrong's life, providing the closest possible match with the era preserved in the rest of the house (Figure 17). This was a period when the room appeared at its most orderly, including a large desk, built-in shelves to house his tapes, and two tape recorders built directly into the walls. Visually seeing the tape boxes (well, reproductions anyway—the originals are at the Archive), provides a unique unveiling as well. After hearing hidden, acousmatic audio throughout the tour, finally we see the original source machines in full transparency. Nevertheless, the recordings we hear again come from hidden speakers, not from the original equipment.

I take no issue with Cosgwell's curatorial choice to re-create this later phase of the den. Personally, however, I remain more haunted by earlier photos of the room from the 1950s, which show Armstrong actively constructing *collages directly on the walls* (Figure 18). Again, pictures of Armstrong are prominent within the collage compositions.

This desire to fill up the walls of the space, as well as the choice to use magazine clippings and other cutouts as source material, calls to mind Zora Neale Hurston's 1934 essay "The Characteristics of Negro Expression," in

FIGURE 18. Louis Armstrong composing collages on the walls of the den. Photo by Charles Graham, courtesy of the Louis Armstrong House Museum.

which Hurston outlines a multigeneric "will to adorn" that connects Black expressive forms of music, drama, visual art, and other realms:

> On the walls of the homes of the average Negro one always finds a glut of gaudy calendars, wall pockets and advertising lithographs. . . . He sees the beauty in spite of the declaration of the Portland Cement Works or the butcher's announcement. I saw in Mobile a room in which there was an over-stuffed mohair living-room suite, an imitation mahogany bed and chifferobe, a console victrola. The walls were gaily papered with Sunday supplements of the *Mobile Register*. There were seven calendars and three wall pockets. One of them was decorated with a lace doily. The mantel-shelf was covered with a scarf of deep home-made lace, looped up with a huge bow of pink crêpe paper. Over the door was a huge lithograph showing the Treaty of Versailles being signed with a Waterman fountain pen.
>
> It was grotesque, yes. But it indicated the desire for beauty. And decorating a decoration, as in the case of the doily on the gaudy wall pocket, did not seem out of place to the hostess. The feeling back of such an act is that there can never be enough of beauty, let alone too much. Perhaps

FIGURE 19. Louis Armstrong's collage wall. Photo by Charles Graham, courtesy of the Louis Armstrong House Museum.

she is right. We each have our standards of art, and thus are we all interested parties and so unfit to pass judgment upon the art concepts of others.[52]

Richard J. Powell has proposed that this notion could point to a broader "collage sensibility" within Black arts.[53] Yet as Hurston also notes, such practices—both in decorative arts and in music—were not always universally appreciated among the Black community, particularly those aspiring toward middle-class status. In this instance, Louis's enjoyment of the wall collages was not shared by the more urbane Lucille, who repeatedly had them removed while the trumpeter was away on tour. Undeterred, he would simply begin anew the next time he returned home—an ongoing flow of cyclical construction, erasure, and revision inscribed directly upon a living space. Is it too much to suggest that this mirrors the structure of jazz itself?

But maybe the collages tell a different story about reproduction, memory, and haunting (Figure 19). Maybe Armstrong's assemblages were simply another way of curating, preserving, and reanimating the past. Maybe he recognized that haunting need not always entail fear or vulnerability.

Instead it provides the basis of all memories—good and bad—as traces of the past that we encounter in the present.[54] One can't always control which traces will last, which are torn down, which fade, and which disappear forever. But we do have some curatorial agency. Agency over what memories we surround ourselves with, and how we position them in relation to one another. History, memory, haunting, the museum itself—all operating in parallel movement: reproductions from the past, curated and conjured in the present, displayed impermanently, like magazine clippings affixed with tape.

CONCLUSION: TO RETURN

Like any good consumer attraction of late capitalism, the tour concludes by returning us to the gift shop. There's a miniature progression of reversal—both spatial and sonic—as we descend back down the stairs, past the living room, and back into the outside world. The street noise opens into us as we step out of the sacred and back into the everyday. If the tour has worked as we hope, these spaces will feel different now. The recordings piped through the speakers are not familiar fragments of a generalized pop music mediascape but transmissions from a figure who you know intimately, domestically. The postcards present pictures of rooms that you have physically stood within. Ms. Selma's still here too—she often spends long portions of the day chatting with the museum staff. You talk with her again, now feeling even more neighborly than before.

・ ・ ・

Taking stock of all we have seen and heard, what are some central takeaways? The first lesson is both a confirmation and expansion of Stanyek and Piekut's theory of deadness. As they argue, the dead do indeed perform labor and generate value in the present. Sound recording's unique ability to capture moments in time and reanimate them is an essential aspect of this operation (the authors' notions of revertability and recombinatoriality). But what becomes clear is how sound and video are not the only possible sources of such impact but are merely two out of many ways that intermundane affect can be generated. In the museum of the dead, we experience the unique sensation of stepping through an embalmed space. The home's perceived function as a time capsule, an unsullied portal into the past (even when it is a re-creation) provides another avenue through which the dead can remain present.

The power of the museum lies in its ability to play these sensory inputs off of each other. Embalmed space, combined with visual representation, and culminating with unexpected and unseen voices, merge to create a multisensory affect of intermundanity that cannot be reduced to a single sense. In relation to the audio clips, we find another instance of sonic encounter that extends its tendrils beyond listening alone. The power of the clips is not generated only by their sound but by the totality of your experiences leading up to their carefully crafted deployment. Your vision, your sense of smell, your body in space—all of these feed into the way that sound is experienced. Sound is not the source of this affect but a tipping point that may push you into an unexpectedly immersive experience of a world beyond. It's this moment of tipping that leads so many visitors to laughter and tears.

The second lesson is that the museum's soundscape of the dead is a decidedly curated and constructed one. The purpose of the audio clips, like most museum audio, is to create a seamless impression of sounds that appear to *belong* in a certain space. This then feeds into a perception of antischizophonia, the sense of a sound being regrafted onto its original source. And although schizophonia is commonly linked with notions of the acousmatic, here we find that *antischizophonia* is equally reliant on acousmatic veiling. The impression of seamless return relies on visitors momentarily being unable to recognize the sound as coming from anywhere other than the walls themselves. In soundwalking the space, we find that our sensory encounters are anything but inevitable. Rather, they have been carefully crafted by a series of curatorial choices from several individuals: particularly Lucille and Louis Armstrong, and Michael Cogswell. These choices might be thought of via the logic of collage: a form that itself was close to Armstrong's heart. Through the juxtaposition of fragments and figments, a coherent construction emerges.

The third lesson is that the sensoria of deadness work most powerfully when they are prepared. This preparation includes not only the felt sensory inputs that we experience (the quiet entranceway, the soft lighting) but also various details of discursive knowledge and background information. Details provided by the stories in the tour script play an essential role, laying the cognitive groundwork that supports the affective impact of the shrine. Visitors must know the great figure's greatness before they can be awed by sharing in his intermundane co-presence. Hagiography itself alters the way we are meant to experience our sensory inputs: this is not merely a bed, it is *the artist's* bed; this is not merely a voice, it is *the artist's* voice. From there, following a common progression of sacred rituals, visitors pass through preparatory liminal sequences before deadness emerges in its final form via the sounding of the audio clips.

Finally, we find that the power of Armstrong's deadness is not merely an ontological relationship between a sound, its source, and its receiver. To the contrary, every element of deadness's affective pull is predicated on radically contextual understandings of who Armstrong was and what he means. This includes his position as the paragon of masculinist "great man" narratives of jazz, narratives that the Armstrongs (both Louis and Lucille) never asked to be inserted into but within which the trumpeter sits at the pinnacle. Indeed, it's hard to experience the total impact of the tour outside of the resonances of gender and domesticity. Everywhere a dichotomy reasserts itself: Lucille's home and Louis's life on the road; Lucille's visual decor and Louis's tapes, Lucille's ornate wallpaper and Louis's rugged wood paneling, and so on. In the end, the den's denouement reinforces a notion that it is Louis who ascends into the pantheon of saints, rising from death in the home's most masculine room. This is, of course, unsurprising. Louis is the musical icon and the reason that tourists flock to the museum. Within jazz's patriarchal paradigm, it is Louis whom visitors come here to seek, despite the museum's efforts to grant Lucille rightful credit. What an immense shame that there are currently so few similar spaces to canonize of any of jazz's female or nonbinary icons—though Ma Rainey's house museum in Columbus, Georgia, provides a happy exception.[55]

. . .

In the end, the deadness of the Louis Armstrong House Museum reveals itself not so much as a static presence but as an interrelated bundle of techniques. As in any séance, spirits do not appear of their own volition; they must be summoned. Like the aesthetic pull of the music itself, deadness's impact is never disconnected from our other senses, our understandings of the world around us, or the stories we tell ourselves.

7   Tape Death

Mourning Sounds We Never Heard

PROLOGUE

At 11 a.m. today, in a midtown Manhattan music studio, a handful of record industry veterans will huddle around a reel of tape they say is an original master from the historic 1954 recording debut of Elvis Presley. Then, after a brief introduction, the tape will be chopped to pieces.

Thus begins a 2004 *Washington Post* article about a minor but curious encounter in the history of recorded sound.[1] The story's origins stretch back to 1992, when an old reel-to-reel tape containing Elvis Presley's earliest recordings on Sun Records was discovered in a Tennessee warehouse.

The reel was sold at a sheriff's auction and proceeded to pass through several sets of hands until the early 2000s, when it came into the possession of a collector named Michael Esposito. Believing the object to be the authentic master tape (and therefore a significant artifact in rock history), Esposito tried to contact the original recording engineer, Sam Phillips, to verify its identity. Unfortunately Phillips died just before they were able to meet. Esposito next pursued other avenues, including contacting RCA records—then the owners of Presley's catalogue—to see if they were interested in buying it, but RCA declined the offer and disputed the tape's authenticity.[2] He made further attempts to sell the tape to institutions like the Rock and Roll Hall of Fame and the Smithsonian, but all were unsuccessful.[3] Undaunted, Esposito instead decided to verify the tape's identity on his own. He hired a team of experienced audio experts to test its authenticity through various means, ultimately producing a detailed "Forensic Report" outlining their findings.[4] Though some of the team's work was later called into question, they ultimately (perhaps unsurprisingly) came to the conclusion that their benefactor's possession was indeed the original, authentic, auratic tape of the Sun Sessions, and was therefore a priceless relic.[5]

To this point, the story reads like a prototypical parable of antiquing culture: the treasure hunter's dream of finding mystical (and, one often hopes, valuable) artifacts shimmering amid piles of unwanted garbage. It's what happened next that infuriated some onlookers. After establishing the tape's authenticity, Esposito and his engineers played it back a single time in order to create a high-quality transfer onto a digital audio tape (DAT).[6] They pledged that this would be the final time the tape would ever be played, claiming that it had "suffered water damage and was too fragile to be played again."[7] With the music dubbed and the artifact's precarity proclaimed, Esposito reconceived and redescribed the tape as "unplayable" and therefore somewhat vestigial. In the absence of playable sound, the silenced media was now transformed, in Esposito's framing, into merely a piece of ephemera—an object significant not for what it contains, but for its sacred status from being touched by Presley himself.[8] He therefore proceeded to make plans to, in his perhaps ironic words, "share the tape."[9]

Forming a company called Master Tape Collection, Esposito announced that the tape would be physically cut up and divided into two-inch slices. Each slice would be mounted under Lucite on an individually numbered commemorative plaque, which could be purchased by Presley fans for $495. The plaque also featured a short text, rendered in (nearly) all caps:

> IN 1954, THE KING OF ROCK 'n' ROLL MADE HIS FIRST RECORDINGS WHICH BECAME KNOWN AS "THE SUN SESSIONS." MOUNTED BELOW IS A VERIFIED AUTHENTIC SEGMENT OF THE ACTUAL MASTER TAPE FROM THOSE EARLY RECORDING SESSIONS. IT IS AN ORIGINAL PIECE OF THE TAPE THAT CAPTURED AN HISTORICAL MOMENT IN TIME.[10]

This brief text emphasizes the auratic significance of the tape in every possible phrasing, at every possible turn: "verified," "authentic," "actual," "master," "original," "historical moment in time." The sale was even authorized and licensed (presumably for a fee) by the Presley estate, although their official statement on the matter reflected a degree of ambivalence: "We do not own the tape.... It was not our decision to make. The project would have happened with or without us. Our licensing department's decision was whether to grant the requested licensing cooperation."[11]

Unsurprisingly, many fans who heard about the sale failed to see the benevolence in Esposito's "sharing." To the contrary, deep-seated tension around the sale was reported in every news story that covered it. If the *Post*'s introductory paragraph wasn't clear enough in conveying the absurdity, the article went on to note how the sale caused an uproar in online fan forums:

> [T]he project has, nonetheless, earned [Esposito] a legion of new enemies. Message boards on Presley fan sites have been filled with slashing posts by collectors who consider Master Tape's cut-and-mount concept an outrage.
>
> "Next they'll be selling little bits of the Mona Lisa," huffed someone identified as Greg on the elvis-collectors.com message board, "or maybe a slice of the U.S. Constitution or the dead sea scrolls."
>
> "If this is real, I'm pretty sure that God made a commandment against doing this kind of thing!!" fumed "elvis fan" on the same page.[12]

A *New York Times* story took a similar angle, though instead of quoting fan forums, it obtained a statement from Presley biographer Dave Marsh:

> Mr. Marsh called the decision to destroy the tapes outrageous. "If they were cutting up something that was purported to be the original copy of the Declaration of Independence or an original copy of 'Moby Dick,' we wouldn't even be asking, 'What's the big deal?'" Mr. Marsh said yesterday. "They're destroying something forever that in the future could have real value." . . .
>
> "This is about one thing," Mr. Marsh said. "This is about money."[13]

The event caused a minor furor for several weeks, with articles in several prominent publications. But within about a month the news thread eventually dried up. It's unclear how many of the plaques actually sold. Web captures of the Master Tape Collection website show that by October (following the January press announcement), the company was selling a more modest version for just $125. The final web capture of the company's site from the Internet Archive was taken in March 2005.[14] As of the summer of 2019, no copies of the plaque seem to be for sale on eBay or from other online secondhand sellers, and the very occasional references to the episode generally seem to frame the incident as a fakery.[15]

TAPE DEATH

Why do we pause here to ruminate on this bizarre, possibly fraudulent, and immediately forgotten footnote in the history of popular music? Unlike those quoted in the news stories, I don't raise it to reflect on the actions taken by Esposito (distasteful though they may be). I'm more interested in the types of impassioned responses that the episode elicited from both audio specialists and the larger public. I suggest that these responses are not unique to this case but are emblematic of a broader category of sonic encounter that I refer to as "tape death." I define tape death as the loss, deterioration, or destruction of recorded sound (regardless of the actual physical media on which it is stored). News stories on the subject tend to recur every few years in various guises, usually in regard to the loss of original studio masters by celebrity musicians. Some of these stories describe losses that have already taken place, while others are proactive efforts aimed at generating support for restoration projects. Somewhat like actual death, many forms of tape death can be prevented (or at least delayed)— but only if one can afford expensive treatments.

In considering this phenomenon as a form of death (rather than using a more neutral term like "loss"), I wish to foreground the types and degrees of affective impact that an encounter with tape death can elicit: a thick admixture of mourning, outrage, bargaining, and other responses typical of grieving. While most instances don't go as far as the Presley case in generating a literal "forensic report," these overtones of grieving are nearly always present.[16] Other recurring themes (each of which is discussed in greater detail in this chapter) include the auratic quality of tape as a visceral, material connection to lost heroes; tape's assumed (yet frequently overstated) fragility as a preservation medium; comparisons between the presumed neglect of audio archives in comparison to other sorts of artifacts (the Mona Lisa, the Declaration of Independence, Moby Dick); and the ongoing tensions between archival obligations and capitalist profit motives. In short, tape death speaks to a certain affective investment we maintain for sound recordings as embodiments of particular figures and moments in time. These investments remain strong even in cases (maybe especially in cases) in which we have never even heard the sounds in question, and perhaps never will.

This chapter enters into dialogue with a recent uptick in scholarship about the medium of tape itself. In the introduction to a special issue on tape in the journal *Twentieth-Century Music,* Andrea Bohlman and Peter McMurray argue that tape traces a crucial medial and cultural thread throughout the twentieth century. They suggest that this thread is arguably even more compelling than the more thoroughly theorized technology of the phonograph. Bohlman and McMurray trace what they call a "phonographic regime" within media studies literature, which begins with the bold pronouncements written by inventors like Thomas Edison and Emile Berliner, and continues into the work of cultural theorists like Theodor Adorno and Friedrich Kittler. Proponents of the phonographic regime tend to frame sound recording in language that suggests a "utopian vision of eternal preservation, perfected memory, and a technological sense of manifest destiny."[17] The phonograph therefore provides a model that frames recording as a practice grounded in the notion of faithfully and accurately capturing a moment, indeed a freezing of time itself. For adherents, "the phonograph is the ultimate promise of presence, coupled with a perfect, infinite inscription of that presence."[18]

Tape, however, Bohlman and McMurray argue, carries a number of key affordances that allow it to function very differently. These include manipulability, erasability, portability, splicing, looping, rewind/fast-forward, and ease of copying and circulation.[19] All of these characteristics became crucial to the way tape functions both at the point of production (via studio production practices, multitracking, tape effects, electronic music, etc.) and at the point of consumption (particularly through the emergence of the cassette, a format that was erasable/recombinatorial/mixtapable in an era when vinyl records were not). Tape therefore offers a lens for considering sound recording not merely as a faithful preservation of a single moment but as a continually reshaped processual entity.

On the surface (and of course, taped data is always adhered atop a surface[20]), it might seem like a chapter on tape death would mark a return to older ways of thinking about audio recording primarily as a media of capture—a return, in other words, to the same phonographic regime critiqued by Bohlman and McMurray. The anxieties around tape death hinge, after all, upon rhetorics about the preservation of the dead and the fear of losing that singular, auratic trace: the "historic moment in time." Indeed, most of the instances of tape death that I describe in this chapter focus not on copies or manipulated media but on so-called "master" recordings: the original source material that exists prior to postproduction processes of editing, layering, equalizing, and adding other effects. To lose a mere copy would obviously be less fraught. The tapes that commentators seem to most fear losing are those that (a) exist in only one copy, (b) contain material that did not receive widespread circulation (lost tracks and the like), or (c) are the original source capture—the physical relic actually touched by the hand (or voice) of the artist, and which are therefore preserved in the truest fidelity.

With these points in mind, the weight of tape death can actually be seen as deeply intertwined with the tapely affordances outlined by Bohlman and McMurray. The very fact that tape is manipulable, enhanceable, copyable, and, especially, erasable *does not* eliminate the sense of auratic quality that adheres to the original. If anything, it heightens it. In cases involving the loss of famous, widely sold items (such as the Presley tape), the fact that so many copies circulated only seems to make the fetishization of the original that much more potent. As a result, if one wishes to consider tape death as emblematic of a desire to return to a more "pure" phonographic logic of capture, preservation, and playback, two points seem relevant. First, this desire to return to an original is nearly always partial. Few would wish to return to a time before tape and post-tape medial logics and interfaces (such as fast-forward and rewind, studio effects, ease of circulation, etc.). The desire for Presley's pre-reverb master, for instance, does not mean that listeners want to discard the finished mix, which spread across the world and provoked its own effects and affects. It does, however, create certain possibilities for reformulation/recombinatoriality/remix of the elements contained therein (the endless stream of remastered versions of classic recordings, for example).[21]

Second, the idea of returning to an original is only possible because there is a sense that something has been left behind. In fact, tape's profound move away from logics of preservation and toward those of manipulation point to the fickleness of preservation itself. If one wants to hold on to some sort of "truth" about the past, tape can be something of an unreliable narrator, since the very logic of the media encodes the potential for manipulation. Only an original, pre-effects master can even begin to fill this role (and even that will only be partial). The logic of lossy reproduction—the idea that fidelity suffers with each copy that is made—may also give lie to the premise that preservation can be achieved simply by making additional copies. To the contrary, the fetishization of tape masters makes it ontologically impossible to make a true "copy": by definition any copy will no longer be the master. Ironically, the master tape is both the source of all copies, and itself is fundamentally uncopyable.

• • •

The chapter proceeds in two sections. The first addresses encounters with tape's fragility, focusing on a form of archival deterioration known as "sticky shed syndrome." Despite being a treatable affliction with known remedies since the 1990s, the rhetoric used in articles on sticky shed reveals deep anxieties surrounding tape's archival status, framing it as a medium that is always under threat. I offer a tentative (and a bit playful) reading of these anxieties via the myth of Eurydice and Orpheus, which pivots around similar issues of loss, access, and failed recovery. The second section turns to the story of a massive fire that took place in the tape vault of the Universal Music Group in 2008, a catastrophic event that led to the loss of more than one hundred thousand tapes. I consider the incident from several directions. These include (1) the fraught relationship between recording artists—

particularly Black artists in the United States—and capitalist profit structures; (2) ontological distinctions between "vaults" and "archives"; and (3) various assessments of value (financial and otherwise) surrounding audio media.

Central to both of these sections (and connecting to the themes of this book) is the premise that the traumatized responses to encounters with tape death point to an ongoing affective investment in absent sounds. By this I mean sounds that are not physically present but may (or may not) be revived via future playback. This is, in a sense, what recording always intends to do: to allow the repetition of (some version of) a moment from a sonic past. But perhaps the most fascinating cases are those in which the lost recordings are unreleased, unknown, and/or vaulted (i.e., physically restricted from being played). The sounds that are mourned in such cases are sounds that not only will never be heard again but perhaps sounds that were never heard at all. Instead, what is mourned is a certain unrealized potential for a pastness that never actually resonated in a physical, vibrational form—at least not beyond its original utterance. Here, we mourn sounds that we have never heard (or that we have been explicitly kept from hearing).

ORPHEUS UNGLUED: STICKY SHED SYNDROME AND TAPE'S ARCHIVAL ANXIETIES

Sticky shed syndrome is a form of archival decay. It is a deteriorative condition that affects numerous reel-to-reel tape stocks manufactured in the 1970s and 1980s. The problem arises in a substance known as the binder, an adhesive glue used to attach the magnetic oxide (where the audio or other data is stored) to the polyester backing material of the tape itself (Figure 20). Starting in the early 1970s, manufacturers began experimenting with new binder formulas in an effort to improve tape's frequency response. While they succeeded in achieving better sound, major problems began to surface when the tapes were kept in long-term storage. Over time, the new binders absorbed moisture from the air, transforming the solid adhesive into a viscous, gummy goop. In minor occurrences the gluey backing simply prevents the tapes from being played; the layers of tape stick together and the reel refuses to turn. But in the most extreme cases, playing the tape will actually cause the oxide layer to flake away or "shed" from its backing, permanently and irreparably destroying the recording. This disintegration is often accompanied by a distinctive, high-pitched squeal from the playback deck—a sort of magnetically mediated death rattle.[22]

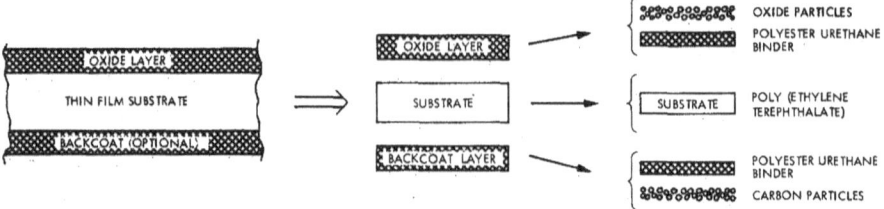

FIGURE 20. Basic physical structure of magnetic tape. Reprinted with permission from H. N. Bertram and E. F. Cuddihy, "Kinetics of the Humid Aging of Magnetic Recording Tape," *IEEE Transactions on Magnetics* 18, no. 5 (September 1982): 994, DOI: 10.1109/TMAG.1982.1061957.

Luckily, a shedding tape is not a death sentence. In fact, most affected tapes remain perfectly stable unless you do one thing: attempt to play them. To address the condition, engineers have devised numerous ways to recover information from affected tapes. Even the very earliest printed references to sticky shed (in audioengineering trade publications from the early 1990s) already suggest makeshift methods for addressing the problem. One of the most frequently cited articles is a 1990 piece from *Mix Magazine*, in which engineer Philip De Lancie describes repairing shedding reels in a homemade heating chamber consisting of a hair dryer inserted into a hole cut in a cardboard box (Figure 21).

Tape manufacturers were already well aware of the condition. A year before De Lancie's article, the Ampex Corporation had applied for a patent for a heating process designed to stabilize shedding reels.[23] A few months later, the tape company AGFA launched a service that offered to repair affected tapes, with prices starting at $280 per reel.[24] Rather than paying these high prices, however, many engineers devised their own solutions, often using tools only slightly less improvised than De Lancie's. The most common techniques over the years have been to either bake the tapes in a convection oven (yes, a regular kitchen convection oven[25]) or run them through a food dehydrator (yes, a regular kitchen food dehydrator[26]). Both of these treatments have the effect of literally *curing* the tapes by drawing out moisture, a temporary fix that allows one to make a duplicate copy before the condition returns. A more recent—and decidedly more controversial—technique involves treating the tapes with a particular brand of car polish (yes, regular commercial car polish[27]), which contains a chemical that proponents claim can permanently restore the bond. Meanwhile, more scientifically rigorous studies addressing the problem continue to appear in the journals of professional audio preservation societies.[28]

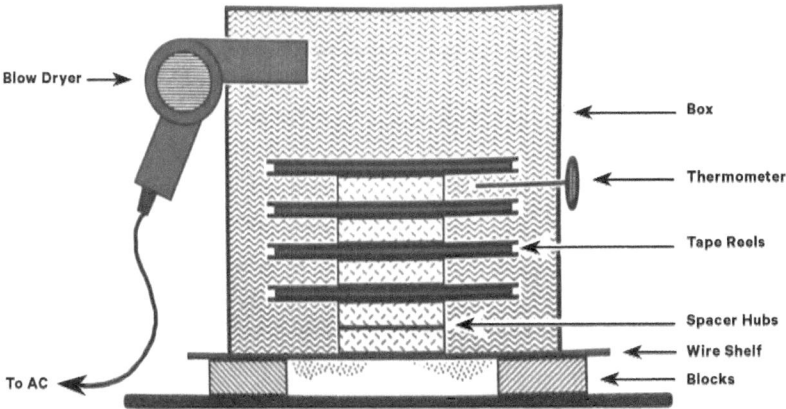

FIGURE 21. Philip De Lancie's hair-dryer heating chamber. Image from Philip De Lancie, "Sticky Shed Syndrome: Tips on Saving Your Damaged Master Tapes," *Mix: The Recording Industry Magazine*, May 1990, 148. Courtesy of *Mix Magazine*.

But despite the fact that engineers have had effective treatments for more than thirty years, news reports about sticky shed continue to crop up at regular intervals, often presented with a noticeable tone of alarmism. Throughout the 1990s one could encounter headlines like "Magnetic Tape Deterioration: Tidal Wave at Our Shores"[29] or "Industry's Catalog at Risk: Archived Tapes Could Be Lost to Binder Problem."[30] As recently as 2015, the Smithsonian warned that "History and Culture of the 1960s to 1980s Is Disintegrating with the Tapes That Recorded It."[31] These accounts often paint a picture of doom that involves various combinations of several core metaphors. Some quotes illustrate a few of the most common:

1. Disease / medicine: "It is commonly believed that Sticky Shed Syndrome is an incurable problem that reduces the useful life of most tapes to ten years or less."[32]

2. Natural disaster / humanitarian crisis: "The threat to nearly all magnetic tape is dire, and recordings from as little as ten years ago may be in danger due to the instability of [the] medium."[33]

3. War: "'We're in our infancy as far as understanding the scope of preservation in the digital age,' says preservationist Bill Ivey, who paraphrases Defense Secretary Donald Rumsfeld: 'There are things you know, things you know you don't know and there are things you don't even know you don't know.'"[34]

Writers sometimes combine these metaphors as well. The notion of performing "triage" on collections comes up somewhat frequently, evoking both medical and military language. In my own ethnographic work in the 1970s tape archive of percussionist Juma Sultan, I found that fellow archivists would often speak to me as if I have a relative in the hospital: "You're working on a collection from the '70s? How's it doing? Is there shed? Is it dire? What's the diagnosis?"[35] The existential threat generated by sticky shed has occasionally even pushed authors into delightfully mixed metaphors: "Like so many lemming[s] leaping off a cliff, hopeful technicians continue the search for a single 'Holy Grail' cleaning solution for master recordings."[36]

How might we interpret the anxiety that pervades these discussions of sticky shed, a slowly progressing problem with a widely known solution? One is to consider them through the lens of institutional challenges surrounding audio restoration projects in general, especially those that involve physical media that are perceived as obsolete. These issues become particularly challenging as many libraries and archives shift their focus toward digital collections. There is no question that addressing shed in large archives is both a time- and funding-intensive process. Nor is there any disagreement that a great deal of twentieth-century culture is preserved within the oxide of magnetic tape. Taken in total, the anxiety surrounding sticky shed seems to pivot upon a combination of: (a) tape's unique materiality as an archival object (its physical needs, affordances, and shortcomings), and (b) larger preservationist anxieties that surround *all* archives, in which the archivist desires to preserve everything, but limitations always force them to make difficult choices due to issues of space, time, funding, staff expertise, equipment maintenance, and so on.[37] The specter of shed—especially those most feared, worst-case instances in which a tape irreparably destroys itself—suggests the possibility of a double failure: a failure of the physical medium (the tape that crumbles) and a failure of the discipline itself (the archive that fails to preserve). Sticky shed represents both a failure of means and a failure of ends.

It seems significant that the precise location of these failures is in the binder, that profoundly liminal substance that marks the point and mode of contact between encoded data and physical substrate. The role of the binder speaks to one of tape's more profound epistemological shifts. In many ways a tape recording is not what would generally be called an *inscription*. There is no physical cut or impression on a surface that reshapes matter into an object of memory. Echoing McMurray's account of tape in terms of superfice, I suggest that the archival potentials of tape rely on a modality of *adhesion:* a sticky, gluey affixing of data (in this case oxide) on top of an exterior ground (the polyester, plastic, or paper backing).[38] When a tape functions properly, everything (data and substrate) sticks firmly in place. Oxide is neither added nor removed but merely reoriented—coaxed into changing its direction at the molecular level. This has several implications. On the one hand, it allows (in theory at least) for infinite erasability and re-recordability—a factor that enabled tape to become such a widely circulated global media throughout the late twentieth century. On the other hand, it also allows for infinite flexibility regarding what types of data can be encoded. Sound, of course, is not the only option. This flexibility allowed tape to function (from quite early in its history) for myriad other applications, including video and computing.[39]

As long as the glue holds, tape's adhesive underpinnings remain concealed. It appears to function like any other media, dutifully storing whatever we choose to write onto it. But sticky shed disrupts this invisibility, laying bare the fragility of the adhesive mode. Data is wrenched off of polyester, out of the physical world, never to be heard again. I call it "data," but we could just as easily say "voice," or "music," or whatever else we desire so desperately to hold onto. In the squealing death rattle of shed, tape ceases to function as memory or archive. It becomes instead a performance: an ephemeral, unrepeatable action that fades into (and out of) memory as soon as it occurs. It is this instantaneous, irreversible transformation that makes shed so fraught. It is not so much that it elicits a new form of anxiety but rather a reemergence of the anxiety of loss that surrounds *any* performance, an anxiety that tape (like all archival media) was supposed to quell by transducing memory into physical form. The fact that shed occurs at the point of playback seems particularly poignant. The archive breaks down at the very instant we wish to hear it.

Perhaps we can think of this loss in terms evoked by the Greek myth of Eurydice and Orpheus.[40] To summarize the tale: following the death of his beloved Eurydice, Orpheus travels to the underworld, where he uses the wondrous sounds of his music to charm Hades and convince the god to allow Eurydice to return to the world of the living. He asks Hades, in a phrase that itself echoes tape, to "reweave, I implore, the fate unwound too fast."[41] (How fitting that winding a reel too fast is one factor that leaves tapes susceptible to shed!) Hades obliges, but he demands that Orpheus walk out in front of Eurydice, not looking back until they have both emerged above the ground. Orpheus, of course, does not obey. He looks back too soon and watches his beloved fade away into the darkness. To quote Ovid's rendition:

> [She] breathed a faint farewell, and turned again
> Back to the land of spirits whence she came.
>   The double death of his Eurydice.[42]

Orpheus, son of the highest muse and grandchild of memory herself, simply cannot bear the weight of mere remembrance. He lacks the faith that Eurydice remains with him at moments when he cannot sense her presence. In some versions of the story, Orpheus looks because he is troubled by the suspicion that he cannot trust the sound of the footsteps behind him, a telling commentary on the ancient Greeks' valuation of sight above hearing. In the end he must look, must perceive, must allow his gaze to possess Eurydice in the present. For the quest is never really about Eurydice, the woman whose only role in the story is to be looked at, to be married, and to die. It is entirely about a fragile man's need to look, to perceive, to be bound. "If only he hadn't looked back," we cry! But obviously this can never be. Orpheus's only desire for Eurydice is the desire to perceive her, not to remember what was. If he cannot do so, she is already lost to him.

Similar stories exist in other mythic traditions as well. Examples include the biblical story of Lot's wife (this time the woman is not even granted a name in the text) who transforms into a pillar of salt, or the Japanese goddess Izanami who implores her husband Izanagi not to look at her in the underworld—when he does, he finds her body being consumed by maggots.[43] Although the details and moral lessons differ in these various versions, all revolve around patriarchal needs to perceive objects of desire in the present when memory is not enough. And all three end in failure, destruction, and a second death (of women, in all three cases) that this desire provokes. The destruction wrought by sticky shed takes place at precisely the same perceptual moment. The very instant that we look—or in this case listen—is the moment where the object of our desire dissolves into thin air. The shedding tape's squeal provides its "breath . . . of faint farewell," and it too is lost to a double death. A past performance of sound—so precariously adhered to this world in oxide, polyester, and glue—passes into ephemerality once again. The bind is broken, and we are left with nothing but imperfect memory.

If only we leave the reel on the shelf, all remains intact. Eurydice is still there behind us, if just out of our grasp. But of course, the fundamental impulse of the archive makes it next to impossible to never look, or listen, again. Our memory alone is never enough. For the archivist, what is the point of a tape we cannot hear?

NECRO-TECHNOPOLITICS AND THE VAULT: THE UNIVERSAL MUSIC GROUP FIRE AND ONTOLOGIES OF SONIC IMPRISONMENT

"It was the biggest disaster in the history of the music business—and almost nobody knew."

As we did at the start of this chapter, we begin once again with a news story, written by reporter Jody Rosen in the *New York Times Magazine* in 2019.[44] The ten-thousand-word exposé reported on a massive 2008 fire that engulfed a warehouse of the Universal Music Group (UMG), one of the "big three" labels of the music industry. At the time, UMG held an enormous quantity of masters from some of the best-known artists of the twentieth century. A brief recap of the details provided by Rosen illuminates the tragedy.

According to the article, the fire began early in the morning of June 1. It started on a nearby movie set (the Universal lot combines movie production studios, offices, storage facilities, and a theme park), but flames soon spread to nearby buildings. Among these was Building 6197, known to employees as the "video vault," but which was also home to UMG's repository of audio tapes. When the fire couldn't be contained by conventional methods, firefighters bulldozed the entire structure to clear obstructions to extinguishing the blaze. It was nearly twenty-four hours before the fire was finally put out.

In the days that followed, the company claimed in official statements that little to no irreplaceable material had been destroyed; one UMG spokesperson emphatically claimed: "We had no loss."[45] Yet Rosen's story presents a very different account of the losses as well as of the company's ongoing evasiveness. An internal UMG memo from 2009, for example, suggested that a staggering 118,230 objects were destroyed. Rosen's primary informant for the piece—an audio engineer named Randy Aronson who worked in the vault at the time of the fire—places the number even higher: around 175,000. And extrapolating to the level of individual songs, another UMG report claimed that an estimated 500,000 titles were destroyed. These estimates are complicated by the facts that (a) no comprehensive inventory existed of the warehouse (itself a disturbing admission), and (b) the company offered very different numbers in different contexts. In PR statements, where it behooved UMG to downplay losses in order to maintain their image as a worthy steward of audio culture, the company implied that that minimal loss occurred. They purposefully conveyed this narrative to artists as well, many of whom were told that none of their work was destroyed. But the company's insurance claims and legal records (including a lawsuit against the landlord of the warehouse) gave very different numbers, there claiming that losses stretched into the hundreds of thousands. In these contexts, of course, the company had an incentive to maximize the impression of loss to get the largest possible judgment.

Drawing from Aronson's accounts, the article provides a disheartening litany of artists whose work was destroyed: figures ranging from Billie Holiday to Louis Armstrong to Chuck Berry to Patsy Cline to Nirvana to Mary J. Blige. Photos of these artists, altered to appear as if they are being consumed by flames, accompanied the article to drive home the emotional point. This list was expanded further in a follow-up piece from Rosen a few weeks later, which printed the company's internal so-called "God list" (a striking name for a list of materials that were destined to die) of all artists who had material lost.[46] The list of over eight hundred names is sobering to read.

By any measure, there's no denying the scope of the loss incurred in the UMG fire. I wish, however, to start a few steps further back in the histories of these ill-fated tapes. I wish to ask about their status before the flames, during the years when they sat unplayed in the back lot of a theme park. They rested on silent shelves, often hundreds of miles from their point of origin, and several mergers and acquisitions removed from being the legal property of the artists. I propose two key questions: (1) What is the ontological status of a vaulted tape? and (2) How should we interpret the various assignations of value (financial, cultural, and otherwise) placed upon them?

ONTOLOGIES OF THE VAULT

Grappling with such a massive encounter with tape death requires close consideration of the imbrication between audio recording and cultural streams of twentieth-century modernity. In particular, it requires considering of the role of Black American sonic culture to discourses of modernity over that time. In his book *Phonographies*, Alexander Weheliye argues that sound technology has long constituted a critical medium through which Black diasporic subjects have engaged with modernity's techno-informational flows. Revising previous scholarship that treats Black music and Black culture as static entities, Weheliye traces an evolving tradition of technicities that create "new styles of technological folding" and give rise to "a plethora of practices and objets d'art that (re)mix the divide between the ephemerality and materiality of technologized sound in the twentieth century."[47]

In critical ways the role of recording within techno-sonic culture dematerializes Black (and other) voices by displacing the voice from the body and encoding it onto discrete media objects. Yet Weheliye argues that this rupture (between body and voice) is not an originary rupture but "a radical reformulation of their already vexed codependency."[48] Thus modernity's continually recurring commodification of Blackness—emblematized most horrifyingly in the transatlantic slave trade but continued in myriad other systems of oppression—is seen as an ominously looming co-presence that underlies, opposes, informs, and feeds back upon the creative forms of resistance embedded in Black sonic cultures. These forces are not solely musical but are sonic in a broader sense. That is, they are as deeply engaged with the technological advancements surrounding sound recording as they are with the aesthetic advancements relating to musical style.

The ontological, social, and political impact of recording's disembodiment of Black voices provides an ongoing concern throughout Weheliye's writing. He asks: "What happens once the black voice becomes disembodied, severed from its source, (re)contextualized, and (re)embodied and appropriated, or even before this point?"[49] What happens, in other words, when Black voices can be transformed not only into performances on a stage but into material objects that can be held in a hand, sold in a store, transferred online, or left to languish on a back shelf? Ownership of these medial objects therefore becomes a key battleground for questions of resistance. Taking Stanyek and Piekut's argument that a recording constitutes a resurrect-able form of dead labor (see chapter 6), the recording becomes not only the means through which Black musical labor can be exploited in the present but also held as a commodity for future use. Perhaps a more succinct version of this idea is crystalized in a statement from the artist Prince, quoted in Rosen's article: "If you don't own your masters, your master owns you."[50]

Weheliye's and Prince's observations on disembodiment, commodification, and modernity are deeply relevant to any consideration of the losses wrought by the UMG fire. Crucially, it should be remembered that, by and large, most of the tapes that were lost no longer "belonged" to the artists in most practical or legal senses, at least as defined under US law. For recordings made prior to the 1972 copyright revisions, record companies often owned both the masters and the performances on them outright. This was due to the fact that record contracts pressured musicians to cede any rights directly to the recording company in perpetuity, often for paltry fees. Historian Maxine Gordon describes an example encountered by saxophonist Dexter Gordon in the 1940s:

> Dexter signed his first contract with Savoy [Records] on October 15, 1945. He was paid sixty dollars for the session with an option for Savoy to extend the contract for four more recordings. The sidemen were paid forty dollars each per session. For the future recordings, Dexter would receive seventy-five dollars. The contract also called for "all original tunes to be given to Savoy Music Co. as publisher and 1 cent royalty to composer." This meant that Savoy Records had its own publishing company, which would be the legal owner of any original composition recorded on its label. Savoy agreed to pay one cent from each sale of the recording to the composer. You can be sure that no royalty was ever received by Dexter. This contract was exclusive, meaning that at the age of twenty-two Dexter was locked into a binding contract that gave away ownership of his compositions to the label for a very small amount of money, and forbade him from recording anything else for any other company. The contract term was "in perpetuity," meaning that the label would own the recordings forever and could sell them to other companies. There was never a provision for the rights to return to the musicians. We know now that this was standard practice in the recording industry and was supported by the American Federation of Musicians. But it gives us pause to think how it affected the economic situation in the lives of jazz musicians.[51]

Such manipulative practices have been especially common in the industry's treatment of Black artists, despite the unequaled prominence of Black genres within American popular music. The history of the industry contains a litany of stories in which artists were pitifully compensated for recordings that generated staggering amounts of money.[52]

The situation changed only slightly after the copyright revisions of the mid-1970s, with many artists still being pressured into inequitable contracts that forfeited their licensing rights.[53] One small change is that for records made since 1978, such deals are no longer enforceable in perpetuity but are subject to a "termination of transfers" limit of thirty-five years, after which time they can be reclaimed or renegotiated. This thirty-five-year limit has itself been subject to numerous attempts by record companies to dismantle or extend it.[54] But suffice it to say, the majority of the materials destroyed in the 2008 fire were firmly under the control of UMG, whether through outright ownership or through the sharecropping logic of long-term licensing. The company had final say over where, when, and how to release, repackage, or otherwise exploit the materials (and yes, "exploit" is the actual term used within the industry).[55] Over several decades UMG had also acquired back catalogues of numerous other companies, such as the legendary blues label Chess, jazz labels Decca and Impulse, and wide-ranging pop music imprints such as MCA, ABC, A&M, Geffen, and

Interscope.[56] These mergers created even greater distance between the artists who created the music and legal ownership of the masters.

In many ways the UMG vault was itself emblematic of the forms of sonic disembodiment, appropriation, and monetization suggested by Weheliye and Prince. The loss of these materials certainly represents an unparalleled loss of culture, to be sure. But we should also remember that long before the fire, the material had *already* been taken out of the hands of artists, out of the hands of the communities making the music, and out of the hands of listeners. Instead, the recordings were held in waiting within the walls of a corporation's vault. The company's stated mission (like that of all commercial entities) was not merely to preserve or disseminate these materials but *explicitly* to profit from them. Such vaults are therefore not publicly accountable stewards of the treasured "musical heritage" that they contain. They are, instead, repositories of stored and/or dead labor that has been inscribed and held in abeyance within a physical object, waiting to be deployed for corporate profit.

It is worth pausing to consider several essential distinctions between a vault and an archive, two very different types of repositories that are frequently conflated in discussions of tape death. A key distinction between the two—and there are many gray areas between them—lies in questions of access. Although details vary, archives are generally conceived as spaces to provide access to preserved materials. This access is often not universal. For many archives it requires approved forms of affiliation and/or administrative registration, which may be unequally distributed. But at its core, facilitating access to users remains an important purview of archival practice. This emphasis becomes clear in the administration of archival grants by organizations like the National Endowment for the Humanities, in which a plan for access (the wider the better) is a key requirement that must be described in grant proposals. This is also a reason why many official archives (especially in universities) keep close statistics regarding usership (the more users the better) to justify their continued existence. When archivists ask patrons to sign-in to a collection, it is not merely a security precaution. It is also to log them for the institution's own record-keeping, which are compiled in year-end reports, budget projections, and the like.

The logic of the vault is something else altogether. From banks to tape collections, vaults are predominantly structured not around letting people in but around *keeping people out*. The vault provides a secure location for objects to be stored away from prying ears, only be accessed by a much smaller number of specific individuals and/or in specific circumstances. To reiterate: this distinction is not hard and fast but one of degrees. If we conceive the two entities as ends of a preservational spectrum, we might conceive of the archive as placing greater emphasis on *facilitating future access* (by authorized users), while the vault foregrounds *prohibiting present access* (by unauthorized users). A second distinction can be found in conceptions of value perceived within the preserved materials themselves. In a discussion of business archives, for instance, Sven Spieker discusses how documents are sent to the archive only at the point when they are no longer perceived as having direct financial or organizational value to a company, when they have literally become "garbage."[57] Vaults, however, are spaces for placing and protecting objects perceived to have *enormous* value: diamonds, irreplaceable documents, and so on. This spectrum can be illustrated as follows:

ARCHIVE ←←←←←←←←← →→→→→→→→→ VAULT	
Emphasis on facilitating authorized access in the future	Emphasis on preventing unauthorized access in the present
Belief that materials have exhausted their primary value	Belief that materials hold tremendous untapped value

I realize that this distinction lies on shaky epistemological ground. There's a sense in which the terms constitute two sides of the same coin: every archive is a vault, every vault an archive. Access philosophies can shift, as can assignations of value (discussed further below). Yet I suggest that thinking through the distinction between archives and vaults, *or archived material versus vaulted material,* is instructive in thinking through the ethical ramifications of the UMG fire and the company's perceived role as stewards of culture.

The UMG collection did indeed function as a vault in more than merely name alone; it directly followed the logic of vaults, rather than that of archives. Rosen's reporting points out, for example, that the company allocated minimal time and expense to maintaining, organizing, or cataloguing the materials. This detail is laid bare most clearly by the fact that there was no inventory of the collection, and even those who worked there—such as Aronson—had no idea what was on many of the tapes. This fact alone may not be as shocking as one might think. Cataloguing is a time- and labor-intensive process, and many repositories have perpetual backlogs of unprocessed materials.[58]

Yet in Aronson's account, UMG seemed to have no systematic approach to cataloguing at all, and no particular desire to create one. This is not an indictment of the company's small preservation staff but rather reflects the priorities of the company itself. If the company desired a complete catalog, it would be a relatively simple (if also somewhat costly) matter to create one by hiring specialists with experience tackling similarly massive collections—a task that has been accomplished in numerous university and institutional settings. And if the primary purpose of the collection was to create broad avenues for future use (the archival side of the spectrum), then such an initiative would make perfect sense. However, if instead the primary goal was to prevent access except in cases with large profit potential (the vault side), then it's no wonder that this might be seen as an unnecessary expense. Bringing users into an archive can be a costly proposition, but keeping them out of a vault can be as simple as tucking things away on a back lot.

What becomes clear in this discussion is that much of the financial logic of major record companies centers not on *providing* access to music but on *restricting* it. From the perspective of capital, recordings can only function as profitable commodities when they are accessible only to paying customers who have purchased the officially licensed media and/or access credentials. While this was a relatively simple matter in the phonograph era (i.e., when only the companies themselves possessed the necessary hardware to make duplicate copies), it became significantly thornier with the advent of consumer-level duplication—first via cassette and more recently via digital sharing.[59] The past several decades have seen record companies involved in a series of legal efforts to prevent unauthorized access—from the infamous Napster lawsuits, to debates over CD-burning hardware, to the creation of new forms of digital rights management (DRM), to the launch of subscription services like Spotify and Apple Music. The reasons for these efforts are not hard to understand: unrestricted access would disrupt the entire revenue stream upon which the industry is based. Taken to its extreme, the standard record contract can perhaps be conceived not purely as an agreement to disseminate an artist's music (thought that is undoubtedly the motivation for the artists) but also as *an agreement to allow one's music to be vaulted*, shunted away at such a time when it no longer serves the company's interests. The contract signs away rights to self-distribution in favor of letting the company dictate when, where, and how the music will be sold, with the primary determining factor being profitability to the company. In return, the artists must hope to benefit (albeit temporarily) from the company's networks of distribution and promotion.

The UMG vault followed this very same logic. For all of the public outcry after the fire about the loss of potential unheard treasures, it is useful to think about why these items remained unheard in the first place. It's not only because the master tapes contained unfinished or unnecessary material that didn't make it onto published albums. It's that this material was intentionally hoarded away, kept in a secure location that is *designed to prevent it from being heard.* In the most generous light, this could be framed as a way of protecting the artists' vision; it allows the artist to present the packaged, polished final product of a recording rather than rough or unfinished drafts. But in practice, protecting the company's assets (including speculative future assets) seems an equally important impetus. There are countless instances (especially in jazz, though also in rock and pop) of labels releasing alternate takes, false starts, studio conversations, and the like, and selling them within new reissues of otherwise previously released material. If we understand vaulted tapes as ghostly artifacts of deadness—hauntological vestiges of past labor that continue to exert influence over the present—then we find that these ghosts are both imprisoned and conscripted into a sort of servitude. They remain under lockdown until such time as they can benefit their captors, or until some accident destroys them entirely.

One might even question when exactly the moment of tape death occurs? Is it truly during the fire, that final moment of irrecoverable loss? Certainly that is how archivists like Aronson frame it, being, as they were, among the select few with the privilege of accessing the material. Yet what do we make of the earlier decision to vault the tape in the first place? To place magnetized sound on a shelf, where it will never be accessed again, until it is destroyed? Is the tape truly alive while in this holding pattern? In this state of stasis awaiting reanimation or destruction? If a tape is put away in 1958, never played again, and then destroyed in 2008, when was the last time it was truly functioned as a recording? When was the last time the tape lived?

Achille Mbembe's theory of necropolitics can provide a possible avenue for thinking through this question. Focusing not on sound but on questions of political sovereignty and the oppressive power of state governments, Mbembe updates Michel Foucault's theory of biopower to outline the ways in which "the ultimate expression of sovereignty resides, to a large degree, in the power and the capacity to dictate who may live and who must die."[60] This control over the power of death is what allows states to control and suppress large portions of their population, often by differentiating between subgroups of people, controlling essential resources, and issuing ongoing threats of pain and/or death as a means of maintaining control. In addition to the moment of death itself, the constant *threat* of death allows the state to reduce certain populations (enslaved people, for example) into conditions of "death-in-life," or "social death," which Mbembe describes as attempts at a veritable expulsion from humanity altogether.[61] Though systems such as slavery, colonial occupation, and apartheid are the paradigmatic examples, Mbembe points to variations of such processes existing throughout the systems of power that have emerged in late capitalism.

Mbembe engages with topics far graver than record company holdings, and I hesitate somewhat to bring his theory to bear on what might seem to be a more benign topic. I raise it, however, for a few instructive insights. First, record companies always retain a degree of control over tape death. We might see this this as a form of necro-technopolitics, or the power of corporate entities to decide which media objects are permitted to circulate, which are left to languish, and which are destroyed. We should note that not all instances of tape death are accidental. At various points in the history of recording, companies have made conscious choices to destroy their archives to save on storage costs (a point referenced by Rosen and explored further below). They also maintain authority over what level of care and/or neglect is undertaken by preservation initiatives. Lastly, the companies regulate all forms of access to the materials—the allowance for playback that we might call tape life. This includes power over when a recording is released commercially, when it is made available to researchers or the general public, and when it remains silent and unreachable. Like the examples discussed by Mbembe, tapes are only allowed to live when their life benefits the needs of the power structure and are otherwise are left to fester. Vaulted tapes, then, might be seen as analogues to what Mbembe describes with the phrase "death-in-life." They have not been killed but remain silent and out of reach, unable to tell a story or articulate their own value.

Coming back to the fire: What is mourned when we mourn the unheard tapes that were destroyed? For we are not mourning sounds that we have encountered in any literal or straightforward sense—the very definition of an unheard tape is that it has not been heard. Instead, we mourn something like a potential for replayed sound that we wish for, but that (for most intents and purposes) never existed at all. It is sound that was captured and never released. It was preserved with the thought that it might generate future value, but its vibrations were never allowed to re-resonate. It is sound beyond our ear, beyond any ear, but only because it is sound that was deliberately placed out of our ear's reach. The sounds that we imagine "we" "lost" in the UMG fire were not lost in 2008 but were purposefully kept away for decades, with no real intention of ever resurrecting them.

VALUATION AND WRITTEN NARRATIVES OF TAPE DEATH

Like much writing on tape death, Rosen's article speaks to conflicting perceptions of value surrounding tape collections. He notes, for instance, that for some record executives "masters were not seen as capable of generating revenue. On the contrary: They were expensive to warehouse and therefore a drain on resources. To record-company accountants, a tape vault was inherently a cost center, not a profit center."[62] The exception to this only occurs when vaulted material is reissued in new editions, an occasional and somewhat cyclical pattern in the industry's history. Depending on one's perspective, these reissues can be understood as (a) a chance to expand, enhance, or increase access to recordings from the past, allowing old fans to hear them again or new generations to experience them for the first time; or (b) a chance to squeeze more capital out of the collection's stored labor by compelling the public to pay once again for music that has already been available for years. The biggest boons for such "back catalog" sales happen when there are shifts in consumer audio formats, as listeners scramble to rebuild their collections on the favored new media. The CD boom of the 1980s and 1990s was perhaps the most lucrative example, a period that saw the digital remastering of huge amounts of older material.

Such descriptions obviously frame the tapes' value primarily in monetary terms. But as Rosen and others have suggested, this view often comes into conflict with alternative ideas of value based on historical, cultural, or auratic factors. Archivists are quite familiar with the challenging process of appraising material based on somewhat abstract notions of long-term historical value that loom large in the branch of the field known as appraisal theory.[63] Theodore Schellenberg, an influential figure in the field during the mid-twentieth century, approached the question by identifying a life cycle of archival records. These included a distinction between an item's "primary value" (the use for which it was originally designed—so in the case of master tapes: as source material for finished commercial recordings) and its "secondary value" (later uses, particularly by historians and researchers).[64] What is unique about record company vaults is that despite containing tremendous potential for secondary use, their ongoing ownership by commercial entities keeps them tethered to their original primary use: generating profit for the record company. A reissue on a new format, for example, would not (in Schellenberg's terms) be an example of secondary value but of primary value (i.e., using the tapes as source material for commercial release). And, indeed, the very logic of the vault (as opposed to the archive) is based on ensuring that secondary users are not only minimized but explicitly prohibited. Popular music historians have long found record company holdings to be extremely difficult to access, despite their containing enormous potential for historical insight.

Perhaps the most common points of tension in discussions of tape death appear at moments when these two value systems (monetary value versus cultural/historical value) are pitted against each other. In some news stories this is depicted as a battle between bean-counting record executives on one side and *true* lovers of art on the other, who appreciate the materials not for their revenue potential but for their innate/aesthetic/cultural value. Interestingly, the defenders that are depicted in many journalistic accounts are not the artists themselves (whose labor is, sadly, too often framed as being dead and passed).[65] Instead, the defenders presented are often the engineers, archivists, and reissue producers employed by the companies, who are presented as literally rescuing cultural treasures from being thrown in the scrap heap.

Rosen's writing does not merely extend this tradition, it explicitly identifies it *as* a tradition in writing about sound archives. He points to a key predecessor in "a two-part exposé, published in *Billboard* in July 1997" by journalist Bill Holland.[66] Framed as an account of the overall "state of the industry's recorded music archives," Holland explores the topic through a series of interviews with archivists and engineers at BMG, Capitol, Universal, and Warner Brothers. The piece is particularly instructive in that it comes from the late 1990s, a period just after the height of the CD reissue boom. Perhaps for this reason, and perhaps because Holland's informants were actively employed by the companies, the article paints a generally optimistic picture of industry archives, even while bemoaning the missteps of the past. He reports that most of the major companies had significantly bolstered their archival departments at the time, seeing renewed value in maintaining organized collections as they sought out material for reissue. Sony and BMG are particularly commended for their attention to detail, and only Atlantic is criticized for having "appalling" conditions. UMG is mentioned only in passing, with its inventory quoted to number at about five hundred thousand items. Read in hindsight, the figure stands as a foreboding foreshadow, as the same number is given by Rosen as the number of items later lost in the 2008 fire.

Despite their general tone of optimism, Holland's two articles overflow with cautionary tales of tape death and/or threats that were narrowly averted. These are primarily framed as specters from an unenlightened past, when companies did not yet understand the true value preserved within their collections. Holland tells of producers at Columbia rescuing one-of-a-kind Louis Armstrong tapes that were marked to be thrown away; of plans at MCA to destroy the original metal parts of pre-1950s master recordings; of "some administrator" at CBS who ordered that they discard all monophonic tapes in the vault and only save those in stereo; of lacquer discs that were irreparably damaged by storing them in stacks hundreds of objects high. At one point, Holland describes CBS employees literally taking a band saw to a stockpile of masters to cut them down for scrap metal, using the logic that "for every tape they got off the shelves, they saved the company a nickel a month."

And, of course, Holland tells stories of earlier fires as well, such as those that had ravaged the archives of Atlantic and MGM. Perhaps the article's most dramatic tale is a decision by RCA in the early 1960s to simply demolish an entire warehouse—building and all—that contained four floors of recordings. A few subsidiary companies and collectors were let in beforehand to salvage what they could, but the rest was detonated and then "bulldozed into the Delaware River. A pier was built on top of the detritus."[67] Engineers and archivists repeatedly emerge in these stories as internal resistance fighters who push back against the destructive process from the inside. Framed as the inverse of executives, they are depicted as desperately working to preserve precious material, either because they alone possessed the necessary technical expertise or simply because they saw its deeper value, a value more profound than can be measured in nickels per month.[68]

The narrative tradition in how tape death is written about extends into the present. We see it not only in published articles like Rosen's but also in the responses generated by those articles. A Facebook post written in the wake of Rosen's piece by former jazz reissue producer Carlos Kase is particularly instructive, worth quoting here in full:

> If you care about any music made in the 20th century, you need to read [Rosen's] article. I worked at this archive before the 2008 fire and I can attest to the truth of the author's claims, and to the statements of Randy Aronson (a guy I worked with and the primary source for this author's research). The 2008 fire at the Universal backlot eviscerated the history of recorded music.
>
> There are many takeaways here. Please take the time to read the article yourself, but here are a few things that I want to emphasize:
>
> 1) Most of the music recorded for these labels will never sound as good as it did on earlier releases and reissues because many of the LP masters and virtually all of the session tapes burned to the ground. (For the most popular material, backup safeties exist, but they are likely dubs of dubs of dubs of dubs.) From the pre-fire Universal lot, I once played a

30 i.p.s. mono session tape of Billie Holiday on Decca that sounded better than any other tape I had ever heard in my life. Those tapes likely burned, though their contents may have been considered "safe" because the same music existed on a crappy 15 i.p.s. dub or, worse, some digital "master" in the black hole of culture that is Iron Mountain.[69]

2) In almost every case, it will not make sense to buy a reissue released by this family of labels ever again. I saw and played the 2-track Coltrane LP masters, which were held on the shelves of the Universal backlot, and which we used in our transfers when we released his music. Even if "safety" dubs were made, new digital transfers of those safety dubs will never compete with earlier transfers of superior, first-generation, analog sources. The label may claim that the LP masters were already safe in Iron Mountain, but I, like the author of the article and the other former-Universal employees interviewed, strongly doubt that claim. I am almost positive that the future history of all reissues by these labels will be dubs of LPs or CDs or digital transfers made by outsourced engineers, with little archival understanding of audiotape, from crappy third-generation "safeties."

3) Only 18% of music ever recorded is available in digital formats. This means that roughly 80% of music once recorded for the Universal Music Group (which includes Chess, Impulse, A&M, Decca, etc.) will never be accessible again (other than through old LPs), because the original tapes are gone. This figure does not even take into account the new impossibility of ever hearing unissued music from these labels: Almost all of the unissued music on all of these labels was incinerated in the fire of 2008.

4) Related to #3 above, virtually all multitrack tapes owned by UMG are gone. I drooled over a dozen session tapes for ELECTRIC MUD in 2000, and imagined a two-disc reissue of that beloved psych-funk-blues wonder with every scrap of Pete Cosey's fuzzy energy intact. That can never happen now. Every single one of Muddy Waters' session tapes turned to smoke. (There are related issues concerning the Edison, NJ flood discussed in the article, which may have destroyed a number of tapes I saw in the late 90s, such as the session multitracks for Tom Waits' RAIN DOGS or Tony Williams' Lifetime's TURN IT OVER, but that's another conversation . . .)

5) A lot of what was lost was black music, some of it obscure, but amazing. Labels like Argo had gems, and nobody cared much about rescuing that stuff when they had Steely Dan to contend with (even though the Carpenters and Steely Dan too suffered irreplaceable losses, as the article indicates). Still, the loss of every single Chess session tape is something that should make any music fan at least a little bit sad.

"Remastered from the original analog master tapes" is rarely a reliable claim. If you hear if from the Universal family of labels in the future, it will, in many cases, be an outright lie, an impossibility. And, to reiterate, it is an almost absolute certainty that there will never be another studio outtake, unissued masterpiece, or unknown record by an obscure artist ever issued by these labels ever again. A massive chunk of music history burned to the ground in 2008 and almost nobody knows about it.[70]

Kase's Facebook post, like so many other writings on tape death, is equal parts eulogy, accusation, and cautionary tale. As one of the privileged few who had been blessed with access to these original materials—a curatorial curate—Kase speaks to the power of the audio objects, the importance of their fidelity, and he lambasts the companies who continually fail to understand this power. He warns against trusting future forgeries, pretenders to sacred status, who can never match the affective power of what was lost. Finally, Kase points to the power imbalances implicit in the tremendous loss of Black music culture within the collection, an additional erasure of Black musical labor that had already been long co-opted by record company practices.

CONCLUSION

One of the more poignant turns of phrase in Rosen's article appears almost about a third of the way through the piece: "The act of listening again has defined music culture for a century."[71] Here he points to a deep power of recorded music, and thus to the sense of loss expressed so frequently at moments of tape death. To destroy a tape is to eliminate the very possibility of "listening again," returning sound to a state of profound and precarious ephemerality. At tape death—sound's second death—repetition ceases.

But despite the importance of repetition, Rosen's article concludes powerfully with an intentionally obscure example—an example that might have never been heard in the first place. In the final paragraphs, Rosen describes his own efforts to hunt out recordings whose masters were destroyed in the fire, pausing particularly on a somewhat obscure singer named Don Bennett. He describes Bennett as "a singular musician who left behind so few traces," and notes that today Bennett has almost no online footprint.[72] In order to hear Bennett's music, Rosen resorted to paying seventy-five dollars for an original issue LP, which arrived in pristine (and therefore minimally played) condition. He describes the impact this recording has on him—a sonic impression that clings so precariously to the world through only a few imperfect, decentralized copies. The implication of Rosen's gesture is clear. The losses of tape death are not only (or perhaps not primarily) about famous records, which already exist in millions of circulated copies. The more troubling, if perhaps less discernable, losses may be those materials that never circulated so widely, or perhaps never circulated at all. This is the loss of the obscure, the hidden, the interstitial, the studio chatter, the unissued, the alternate take.

When we mourn tape death, we are not only mourning what we have heard before and wish to hear again. We are also, perhaps more existentially, mourning sounds we never encountered at all. Sounds whose potential was locked away on a silent shelf. Counterfactual sounds. Sounds that might have been but were not. Sounds that were captured from their creators and hoarded away. Sounds that we thought we had stored in the miraculous memory prostheses that we imagine our media to be but that were never actually allowed to resonate. Sounds that are little more than the memory of a memory.

Acknowledgments

As with any project of this scope, this book could never have come about without the help and support of countless colleagues, friends, and loved ones. I begin by thanking my family, particularly my wife, Charlie, and daughter, Perry. Especially amid the years of pandemic lockdown, having our loving baseline of home has been more important than ever. As tragic and difficult as the years have been, working from home allowed me to enjoy more time with these most important people in my life. I love you beyond measure, and thank you endlessly for your support and companionship. Other ever-present sources of love and inspiration are my mother, Kathy Heller; mother-in-law, Kap Han Kim; siblings, Chris and Patrick; and my late father, Richard Heller.

The earliest seeds of this book were sown in 2007, during two graduate seminars taught by Jason Stanyek (on sound studies) and Carolyn Abbate (on opera). As I had come into graduate school with almost an exclusive focus on jazz (which still sits at the center of my scholarship), these two classes expanded my awareness of what music and sonic studies could be. The term papers I wrote for those classes became the basis for chapters 1 and 4 of this book, and I remain ever grateful to both professors for my experiences in those courses.

Other chapters emerged from collaborations that took place in the years that followed. For chapters 2 and 3, I'm deeply thankful to Peter McMurray, who first introduced me to the archives of the Harvard acoustics labs and got me interested in the anechoic chamber. I cherish those hours we spent together digging through the archives, talking about the project, and eventually building our own small anechoic chamber. Taking that portable chamber on tour with Matthew Battles, James Yamada, and other folks from the Harvard metaLab remains one the most fun research trips I've ever taken. But more than that, I'm grateful for the time we spent exploring the topic together, even without (at that time) a concrete output in mind. We had always hoped this would be a collaborative writing project, but life and careers took us other places, so I hope these chapters can do justice to some of that work. And maybe someday we can resume it in a more directly collaborative way (maybe that ethnography of the *Lab Echo* we were always talking about!)

Chapter 7 also owes thanks to Peter as well as to Andrea Bohlman, since the first part of the chapter emerged out of the panel on tape that they both organized at the American Musicological Society conference in 2015. Even though the article never made it into the issue of *Twentieth-Century Music* they edited (I know they tried!), I remain thankful for the invitation to write it. But infinitely more important, I am thankful for our ongoing friendship through these many years.

Chapter 6 is indebted to my friends and colleagues at the Louis Armstrong House Museum, especially Deslyn Dyer, Ricky Riccardi, and the late Michael Cogswell and Selma Heraldo. Ricky deserves special thanks for reading and offering feedback on a draft of this chapter. Thank you as well my fellow docents from my year working at the museum, including Patricio Canela, Carolyn Carter-Kennedy, Francis Lunzer, and others. So many years later, my time at the Armstrong House remains such a treasured memory.

This book would never have been possible without the endless support of my colleagues at the University of Pittsburgh, beginning always with the great Geri Allen. Geri taught me so much in the short time we got to work together before her passing—about how to be strong and steadfast, to advocate and activate, while simultaneously remaining present and supportive toward students and colleagues. Thank you, Geri, for giving me the opportunity to work at Pitt. I continue to try to live up to the faith that you had in me when I was hired in 2015. We miss you every day.

Aaron Johnson has been equally important in my time at Pitt, and I am continuously grateful for our time working together. We've been through a lot, not least of which was losing Geri in 2017 and keeping the program together as junior faculty, but I can't think of anyone I would rather have done it with. Equal thanks and praise are due to Nicole Mitchell, our subsequent director of Jazz Studies and a daily inspiration. Additional thanks go out to all of my wonderfully supportive Pitt colleagues, especially department chairs Andrew Weintraub, Deane Root, Mathew Rosenblum, and Adriana Helbig. The entire faculty of the music department has simply been a joy to work with. One hears so many horror stories of other academic departments filled with toxic personalities and petty politics, and it only makes me more grateful for the opportunity to work with colleagues I adore. Thank you to Dan Wang and Jiyoon Au for inviting me to present chapter 5 as part of the department's workshop series—I don't think I would have ever finished it without the feedback from the group that day!

Thanks are also due to all of the graduate students I've had the honor of working with, who continue to inspire and challenge me. My doctoral advisees deserve special mention: Ben Barson, Samuel Boateng, Lee Caplan, YuHao Chen, Adam Lee, Mike Mackey, John Petrucelli, Warner Sabio, Billy D. Scott, Jeff Weston, and Deanna Witkowski. Thanks as well to the students in my Writing About Music Seminar in Spring 2023. Our weekly discussions of the writing process were a constant source of strength in the final months of preparing the manuscript.

I am deeply thankful to the University of Pittsburgh administration, especially Dean Kathleen Blee, for providing sabbatical support to complete this book in Fall 2018 and Spring 2022. I extend deep thanks to the American Council of Learned Societies (ACLS) for supporting a research leave in Spring 2019. Much gratitude is directed to Frank Hammond and Lauren Upchurch, Pitt's jazz program assistants, for their ongoing administrative support over many years. And thank you as well to all of the inspiring authors and contributors to our journal *Jazz and Culture*. Editing a journal has been a humbling and enlightening experience and it has been a joy to work with all of you.

Thank you to the many people who offered feedback on chapters and excerpts of this work, including William Chang, Ellie Hisama, Carlos Case, Emily Richmond Pollock, and the aforementioned Ricky Riccardi, Peter McMurray, and Andrea Bohlman. I extend my gratitude to Robert Lublin and Eric Gidal, who offered feedback on an earlier version of the introduction that discussed Mary Shelley's *Frankenstein* (although this didn't end up making the cut, I deeply appreciated the feedback!). Thank you to my peer reviewers Ben Tausig and Marina Peterson for supporting the project and offering insight and feedback at several points. And thank you as well to Michael Bull and Veit Erlmann of the journal *Sound Studies*, which published earlier versions of two of the chapters. Very special thanks to the archivists who provided support for this project, including Timothy Driscoll, Ed Copenhagen, and the rest of the staff of the Harvard University Archives discussed in chapter 2 as well as the wonderful staff of the archive discussed in chapter 5. While the final chosen format of that chapter makes it impossible for me to thank you by name here, I am enormously thankful for your help and support.

I offer eternal thanks to the editorial staff at the University of California Press, especially the brilliant Raina Polivka. You are simply a delight to work with, and you always went above and beyond to fight for this project in every way that it needed. Thank you as well to editorial assistant Sam Warren and project editor Francisco Reinking for shepherding the manuscript through the production process. And tremendous thanks to copyeditor Amy Smith Bell for your close attention to detail and for reining in my terrible comma and hyphen habits. As someone who comes from a family of copyeditors, I know the priceless value of a close eye, and I deeply appreciate your meticulous work. Finally, I extend enormous gratitude to Bill Mazza for the absolutely gorgeous artwork that appears on the cover, and to Kevin Barrett Kane for his impeccable design work.

I close with a thank you to figures of more general inspiration in my life and career, including the ever-uplifting Juma Sultan. You are an icon for your ability to always fight for truth and justice while remaining a positive and loving force to everyone around you. I couldn't be more excited for the next book project that you and I are embarking on together. Thanks as well to Stephen Farina and Johndan Johnson-Eilola, two fellow travelers whom I neglected to thank in the last book but am making sure to honor here. And finally, thanks to my many teachers and mentors at every stage of my life, including Patricia Nicholson Parker, Ingrid Monson, Robin Kelley, Kay Shelemay, and Phil Schaap. Thank you all for making me the person I am.

Notes

INTRODUCTION

1. I haven't been back to Notre Dame since (and recordings offer only a pale comparison), but I can't help thinking that their chaotic discrepancies were integral to the power I experienced that afternoon.

2. Maïa de la Baume, "A Melodic Emblem Falls out of Tune," *New York Times*, October 19, 2011, www.nytimes.com/2011/10/19/world/europe/in-paris-bells-at-notre-dame-will-be-replaced.html; Eleanor Beardsley, "New Bells Chime with Modern Pitch at Notre Dame Cathedral," *NPR*, March 24, 2013, www.npr.org/2013/03/24/175173103/new-bells-chime-with-modern-pitch-at-notre-dame-cathedral.

3. James G. Mansell, "Hearing With: Researching the Histories of Sonic Encounter," in *The Bloomsbury Handbook of Sonic Methodologies*, ed. Michael Bull and Marcel Cobussen (New York: Bloomsbury, 2020), 98.

4. Marie Thompson, "Whiteness and the Ontological Turn in Sound Studies," *Parallax* 23, no. 3 (2017): 278. See also Anahid Kassabian, *Ubiquitous Listening: Affect, Attention, and Distributed Subjectivity* (Berkeley: University of California Press, 2013); Brian Kane, "Sound Studies without Auditory Culture: A Critique of the Ontological Turn," *Sound Studies* 1, no. 1 (2015): 2–21; Annie Goh, "Sounding Situated Knowledges: Echo in Archaeoacoustics," *Parallax* 23, no. 3 (2017): 283–304.

5. Nina Sun Eidsheim, *Sensing Sound: Singing and Listening as Vibrational Practice* (Durham, NC: Duke University Press, 2015); Nina Sun Eidsheim, *The Race of Sound: Listening, Timbre, and Vocality in African American Music* (Durham, NC: Duke University Press, 2018); Anthony Braxton, *Tri-Axium Writings*, rev. ed., 3 vols. (Lebanon, NH: Frog Peak Music, forthcoming 2023).

6. For another example of scholarship that pushes against reduced listening and argues for a more intersensorial understanding, see Steven Connor, "Edison's Teeth: Touching Hearing," in *Hearing Cultures: Essays on Sound, Listening, and Modernity*, ed. Veit Erlmann (Oxford: Berg, 2004), 153–72.

7. Braxton, *Tri-Axium Writings*, vol 1., "Introduction," i–xx.

8. Other examples of the powerful work in this wave include Daphne Brooks, *Liner Notes for the Revolution: The Intellectual Life of Black Feminist Sound* (Cambridge, MA: Belknap Press, 2021); Deborah Kapchan, *Theorizing Sound Writing* (Middletown, CT: Wesleyan University Press, 2017); Carter Mathes, *Imagine the Sound: Experimental African American Literature after Civil Rights* (Minneapolis: University of Minnesota Press, 2015); Matthew D. Morrison, "Race, Blacksound, and the (Re)Making of Musicological Discourse," *Journal of the American Musicological Society* 72, no. 3 (2019): 781–823; Fred Moten, *In the Break: The Aesthetics of the Black Radical Tradition* (Minneapolis: University of Minnesota Press, 2003); Tavia Nyong'o, "Afro-Philo-Sonic Fictions: Black Sound Studies after the Millennium," *Small Axe* 18, no. 2 (2014): 173–79; Ana María Ochoa Gautier, *Aurality: Listening and Knowledge in Nineteenth-Century Colombia* (Durham, NC: Duke University Press, 2014); Fumi Okiji, *Jazz As Critique: Adorno and Black Expression Revisited* (Redwood City, CA: Stanford University Press, 2018); Kevin Everod Quashie, *The Sovereignty of Quiet: Beyond Resistance in Black Culture* (New Brunswick, NJ: Rutgers University Press, 2012); Dylan Robinson, *Hungry Listening: Resonant Theory for Indigenous Sound Studies* (Minneapolis: University of Minnesota Press, 2020); Gavin Steingo and Jim Sykes, eds., *Remapping Sound Studies* (Durham, NC: Duke University Press, 2019); Jennifer Lynn Stoever, *The Sonic Color Line: Race and the Cultural Politics of Listening* (New York: New York University Press, 2016); Benjamin Tausig, *Bangkok Is Ringing: Sound, Protest, and Constraint* (New York: Oxford University Press, 2019); Alexander G. Weheliye, *Phonographies: Grooves in Sonic Afro-Modernity* (Durham, NC: Duke University Press, 2005).

9. Melissa Gregg and Gregory J. Seigworth, "An Inventory of Shimmers," in *The Affect Theory Reader* (Durham, NC: Duke University Press, 2010), 2.

10. Brian Massumi, *What Animals Teach Us about Politics* (Durham, NC: Duke University Press, 2014), 6.

CHAPTER 1

1. Ezer Griffiths, "George William Clarkson Kaye. 1880–1941," *Obituary Notices of Fellows of the Royal Society* 3 (December 1941): 889.

2. Llewelyn S. Lloyd, "What Are Phons?," *The Musical Times* 93, no. 1308 (1952): 62–63.

3. For several examples, see Edward Fischer Brown et al., eds., "City Noise: The Report of the Commission Appointed by Dr. Shirley W. Wynne, Commissioner of Health, to Study Noise in New York City and to Develop Means of Abating It," New York Noise Abatement Commission, Department of Health, New York, 1930.

4. Emily Ann Thompson, *The Soundscape of Modernity: Architectural Acoustics and the Culture of Listening in America, 1900–1933* (Cambridge, MA: MIT Press, 2002), 115–68; Karin Bijsterveld, *Mechanical Sound: Technology, Culture, and Public Problems of Noise in the Twentieth Century*

(Cambridge, MA: MIT Press, 2008), 104–10. Similar usages of decibel charts would be revisited extensively in the 1970s in the ecological work of R. Murray Schafer. See R. Murray Schafer, *The Soundscape: Our Sonic Environment and the Tuning of the World* (Rochester, VT: Destiny Books, 1993), 74–77, and elsewhere throughout the book.

5. R. L. Wegel, "The Physical Examination of Hearing and Binaural Aids for the Deaf," *Proceedings of the National Academy of Sciences of the United States of America* 8, no. 7 (1922): 156 (emphasis mine).

6. R. L. Wegel, "The Physical Characteristics of Audition and Dynamical Analysis of the External Ear," *Bell System Technical Journal* 1, no. 2 (1922): 56–68, 58, https://doi.org/10.1002/j.1538-7305.1922.tb00389.x; "The Audiometer: An Instrument for Measuring the Acuity and Quality of Hearing" (Warren, NJ, circa 1923), AT&T Archives #DOC-0207–000576 (B03 03), 5–6; R. R. Riesz, "The Relationship between Loudness and the Minimum Perceptible Increment of Intensity," *Journal of the Acoustical Society of America* 4, no. 3 (1933): 212–13, https://doi.org/10.1121/1.1915601; Harvey Fletcher and W. A. Munson, "Loudness, Its Definition, Measurement, and Calculation," *Bell System Technical Journal* 12, no. 4 (1933): 377–430, https://doi.org/10.1002/j.1538-7305.1933.tb00403.x, 394.

7. Karolina Smeds and Arne Leijon, "Loudness and Hearing Loss," in *Loudness*, ed. Mary Florentine, Arthur N. Popper, and Richard R. Fay, Springer Handbook of Auditory Research 37 (New York: Springer, 2010), 223–59, 236.

8. Wegel, "Physical Examination of Hearing and Binaural Aids," 157.

9. Among acousticians and psychologists, the term "loudness" is strictly differentiated from "volume," with the latter referring to "the subjective size of a sound, not its perceptual strength" (see Florentine, Popper, and Fay, *Loudness*, 6). To these researchers, the vernacular tendency to conflate the two concepts presents an understandably frustrating source of confusion, since they require very different approaches to measurement and experimental design. While I am sympathetic to this concern, I have found a small amount of terminological slippage to be unavoidable in this chapter for two reasons. First, much of the discussion considers reports of loudness experience offered by everyday listeners, outside of the lab setting. I have found it necessary to account for the scientific imprecision of these largely nonscientific writings, which tend to treat the two terms as synonymous. Second, many forms of sonic deployment involve efforts to make sound permeate space *and* penetrate/resonate within bodies. These characteristics, which are often closely linked, seem to fall somewhere between the clinician's differentiation between perceptions of space (volume) and those of strength (loudness). Their close imbrication acts as a key component of loudness's politico-aesthetic power, making it difficult to neatly disentangle them. While such a project would make a fascinating topic for further study, it will only be only obliquely referenced here.

10. Melissa Gregg and Gregory J. Seigworth, "An Inventory of Shimmers," in *The Affect Theory Reader* (Durham, NC: Duke University Press, 2010), 1.

11. Gregg and Seigworth, "Inventory of Shimmers," 2.

12. Curtis Roads, *Microsound* (Cambridge, MA: MIT Press, 2001), 7–8.

13. Hermann von Helmholtz, *On the Sensations of Tone as a Physiological Basis for the Theory of Music*, trans. Alexander John Ellis (London: Longmans Green, 1875), 7–25.

14. Florentine, Popper, and Fay, *Loudness*, 4.

15. Lawrence E. Marks and Mary Florentine, "Measurement of Loudness, Part I: Methods, Problems and Pitfalls," in Florentine, Popper, and Fay, *Loudness*, 21.

16. Jean-Luc Nancy, *Listening*, trans. Charlotte Mandell (New York: Fordham University Press, 2007), 14.

17. David Novak, *Japanoise: Music at the Edge of Circulation* (Durham, NC: Duke University Press, 2013), 46.

18. See also Robert Walser, *Running with the Devil: Power, Gender, and Madness in Heavy Metal Music* (Middletown, CT: Wesleyan University Press, 1993), 45; Paul Hegarty, *Noise/Music: A History* (New York: Continuum, 2007), 145; Jeremy Wallach, Harris M. Berger, and Paul D. Greene, "Affective Overdrive, Scene Dynamics, and Identity in the Global Metal Scene," in *Metal Rules the Globe: Heavy Metal Music Around the World* (Durham, NC: Duke University Press, 2011), 12; and Olivia Lucas, "MAXIMUM VOLUME YIELDS MAXIMUM RESULTS," *Journal of Sonic Studies* 7 (2014), http://sonicstudies.org/jss7.

19. Theodore Gracyk, *Rhythm and Noise: An Aesthetics of Rock* (Durham, NC: Duke University Press, 1996), 106.

20. Ian S. Port, "My Bloody Valentine Turns It Down to 11," *SF Weekly*, www.sfweekly.com/sanfrancisco/my-bloody-valentine-turns-it-down-to-11/Content?oid=2827103 (accessed November 7, 2015).

21. Lucas, "MAXIMUM VOLUME YIELDS MAXIMUM RESULTS."

22. Lucas, "MAXIMUM VOLUME YIELDS MAXIMUM RESULTS."

23. Elaine Scarry, *The Body in Pain: The Making and Unmaking of the World* (New York: Oxford University Press, 1985), 33.

24. Scarry, *Body in Pain*, 165.

25. Suzanne G. Cusick, "'You Are in a Place That Is Out of the World . . .': Music in the Detention Camps of the 'Global War on Terror,'" *Journal of the Society for American Music* 2, no. 1 (2008): 1–26; J. Martin Daughtry, "Thanatosonics: Ontologies of Acoustic Violence," *Social Text* 32, no. 2 (2014): 25–51. Steve Goodman, *Sonic Warfare: Sound, Affect, and the Ecology of Fear* (Cambridge, MA: MIT Press, 2010).

26. Novak, *Japanoise*, 47.

27. Lucas, "MAXIMUM VOLUME YIELDS MAXIMUM RESULTS."

28. Novak, *Japanoise*, 47.

29. Walser, *Running with the Devil*, 44–45.

30. Walser, *Running with the Devil*, 44–45.

31. Psychophysicists have observed similar associations between loudness and other stimuli in laboratory settings. In one recent study, recordings of automotive sounds played alongside photos of red sports cars were judged by participants as being louder than those played with cars of other colors, even when

played back at the same level. See Daniel Menzel et al., "Influence of Vehicle Color on Loudness Judgments," *Journal of the Acoustical Society of America* 123, no. 5 (2008): 2477–79, https://doi.org/10.1121/1.2890747.

32. Gracyk, *Rhythm and Noise*, 100.

33. Several scholars have also noted how (particularly in American music) ideas regarding timbre, loudness, and distortion have frequently been mapped onto conceptions of race and Blackness. See Nina Sun Eidsheim, *The Race of Sound: Listening, Timbre, and Vocality in African American Music* (Durham, NC: Duke University Press, 2018); Jennifer Lynn Stoever, *The Sonic Color Line: Race and the Cultural Politics of Listening* (New York: New York University Press, 2016).

34. John F. Szwed, *So What: The Life of Miles Davis* (New York: Simon & Schuster, 2002), 186.

35. Anne Karpf, *The Human Voice: How This Extraordinary Instrument Reveals Essential Clues about Who We Are* (New York: Bloomsbury, 2006), 41.

36. A third definition, sometimes used in musical acoustics, refers to noise as "irregular vibrations in contrast to the periodic sound waves of musical tones" (Bijsterveld, *Mechanical Sound*, 104). This usage will have less bearing on the discussion here.

37. Hegarty, *Noise/Music*, ix.

38. Hegarty, *Noise/Music*, ix; Novak, *Japanoise*.

39. A more detailed survey of recent literature on noise in sound studies and related fields can be found in Bijsterveld, *Mechanical Sound*, 31–41. See also Thompson, *Soundscape of Modernity*; Jonathan Sterne, *MP3: The Meaning of a Format* (Durham, NC: Duke University Press, 2012); Novak, *Japanoise*.

40. Bijsterveld, *Mechanical Sound*, 40.

41. Jacques Attali, *Noise: The Political Economy of Music*, trans. Brian Massumi (Minneapolis: University of Minnesota Press, 1985), 6.

42. Gracyk, *Rhythm and Noise*, 106.

43. William Echard, *Neil Young and the Poetics of Energy* (Bloomington: Indiana University Press, 2005), 87.

44. For further scholarship engaging with debates over music being amplified in public and semipublic spaces, see Tricia Rose, *Black Noise: Rap Music and Black Culture in Contemporary America* (Hanover, NH: Wesleyan University Press / University Press of New England, 1994); Ian Biddle, "Love Thy Neighbour? The Political Economy of Musical Neighbours," *Radical Musicology* 2 (2007), www.radical-musicology.org.uk/2007/Biddle.htm; Wayne Marshall, "Treble Culture," in *The Oxford Handbook of Mobile Music Studies, Volume 2*, ed. Sumanth Gopinath and Jason Stanyek, Oxford Handbooks in Music (New York: Oxford University Press, 2014).

45. Michel Poizat, *The Angel's Cry: Beyond the Pleasure Principle in Opera* (Ithaca, NY: Cornell University Press, 1992), 40–48.

46. Poizat, *Angel's Cry*, 90.

47. Poizat, *Angel's Cry*, 76 (emphasis in original).

48. Poizat, *Angel's Cry*, 77.

49. See also Mladen Dolar, *A Voice and Nothing More* (Cambridge, MA: MIT Press, 2006), 26–42.

50. Poizat, *Angel's Cry*, 87.

51. Poizat, *Angel's Cry*, 89.

52. Fred Moten, *In the Break: The Aesthetics of the Black Radical Tradition* (Minneapolis: University of Minnesota Press, 2003), 6.

53. Moten, *In the Break*, 6.

54. Frederick Douglass, "Narrative of the Life of Frederick Douglass, An American Slave," in *The Classic Slave Narratives*, ed. Henry Louis Gates (New York: Mentor, 1987), 259.

55. Douglass, "Narrative of the Life of Frederick Douglass," 259.

56. Moten, *In the Break*, 22.

57. Moten, *In the Break*, 233–54.

CHAPTER 2

1. For more on pre–World War II acoustic locators, see Gascia Ouzounian, "Powers of Hearing: Acoustic Defense and Technologies of Listening during the First World War," in *Stereophonica: Sound and Space in Science, Technology, and the Arts* (Cambridge, MA: MIT Press, 2021), 37–60; Richard N. Scarth, *Echoes from the Sky: A Story of Acoustic Defense* (Kent, UK: Hythe Civic Society, 1999).

2. "Memorandum: Interference of Echoes," dated October 3, 1944, Records of the Harvard Underwater Sound Laboratory, UAV 859.254.6, Box 1 (Noise and Reverberation), Harvard University Archives.

3. Brandon Gary Shackelford, "When the Noise Signals Change: The Electro-Acoustic and Psycho-Acoustic Laboratories from 1940 to 1945," AB thesis, Harvard University, 1997; Leo Beranek, *Riding the Waves: A Life in Sound, Science, and Industry* (Cambridge, MA: MIT Press, 2008).

4. "Listening torpedoes" differed from torpedoes that used active sonar. The former, rather than emitting and detecting pings, actually did listen for and home in on the sounds of enemy boat engines. One of the countermeasures used to thwart such devices was actually a sonic decoy that was towed behind a boat that generated false propeller sounds. "Status of Special Control Weapons," November 10, 1944, Records of the Harvard Underwater Sound Laboratory, UAV 859.30, Folder 3, Harvard University Archives. See also Robert Gannon, *Hellions of the Deep: The Development of American Torpedoes in World War II* (University Park, PA: Penn State Press, 1996); Frederick M. Pestorius and David T. Blackstock, "Contributions to the Development of Underwater Acoustics at the Harvard Underwater Sound Laboratory (HUSL)," *Proceedings of Meetings on Acoustics* 23, no. 1 (May 18, 2015).

5. Leo Beranek, interview by Michael Heller and Peter McMurray, August 26, 2014, Westwood, MA (audio and video recording).

6. J. Martin Daughtry, *Listening to War: Sound, Music, Trauma and Survival in Wartime Iraq* (New York: Oxford University Press, 2015), 181, 240.

7. Jack Kneece, *Ghost Army of World War II* (Gretna, LA: Pelican, 2001). Beranek, incidentally, was told nothing about the military's intended use of his new speaker technology. Beranek, interview.

8. Leo L. Beranek and Harvey P. Sleeper Jr., "The Design and Construction of Anechoic Sound Chambers," *Journal of the Acoustical Society of America* 18, no. 1 (1946): 140–50, doi:10.1121/1.1916351.

9. Beranek, interview. The large anechoic chamber was one of at least three such chambers that would be built at Harvard during the war years.

10. Ana María Ochoa Gautier, "Silence," in *Keywords in Sound*, ed. Matt Sakakeeny and David Novak (Durham, NC: Duke University Press, 2015), 183, 186.

11. Pestorius and Blackstock, "Contributions to the Development of Underwater Acoustics," 5.

12. Pestorius and Blackstock, "Contributions to the Development of Underwater Acoustics," 5. The abundance of research relating to underwater sound could also reflect the ubiquitous use of water metaphors and maritime imagery that have existed throughout the history of acoustic science. See Tara Rodgers, "Toward a Feminist Epistemology of Sound: Refiguring Waves in Audio-Technical Discourse," in *Engaging the World: Thinking after Irigaray*, ed. Mary C. Rawlinson, 195–213 (Albany: State University of New York Press, 2016), 196.

13. "Interference of Echoes," memo dated October 3, 1944, Records of the Harvard Underwater Sound Laboratory, UAV 859.254.6, Box 1 (Noise and Reverberation), Harvard University Archives.

14. B. Chandrasekaran, John R. Josephson, and V. Richard Benjamins, "What Are Ontologies, and Why Do We Need Them?," *Intelligent Systems and Their Applications, IEEE* 14, no. 1 (1999): 20–26.

15. M. Cristina Pattuelli, Alexandra Provo, and Hilary Thorsen, "Ontology Building for Linked Open Data: A Pragmatic Perspective," *Journal of Library Metadata* 15, no. 3–4 (2015): 265–94.

16. "The Lab Echo 1944–1945," issues 1–12, HUF 859.822, Harvard University Archives.

17. USS *Galaxy* [Logs and Memoranda], Records of the Harvard Underwater Sound Laboratory, UAV 859.295.3 Logbooks of Experimental Vessels, Box 2, Harvard University Archives.

18. USS *Galaxy* [Logs and Memoranda], memo dated June 27, 1945, Records of the Harvard Underwater Sound Laboratory, UAV 859.295.3 Logbooks of Experimental Vessels, Box 2, Harvard University Archives.

19. USS *Galaxy* [Logs and Memoranda], memo dated June 27, 1945, Records of the Harvard Underwater Sound Laboratory, UAV 859.295.3 Logbooks of Experimental Vessels, Box 2, Harvard University Archives.

20. "Highlights of NRL Meeting," December 5, 1944, Records of the Harvard Underwater Sound Laboratory, UAV 859.95.1 Records of the Office of the Director 1941–45, Folder 50, Harvard University Archives.

21. This article is likely also the first time that the term "anechoic" appears in print, and Beranek even offers a footnote informing readers that the term is

"pronounced ăn'-ę-kō'-ĭk, meaning 'without echo.'" Beranek and Sleeper, "Design and Construction of Anechoic Sound Chambers," 140.

22. Beranek, *Riding the Waves*, 1.
23. Beranek, *Riding the Waves*, 66.
24. Beranek, *Riding the Waves*, 215.
25. Beranek, interview.
26. This theme is hardly limited to military research. Sterne details how a central theme throughout the history of acoustics is that the field "[posits] instruments outside the body as more accurate auditors than human ears themselves, even as it also seeks to establish universal regularities in human hearing, the normal, and the pathological." Jonathan Sterne, "Hearing," in *Keywords in Sound*, ed. Matt Sakakeeny and David Novak (Durham, NC: Duke University Press, 2015), 69.
27. Scarth, *Echoes from the Sky*, 5.
28. Tucker's memo is quoted in Scarth, *Echoes from the Sky*, 11.
29. Sterne, "Hearing"; Tom Rice, "Listening," in *Keywords in Sound*, ed. Matt Sakakeeny and David Novak, 99–111 (Durham, NC: Duke University Press, 2015). For more on doubling, see also Massumi's discussion of Bergson and Spinoza in Brian Massumi, *Parables for the Virtual: Movement, Affect, Sensation* (Durham, NC: Duke University Press, 2002), 31.
30. Massumi, *Parables for the Virtual*, 27–8.
31. Ana Pais, "Almost Imperceptible Rhythms and Stuff Like That: The Power of Affect in Live Performance," in *Theorizing Sound Writing*, ed. Deborah Kapchan (Hanover, NH: Wesleyan University Press, 2017), 233–49; Carolyn Abbate, "Music: Drastic or Gnostic," *Critical Inquiry* 30 (Spring 2004): 505–36; Simon Frith, afterword in *The Relentless Pursuit of Tone: Timbre in Popular Music*, ed. Robert Fink, Melinda Latour, and Zachary Wallmark (New York: Oxford University Press, 2018), 367–76.
32. Rice, "Listening," 99.
33. Ben Anderson, "Becoming and Being Hopeful: Towards a Theory of Affect," *Environment and Planning D: Society and Space* 24, no. 5 (October 2006): 737.
34. Stefan Helmreich, "An Anthropologist Underwater: Immersive Soundscapes, Submarine Cyborgs, and Transductive Ethnography," *American Ethnologist* 34, no. 4 (November 1, 2007): 622.
35. See, for example, Rodgers, "Toward a Feminist Epistemology of Sound"; Friedrich A. Kittler, *Gramophone, Film, Typewriter* (Stanford, CA: Stanford University Press, 1999).
36. See Robert Galambos and Donald R. Griffin, "Obstacle Avoidance by Flying Bats: The Cries of Bats," *Journal of Experimental Zoology* 89, no. 3 (April 1, 1942): 475–90; Robert Galambos, "Flight in the Dark: A Study of Bats," *Scientific Monthly* 56, no. 2 (1943): 155–62. Though in published accounts Galambos and Griffin refer to the chamber merely as a "soundproof chamber in the Cruft Physics Laboratory at Harvard" (Galambos, "Flight in the

Dark: A Study of Bats," 156), Beranek confirmed during our interview that this was indeed an EAL chamber.

37. Beranek, interview.

38. John Cage, *A Year from Monday: New Lectures and Writings* (Middletown, CT: Wesleyan University Press, 1967), 134.

39. Kyle Gann, *No Such Thing as Silence: John Cage's 4'33"* (New Haven, CT: Yale University Press, 2010), 110; David Revill, *The Roaring Silence: John Cage: A Life* (New York: Arcade Publishing, 2012), 153.

40. John Cage, *Silence: Lectures and Writings* (Middletown, CT: Wesleyan University Press, 1961), 51.

41. Cage, *Silence*, 70, 81.

42. Michel Poizat, *The Angel's Cry: Beyond the Pleasure Principle in Opera* (Ithaca, NY: Cornell University Press, 1992), 87–89.

43. Cage, *Silence*.

44. The extent of Cage's engagement with Zen Buddhism, however, is called into question in Tracy M. McMullen, "Subject, Object, Improv: John Cage, Pauline Oliveros, and Eastern (Western) Philosophy in Music," *Critical Studies in Improvisation / Études Critiques En Improvisation* 6, no. 2 (December 1, 2010), https://doi.org/10.21083/csieci.v6i2.851. This topic is taken up in chapter 3. Gann, *No Such Thing as Silence*, 121–66.

45. Douglas Kahn, "John Cage: Silence and Silencing," *Musical Quarterly* 81, no. 4 (1997): 556–98, 574.

46. Kahn, "John Cage," 576.

47. Kahn, "John Cage," 581.

48. Cage quoted in Michael Zwerin, "A Lethal Measurement," in *John Cage: An Anthology*, ed. Richard Kostelanetz (New York: Da Capo Press, 1991), 166.

49. The quote appears in Cage, *Silence*, 51, but he repeated the phrase in numerous contexts.

50. Beranek, interview.

51. Orfield quoted in Rose Eveleth, "Earth's Quietest Place Will Drive You Crazy in 45 Minutes," *Smithsonian*, www.smithsonianmag.com/smart-news/earths-quietest-place-will-drive-you-crazy-in-45-minutes-180948160/ (accessed September 29, 2015).

52. Katrine Krøjby, "I Locked Myself in a Soundproof Room and Almost Lost My Mind," *Vice*, September 29, 2017, www.vice.com/en_us/article/gy55z9/i-locked-myself-in-a-soundproof-room-and-almost-lost-my-mind (accessed January 18, 2019).

53. As just a few of the many examples of such news stories from the past few years: A. Pawlowski, "Seeking Silence: What's It's Like in One of the Quietest Rooms in the World," *Today*, June 15, 2018, www.today.com/health/therapeutic-silence-one-quietest-rooms-world-t130981; Alex Wragge-Morley, "What happened when I walked into the world's quietest place," *The Guardian*, December 24, 2018, www.theguardian.com/commentisfree/2018/dec/24/what-happened-when-

i-walked-into-the-worlds-most-silent-place; Eric Adams, "Step Inside the Air Force's Sound-Swallowing Anechoic Chamber," *Wired*, October 26, 2018, www.wired.com/story/air-force-anechoic-chamber-acoustic-study/; Jacopo Prisco, "Inside the world's quietest room," CNN, March 28, 2018, www.cnn.com/style/article/anechoic-chamber-worlds-quietest-room/index.html.

54. One of the most watched of such videos, as of this writing, is titled "Can Silence Actually Drive You Crazy?" The video features a host testing (and disproving) the common myth that one cannot remain in a chamber for more than forty-five minutes. The video has been watched more than twenty million times, as of January 2019. "Can Silence Actually Drive You Crazy?," produced by Veritasium, YouTube, February 18, 2014, https://youtu.be/mXVGIb3bzHI (accessed January 16, 2019).

55. Eveleth, "Earth's Quietest Place Will Drive You Crazy"; George Michelson Foy, "Experience: I've Been to the Quietest Place on Earth," *The Guardian*, May 12, 2012, www.theguardian.com/lifeandstyle/2012/may/18/experience-quietest-place-on-earth.

56. Caity Weaver, "Could I Survive the 'Quietest Place on Earth'?," *New York Times Magazine*, November 23, 2022, www.nytimes.com/2022/11/23/magazine/quiet-chamber-minneapolis.html.

57. To use the language of Gilles Deleuze, one could describe the listener's experience vacillating "from endosensation to exosensation." See Gilles Deleuze and Félix Guattari, *What Is Philosophy?* (New York: Columbia University Press, 1994), 185.

58. Cage, *Silence*, 51.

59. Gann, *No Such Thing as Silence*, 138–39.

60. Beranek and Sleeper, "Design and Construction of Anechoic Sound Chambers."

61. As of this writing, the record is held by a chamber in the Microsoft headquarters in Redmond, Washington. Richard Gray, "Inside the Quietest Place on Earth," BBC Future, www.bbc.com/future/story/20170526-inside-the-quietest-place-on-earth (accessed December 5, 2018).

62. Zwerin, "Lethal Measurement," 166.

63. Revill, *Roaring Silence*, 114.

64. John Mowitt, *Sounds: The Ambient Humanities* (Oakland: University of California Press, 2015), 113–14.

65. Quoted in in Richard Kostelanetz, *Conversing with Cage*, 2nd ed, (New York: Routledge, 2003), 70.

66. This aspect of the experience again matches aspects of audience "silencing" as noted in Ochoa Gautier, "Silence"; and Kahn, "John Cage."

67. Cage himself had varied relationships with such descriptions. Although he sometimes cited the influence of theater, his later accounts would instead describe *4′33″* as a simple act of listening, a tuning-in to the world around you that could be experienced anywhere at any time. See, for instance, Richard Fleming and William Duckworth, eds., *John Cage at Seventy-Five* (Lewisburg, PA: Bucknell University Press, 1989).

68. Gann, *No Such Thing as Silence*, 17–19.
69. "BBC—John Cage Live at the Barbican," BBC, 2004, www.bbc.co.uk/programmes/p013s7yd (accessed December 5, 2018).
70. Quoted in in Kostelanetz, *Conversing with Cage*, 70.

CHAPTER 3

1. Rebecca Y. Kim, "John Cage in Separate Togetherness with Jazz," *Contemporary Music Review* 31, no. 1 (February 1, 2012): 83–84.
2. Georgina Born and David Hesmondhalgh, introduction to *Western Music and Its Others: Difference, Representation, and Appropriation in Music* (Berkeley: University of California Press, 2000), 163–86; John Corbett, "Experimental Oriental: New Music and Other Others," in *Western Music and Its Others: Difference, Representation, and Appropriation in Music*, 163–86; George E. Lewis, "Improvised Music after 1950: Afrological and Eurological Perspectives," *Black Music Research Journal* 16, no. 1 (1996): 91–122; George E. Lewis, "Afterword to 'Improvised Music after 1950': The Changing Same," in *The Other Side of Nowhere: Jazz, Improvisation, and Communities in Dialogue*, ed. Daniel Fischlin and Ajay Heble (Middletown, CT: Wesleyan University Press, 2004), 163–72.
3. See George Lewis, *A Power Stronger Than Itself: The AACM and American Experimental Music* (Chicago: University of Chicago Press, 2008).
4. Richard Kostelanetz, *Conversing with Cage*, 2nd ed. (New York: Routledge, 2003), 239–40.
5. Lewis, *Power Stronger Than Itself*, 129.
6. Kim, "John Cage in Separate Togetherness with Jazz," 79, 81.
7. For further discussion of racially coded and circumscribed constructions of sonic practice, see Jennifer Lynn Stoever, *The Sonic Color Line: Race and the Cultural Politics of Listening* (New York: New York University Press, 2016), 12–14.
8. John Cage, *Silence: Lectures and Writings* (Middletown, CT: Wesleyan University Press, 1961), 18–56.
9. Kim, "John Cage in Separate Togetherness with Jazz," 82, 86[n21.
10. Cage, *Silence*, 43.
11. Cage, *Silence*, 43.
12. Cage, *Silence*, 51.
13. Sun Ra and John Cage, *John Cage Meets Sun Ra: The Complete Concert*, compact disc (Modern Harmonic MHCD-020, 2016 [June 8, 1986]).
14. Russo in "John Cage Meets Sun Ra—A Modern Harmonic Industrial Film Short," YouTube, May 11, 2017, https://youtu.be/fuUS9atx-8o (accessed January 16, 2019).
15. Russo in "John Cage Meets Sun Ra—A Modern Harmonic Industrial Film Short."
16. Jon Pareles, "Music Moves into the Open Air, from Boats to City Streets." *New York Times*, June 6, 1986, C1.

17. Born and Hesmondhalgh, introduction, 16.

18. Howard Mandel, liner notes to Sun Ra and John Cage, *John Cage Meets Sun Ra*, LP (Meltdown Records MPA-1, 1987).

19. John F. Szwed, *Space Is the Place: The Lives and Times of Sun Ra* (New York: Pantheon Books, 1997), 356. The phrase "feeling a draft" refers to feeling unwelcome, often applied to situations of racism.

20. Cited in Szwed, *Space Is the Place*, 356.

21. For example, Cage performed "Empty Words" in Milan at the Teatro Lirico in 1977, at LA's Bing Theater in 1979, at the University of California–San Diego in 1980, and in Hartford, CT, in 1981.

22. Cage speaking at Broward Community College, "Empty Words IV Story," YouTube, July 11, 2012, https://youtu.be/4pnCwmlUQOE (accessed January 16, 2019).

23. Kevin Quashie, *The Sovereignty of Quiet: Beyond Resistance in Black Culture* (New Brunswick, NJ: Rutgers University Press, 2012), 3.

24. Quashie, *Sovereignty of Quiet*, 8.

25. Anthony Braxton, *Silence*, LP (Freedom FLP40123, 1974).

26. Wadada Leo Smith, *Notes (8 Pieces)*, reprint edition (Chicago: Renaissance Society at the University of Chicago, 2015).

27. Smith, *Notes*.

28. Wadada Leo Smith, quoted in Eric Lewis, *Intents and Purposes: Philosophy and the Aesthetics of Improvisation* (Ann Arbor: University of Michigan Press, 2019), 179.

29. Fred Moten, *In the Break: The Aesthetics of the Black Radical Tradition* (Minneapolis: University of Minnesota Press, 2003).

30. Yvonne Rainer, "Looking Myself in the Mouth," *October* 17 (1981): 67.

31. Smith, *Notes*.

32. Smith's reference to silence as space has significant precedent in the Black music tradition as well. Jazz soloists who employ long breaks or pauses between phrases are frequently referred to as "using space." Figures known for their innovative use of space include Thelonious Monk, Miles Davis, Ahmad Jamal, and Billie Holiday.

33. Ruth Frankenberg, *White Women, Race Matters: The Social Construction of Whiteness* (Minneapolis: University of Minnesota Press, 1993).

34. See Douglas Kahn, "John Cage: Silence and Silencing," *Musical Quarterly* 81, no. 4 (1997): 556–98.

35. Pauline Oliveros, *Deep Listening: A Composer's Sound Practice* (New York: iUniverse, Inc, 2005), xxiii.

36. Oliveros, *Deep Listening*, xxiv.

37. "About the Center for Deep Listening," www.deeplistening.rpi.edu/about-us/ (accessed July 15, 2021).

38. Maud Jacquin and Elsa Polverel, "'Dissolving Your Ear Plugs': The Unheard in Pauline Oliveros' Deep Listening Practice," *Auditive Perspektiven*, January 2020, https://edoc.hu-berlin.de/handle/18452/21842.

39. Pauline Oliveros, "The Poetics of Environmental Sound," in *Software for People: Collected Writings, 1963–80* (Baltimore, MD: Smith Publications, 1984), 28. Line breaks reproduced from the original.

40. Oliveros, "But Never Silence," in *Software for People*. All punctuation and formatting maintained from the original.

41. Quote in Peter Dickinson, *CageTalk: Dialogues with and about John Cage* (Rochester, NY: University of Rochester Press, 2006), 172.

42. Later in the same interview, when asked by Dickinson (perhaps a bit condescendingly) if she would feel "lost without [Cage's] example," Oliveros replies: "I don't know if I'd be lost or not, but I certainly would never discount the influence. It was a very important meeting."

43. Oliveros did offer her own direct observations in some writings as well, such as in her essay "Some Sound Observations" in Oliveros, *Software for People*, 17–27.

44. De Re (paraphrasing Oliveros) in Oliveros, *Deep Listening*, 76–77.

45. De Re, in Oliveros, *Deep Listening*.

46. Pauline Oliveros, *Sonic Meditations* (Baltimore, MD: Smith Publications, 1974).

47. Oliveros, *Sonic Meditations*.

48. Oliveros, *Sonic Meditations*.

49. Tracy M. McMullen, "Subject, Object, Improv: John Cage, Pauline Oliveros, and Eastern (Western) Philosophy in Music," *Critical Studies in Improvisation / Études Critiques En Improvisation* 6, no. 2 (December 1, 2010), https://doi.org/10.21083/csieci.v6i2.851.

50. John Cage, "Tokyo Lecture and Three Mesostics," *Perspectives of New Music* 26, no. 1 (1988): 7.

51. Cage, "Tokyo Lecture and Three Mesostics," 7.

52. De Re, in Oliveros, *Deep Listening*, 74.

53. Kusama, in Oliveros, *Deep Listening*, 80.

54. See, for example, Barbara Rose Lange, "The Politics of Collaborative Performance in the Music of Pauline Oliveros," *Perspectives of New Music* 46, no. 1 (2008): 50, 53–54.

55. Kahn, "John Cage," 581.

CHAPTER 4

1. Donal Henahan, "Supertitles: The Eyes Have It," *New York Times*, March 13, 1988, H27.

2. Lotfi Mansouri and Donald Arthur, *Lotfi Mansouri: An Operatic Journey* (Boston: Northeastern University Press, 2010), 144.

3. Mansouri and Arthur, *Lotfi Mansouri*, 144.

4. Mansouri and Arthur, *Lotfi Mansouri*, 146.

5. Other early names for the practice included "transcaps" and "op-trans"—the names often differed from company to company. The Metropolitan Opera's system of displaying titles on seatbacks was named Met Titles upon its debut in 1995.

6. Heidi Waleson, *Mad Scenes and Exit Arias: The Death of the New York City Opera and the Future of Opera in America* (New York: Metropolitan Books, Henry Holt and Company, 2018), 62–63.

7. Numbers from US Opera Survey, as reported in Maria F. Rich, "No Surprises: U.S. Opera Survey, 1983–84," *Opera News*, November 1984; Maria F. Rich, "State of the Art: U.S. Opera Survey, 1984–85," *Opera News*, November 1985.

8. John Rockwell, "City Opera Boasts a Smash Season," *New York Times*, November 15, 1984, C30.

9. The four still abstaining at the time were New York's Metropolitan Opera, Opera Theatre of Saint Louis (which performs using sung English translations), Opera Company of Philadelphia, and the Santa Fe Opera. Patrick J. Smith, "Viewpoint," *Opera News*, May 1990, 6.

10. James Levine, quoted in Will Crutchfield, "James Levine: New Era at the Met," *New York Times*, September 22, 1985, SM38.

11. Rodney Milnes, "Sounding Board," *Opera* (October 1984): 1077.

12. Rodney Milnes, "Response to Letter from Neil M. Henderson," *Opera* (December 1984): 1351.

13. Gundula Kreuzer, *Curtain, Gong, Steam: Wagnerian Technologies of Nineteenth-Century Opera* (Oakland: University of California Press, 2019); Melina Esse, ed., "Mediating Opera," special issue of *Opera Quarterly* 26, no. 1 (January 1, 2010); David Trippett, "Facing Digital Realities: Where Media Do Not Mix," *Cambridge Opera Journal* 26, no. 1 (2014): 41–64.

14. Melina Esse, "Don't Look Now: Opera, Liveness, and the Televisual," *Opera Quarterly* 26, no. 1 (2010): 82.

15. Esse, "Don't Look Now," 81–95.

16. Kreuzer, *Curtain, Gong, Steam*.

17. James Steichen, "HD Opera: A Love/Hate Story," *Opera Quarterly* 27, no. 4 (2011): 443–59; W. Anthony Sheppard, "Review of the Metropolitan Opera's New HD Movie Theater Broadcasts," *American Music* 25, no. 3 (2007): 383–87.

18. Philip Auslander, *Liveness: Performance in a Mediatized Culture* (London: Routledge, 1999).

19. See Atom Egoyan and Ian Balfour, eds., *Subtitles: On the Foreignness of Film* (Cambridge, MA: MIT Press, 2004); Abé Mark Nornes, "For an Abusive Subtitling," *Film Quarterly* 52, no. 3 (1999): 17–34.

20. Amresh Sinha, "The Use and Abuse of Subtitles," in *Subtitles: On the Foreignness of Film*, ed. Atom Egoyan and Ian Balfour (Cambridge, MA: MIT Press, 2004), 173.

21. B. Ruby Rich, "To Read or Not to Read: Subtitles, Trailers, and Monolingualism," in *Subtitles: On the Foreignness of Film*, ed. Atom Egoyan and Ian Balfour (Cambridge, MA: MIT Press, 2004), 157–62.

22. Hans Ulrich Gumbrecht, *Production of Presence: What Meaning Cannot Convey* (Stanford, CA: Stanford University Press, 2004).

23. Carolyn Abbate, "Music: Drastic or Gnostic," *Critical Inquiry* 30, no. 3 (2004): 505–36.

24. For a critique of universalizing tendencies within models of white aurality, see Marie Thompson, "Whiteness and the Ontological Turn in Sound Studies," *Parallax* 23, no. 3 (2017): 266–82.

25. Cited in Ian Crofton and Donald Fraser, *A Dictionary of Musical Quotations* (New York: Schirmer Books, 1985), 105.

26. Michel Poizat, *The Angel's Cry: Beyond the Pleasure Principle in Opera* (Ithaca, NY: Cornell University Press, 1992), 44.

27. Poizat, *Angel's Cry*.

28. Poizat's full text argues that as a whole opera has steadily moved toward elements that obscure or eliminate textual meaning in favor of more pure vocal display, though others have taken issue with this teleology.

29. Carolyn Abbate and Roger Parker, *A History of Opera* (New York: W.W. Norton & Company, 2012), 146–66.

30. Donal Henahan, "Could Supertitles Solve the 'Capriccio' Problem?" *New York Times*, February 2, 1986, H21.

31. Bernard Holland, "An Argument in Favor of Supertitles for Opera," *New York Times*, November 15, 1984, C24.

32. This anecdote is related in Gary D. Lipton, "Everybody's Doing It! Surtitles Are Suddenly the Hottest New Trend in the Opera World," *Opera News*, September 1984, 18. It reappears in several subsequent articles on titles.

33. Holland, "Argument in Favor of Supertitles for Opera," C24.

34. Will Crutchfield, "Crutchfield at Large," *Opera News*, May 1990, 43 (emphasis in original).

35. One of the better-known twentieth-century essays on the subject is Benjamin's "The Task of the Translator," which notes that "all translation is only a somewhat provisional way of coming to terms with the foreignness of languages. An instant and final rather than a temporary and provisional solution to this foreignness remains out of the reach of mankind; at any rate it eludes any direct attempt." Walter Benjamin, "The Task of the Translator," in *Selected Writings, Vol. 1, 1913–1926*, ed. Marcus Bullock and Michael W. Jennings (Cambridge, MA: Belknap Press of Harvard University Press, 1996), 257.

36. These categories were introduced in the 1940s by linguist and translation theorist Eugene Nida.

37. Abbate and Parker, *History of Opera*, 2–7.

38. As Bernard Holland put it in a 1984 editorial: "Elitists won't like [supertitles] one bit." (Holland, "Argument in Favor of Supertitles for Opera," C24.)

39. Will Crutchfield, "Review and Overview of Opera Supertitles," *New York Times*, August 30, 1984, C19.

40. Crutchfield, "Review and Overview of Opera Supertitles," C19 (emphasis in original).

41. Henahan, "Supertitles: The Eyes Have It," H27.

42. Carolyn Abbate and Roger Parker, among others have noted that this was quite common from the seventeenth to the nineteenth centuries. Abbate and Parker, *History of Opera*, 4.

43. Quoted in Donal Henahan, "What's Wrong with Supertitles?," *New York Times*, October 6, 1985, H1.

44. Joan Dornemann, Matthew Epstein, Robert Marx, Francis Rizzo, and Patrick J. Smith, "Around the Table: The Pros and (Mostly) Cons of Projected Titles," *Opera News*, May 1990, 15.

45. Paul A. Robinson, "Reading Libretti and Misreading Opera," in *Opera, Sex, and Other Vital Matters* (Chicago: University of Chicago Press, 2002), 31.

46. Robinson, *Reading Libretti and Misreading Opera*, 48.

47. Will Crutchfield, "Need Librettos Be Really Understood?" *New York Times*, August 19, 1984, H17.

48. Crutchfield, "Need Librettos Be Really Understood?"

49. Katherine K. Preston, "Between the Cracks: The Performance of English-Language Opera in Late Nineteenth-Century America," *American Music* 21, no. 3 (2003): 349–74.

50. Mostel as quoted in Speight Jenkins, "Zero In: An Interview with Comedian Mostel," *Opera News*, February 13, 1971, 15.

51. Crutchfield, "Need Librettos Be Really Understood?" H17.

52. Robinson, *Reading Libretti and Misreading Opera*, 51.

53. Robinson, *Reading Libretti and Misreading Opera*, 51.

54. Mladen Dolar, *A Voice and Nothing More* (Cambridge, MA: MIT Press, 2006), 31.

55. Crutchfield, "Need Librettos Be Really Understood?" H17; and Dolar, *Voice and Nothing More*.

56. David J. Levin, *Unsettling Opera: Staging Mozart, Verdi, Wagner, and Zemlinsky* (Chicago: University of Chicago Press, 2007).

57. Francis Rizzo, "The Reluctant Titlist," *Opera News* (May 1990): 21–22.

58. Barry Laine, "The Subtle Work of Making Supertitles," *New York Times*, July 27, 1986, H26.

59. Patrick J. Smith, "Score to Screen," *Opera News*, May 1990, 24.

60. For other examples of experimental titling approaches, see Matthew Gurewitsch, "Supertitles Are Starting to Become Part of the Act," *New York Times*, February 10, 2002.

61. Ludwig Wittgenstein, *Philosophical Investigations*, trans. G.E.M. Anscombe (Malden, MA: Blackwell, 1997), 193e.

62. Similar systems have been used by the Santa Fe Opera, the Seattle Opera House, the Vienna State Opera, the Komische Oper Berlin, London's Royal Opera House, and the Grand Teatro del Liceu in Barcelona.

63. Quoted in Dornemann et al., "Around the Table," 16.

64. Dornemann et al., "Around the Table," 18.

65. See Kreuzer, *Curtain, Gong, Steam*.

66. Abbate and Parker, *A History of Opera*, 4; Robinson, *Opera, Sex, and Other Vital Matters*, 48.

67. "Text," here, refers not only to the libretto but any conceptions of opera in a fixed form to be decoded via any number of hermeneutic or semiotic processes. Still, scores and libretto have historically been the most frequent points

of entry for gnostic modes of engagement, including much of musicology. Abbate, "Music: Drastic or Gnostic."

68. Will Crutchfield, "On Supertitles and the Joys of Opera," *New York Times*, November 27, 1986, C13.

69. Argento quoted in Dornemann et al., "Around the Table," 18.

CHAPTER 5

1. Death Certificate dated June 4, 1975, in "Correspondence 197X-X," *[The Composer] Collection, [source redacted]*. Further citations from this archive are cited in short form simply as "Composer Collection."

2. High School Yearbook, in "Documents and Ephemera," Composer Collection.

3. Letter from [Glow]'s Parents, July 8, 1975, "Correspondence 197X-X," Composer Collection.

4. Brent Hayes Edwards, "The Taste of the Archive," *Callaloo* 35, no. 4 (2012): 946. For more on the affective impacts of dead ends in the archive, see Saidiya Hartman, "Venus in Two Acts," *Small Axe* 12, no. 2 (July 17, 2008): 1–14.

5. Arlette Farge, *The Allure of the Archives*, trans. Thomas Scott-Railton (New Haven, CT: Yale University Press, 2013), 10.

6. Farge, *Allure of the Archives*, 12.

7. Nina Sun Eidsheim, *Sensing Sound: Singing and Listening as Vibrational Practice* (Durham, NC: Duke University Press, 2015), 5.

8. Documents about [Redacted] Fan Club, in "Correspondence—1960s," Composer Collection.

9. The observation that archival and curatorial choices are not politically neutral and are deeply embedded in larger power structures has been a significant focus of critical archival studies over the past several decades, particularly in regard to issues of race. See, for example, Verne Harris, "The Archival Sliver: Power, Memory, and Archives in South Africa," *Archives & Museum Informatics* 2, no. 1–2 (2002): 63–86; Moya Bailey, "On Misogynoir: Citation, Erasure, and Plagiarism," *Feminist Media Studies: Online Misogyny* 18, no. 4 (2018): 762–68; Mario H. Ramirez, "Being Assumed Not to Be: A Critique of Whiteness as an Archival Imperative," *American Archivist* 78, no. 2 (2015): 339–56; Anthony W. Dunbar, "Introducing Critical Race Theory to Archival Discourse: Getting the Conversation Started," *Archival Science* 6, no. 1 (2006): 109–29; Tonia Sutherland, "Archival Amnesty: In Search of Black American Transitional and Restorative Justice," *Journal of Critical Library and Information Studies* 1, no. 2 (2017), https://doi.org/10.24242/jclis.v1i2.42; Jarrett M. Drake, "#ArchivesForBlackLives: Building a Community Archives of Police Violence in Cleveland," *Medium*, April 22, 2016, https://medium.com/on-archivy/archivesforblacklives-building-a-community-archives-of-police-violence-in-cleveland-93615d777289; Terry Cook, "What Is Past Is Prologue: A History of Archival Ideas since 1898 and the Future Paradigm Shift," *Archivaria*

43 (1997): 17–63; Joan M. Schwartz and Terry Cook, "Archives, Records, and Power: The Making of Modern Memory," *Archival Science* 2 (2002): 1–19.

10. Michael C. Heller, *Loft Jazz: Improvising New York in the 1970s* (Oakland: University of California Press, 2017).

11. My own background is within the American middle class. My mother completed college, my father did not, but both enjoyed stable, if not luxurious, work throughout my upbringing.

12. Marika Cifor, "Affecting Relations: Introducing Affect Theory to Archival Discourse," *Archival Science* 16, no. 1 (March 2016): 15.

13. For overviews of some of these contributions, see Michelle Caswell, "'Owning Critical Archival Studies: A Plea'" lecture, Kent State University, 2016, https://escholarship.org/uc/item/75x090df; Michelle L. Caswell, "'The Archive' Is Not an Archives: On Acknowledging the Intellectual Contributions of Archival Studies," *Reconstruction: Studies in Contemporary Culture* 16, no. 1 (2016).

14. Caswell has been critical of this literature (in "'The Archive' Is Not an Archives'") as minimizing the contributions of actual working archivists and archival theorists from within the discipline. In this chapter, however, I draw from both threads of these critical archival traditions. For some examples of the latter, see Antoinette M. Burton, *Archive Stories: Facts, Fictions, and the Writing of History* (Durham, NC: Duke University Press, 2005); Antoinette M. Burton, *Dwelling in the Archive: Women Writing House, Home, and History in Late Colonial India* (New York: Oxford University Press, 2003); Ann Cvetkovich, *An Archive of Feelings: Trauma, Sexuality, and Lesbian Public Cultures* (Durham, NC: Duke University Press, 2003); Jacques Derrida, *Archive Fever: A Freudian Impression* (Chicago: University of Chicago Press, 1996); Edwards, "Taste of the Archive"; Kate Eichhorn, *The Archival Turn in Feminism: Outrage in Order* (Philadelphia, PA: Temple University Press, 2013); Farge, *Allure of the Archives*; Hartman, "Venus in Two Acts"; Achille Mbembe, "The Power of the Archive and Its Limits," in *Refiguring the Archive*, ed. Carolyn Hamilton et al. (Dordrecht: Springer Netherlands, 2002); Carolyn Steedman, *Dust: The Archive and Cultural History* (New Brunswick, NJ: Rutgers University Press, 2002); Ann Laura Stoler, *Along the Archival Grain: Epistemic Anxieties and Colonial Common Sense* (Princeton, NJ: Princeton University Press, 2009); Diana Taylor, *The Archive and the Repertoire: Performing Cultural Memory in the Americas* (Durham, NC: Duke University Press, 2003); Michel-Rolph Trouillot, *Silencing the Past: Power and the Production of History* (Boston: Beacon Press, 1995).

15. Mbembe, "Power of the Archive and Its Limits," 20.

16. See, for instance, David Scott, "Introduction: On the Archaeologies of Black Memory," *Small Axe* 12 no. 2 (2008), vi.

17. Drake, "#ArchivesForBlackLives."

18. Heller, *Loft Jazz*.

19. Mbembe, "Power of the Archive and Its Limits."

20. Sutherland, "Archival Amnesty," 7. See also George Lipsitz, *The Possessive Investment in Whiteness: How White People Profit from Identity Politics* (Philadelphia: Temple University Press, 2018), 54.

21. Manne has defined "himpathy" as "the exonerating narratives and excessive sympathy of which comparatively privileged men tend to be the beneficiaries." I am grateful to Ellie Hisama for bringing the theory to my attention and for her own work applying the idea to music theory contexts. Kate Manne, abstract for the talk "More Than Fair: How Excessive Sympathy for Him ('Himpathy') Obscures and Causes Misogyny," University of North Carolina Department of Philosophy, 2018, https://philosophy.unc.edu/event/speaker-series-kate-manne-cornell/; Ellie M Hisama, "Getting to Count," *Music Theory Spectrum* 43, no. 2 (October 1, 2021): 349–63, https://doi.org/10.1093/mts/mtaa033.

22. For the former, see, for instance, Cifor, "Affecting Relations"; Tina Campt, *Image Matters: Archive, Photography, and the African Diaspora in Europe*, E-Duke Books Scholarly Collection (Durham, NC: Duke University Press, 2012); Cvetkovich, *Archive of Feelings*; Edwards, "Taste of the Archive"; and A.J. Gilliland and M. Caswell, "Records and Their Imaginaries: Imagining the Impossible, Making Possible the Imagined," *Archival Science* 16, no. 1 (November 7, 2015): 53–75.

23. Letter from "Norman," in "Correspondence [late 1970s]," Composer Collection.

24. Postcard from "Norman," in "Postcards," Composer Collection.

25. Letter from "Norman," in "Correspondence [late 1970s])," Composer Collection.

26. Norman was not unique among white men in contemporary music holding problematic views about commissions won by Black or women composers. As Hisama ("Getting to Count," fn48) points out: "In 1994, [Milton] Babbitt intimated that 'reverse sexism' and 'reverse racism' were behind the National Endowment for the Arts' 'ideological correctness,' and identified 'the most threatened minority groups' as 'the composers and performers who have been on the programmes and on the stage." Quotations from Milton Babbitt, "Brave New Worlds," *The Musical Times* 135, no. 1816 (1994): 330, 332–33.

27. University Alumni Magazine, in "College Documents," Composer Collection.

28. University Alumni Magazine, in "College Documents," Composer Collection.

29. Letter from "Neville," in "Correspondence [late 1970s]," Composer Collection.

30. Letter B from Composer to "Ted" and "Norman," early 1980s, digital scan on CD Rom, in "Digital Media," Composer Collection. Though the letter lists the cause of death as liver cancer, Neville's premature death comes during the first wave of the AIDS epidemic in New York City, at a time when many AIDS cases were misidentified as cancer.

31. Letter A from Composer to "Ted" and "Norman," early 1980s, digital scan on CD Rom, in "Digital Media," Composer Collection.

32. Susan Sontag, "Notes on Camp," in *Against Interpretation, and Other Essays* (New York: Picador USA, 2001), 279, 286–87.

33. Whereas Cage was known to have approximated *I Ching* practices using coin flips, the Composer used the more traditional yarrow sticks.

34. Letter from [Cellist], 1983, in "Correspondence [early 1980s]," Composer Collection.

35. Program note found in subseries "Programs—Compositions by [Composer]," Composer Collection.

36. "Programs—Compositions by [Composer]," Composer Collection.

37. Composition notes and full scores in subseries "Scores by [Composer]," in Composer Collection.

38. In "Scores by [Composer]," in Composer Collection.

39. A widely cited example of such work from the 1980s is Margo Culley, *A Day at a Time: The Diary Literature of American Women from 1764 to the Present* (New York: Feminist Press at the City University of New York, 1985). For a useful general discussion from the late 1990s of diaries alongside other women's autobiographical genres, see Sidonie Smith and Julia Watson, "Introduction: Situating Subjectivity in Women's Autobiographical Practices," in *Women, Autobiography, Theory: A Reader* (Madison: University of Wisconsin Press, 1998), 3–52. In musicology one of many influential works is Ellie Hisama's research on Ruth Crawford's diaries and Miriam Gideon's journal in Ellie M. Hisama, *Gendering Musical Modernism: The Music of Ruth Crawford, Marion Bauer, and Miriam Gideon*, (New York: Cambridge University Press, 2001). For another recent discussion specifically relating to archival practice, see Heather Beattie, "Where Narratives Meet: Archival Description, Provenance, and Women's Diaries," *Libraries & the Cultural Record* 44, no. 1 (2009): 82–100.

40. [Virtuoso's] Diaries, entry from mid-1970s, in "Documents and Ephemera," Composer Collection (emphasis in original).

41. I allude to a similar phenomenon in Heller, "Archive," in *Loft Jazz*.

42. [Virtuoso's] Diaries, entry from mid-1970s, in "Documents and Ephemera," Composer Collection.

43. All diary quotations in the pages to follow drawn from [Virtuoso's] Diaries, mid-1970s-2000s, in "Documents and Ephemera," Composer Collection.

44. Online obituary of the Virtuoso. Source redacted.

45. See, for example, Lara Pellegrinelli, "Women in Jazz: Blues and the Objectifying Truth," *National Sawdust Log* (blog), 2017, https://nationalsawdust.org/thelog/2017/12/12/women-in-jazz-blues-and-the-objectifying-truth/; Sasha Berliner, "An Open Letter to Ethan Iverson (and the Rest of Jazz Patriarchy)," *Sasha Berliner* (blog), September 21, 2017, www.sashaberlinermusic.com/sociopoliticalcommentary-1/2017/9/21/an-open-letter-to-ethan-iverson-and-the-rest-of-jazz-patriarchy; Tracy McMullen, "Jazz Education after 2017: The Berklee Institute of Jazz and Gender Justice and the Pedagogical Lineage," *Jazz & Culture* 4, no. 2 (2021): 27–55.

46. [Virtuoso's] Diaries, entry from late 1980s, in "Documents and Ephemera," Composer Collection. A more jokey reference to the Composer's

growing stature with age came in a birthday card from the Virtuoso to the Composer early on in their relationship: "For my dearest on his 35th birthday. You may be an old composer, but you're still a young conductor. I love you. [V.]" In "Postcards," Composer Collection.

47. Online obituary of the Virtuoso. Source redacted.

48. Postcards from [Virtuoso], in "Postcards," Composer Collection.

CHAPTER 6

1. "Interpretive Program for the Louis Armstrong House: A Handbook for Docents, Volunteers, and Other Staff of the Louis Armstrong House," October 20, 2003, private document, copy in possession of author, page 14.

2. For a more detailed account of the Armstrongs obtaining the house, see Michael Cogswell, *Louis Armstrong: The Offstage Story of Satchmo* (Portland, OR: Collectors Press, 2003).

3. "Interpretive Program for the Louis Armstrong House."

4. Personal correspondence with Ricky Riccardi, May 13, 2019.

5. Hildegard Westerkamp, "Soundwalking," *Sound Heritage* 3, no. 4 (1974): 18–27. Quoted in Andra McCartney, "Soundwalking," in *The Oxford Handbook of Mobile Music Studies*, ed. Sumanth Gopinath and Jason Stanyek (New York: Oxford University Press, 2014), 5.

6. McCartney, "Soundwalking."

7. The chapter's structure is inspired in part by Diana Taylor's digital essay/book "Villa Grimaldi," which centers around the experience of participating in guided tours of the infamous Chilean detention center, led by survivor Pedro Matta. Diana Taylor, *Villa Grimaldi (From History to Memory: Walking through Villa Grimaldi)* (Hemi Press, n.d.), http://villagrimaldi.typefold.com/.

8. Alison Martin makes important points regarding the crucial role of situated listening (and the pitfalls of supposedly "objective" methods) within her development of a Black feminist soundwalking practice in "Hearing Change in the Chocolate City: Soundwalking as Black Feminist Method," *Sounding Out!* (blog), August 5, 2019, https://soundstudiesblog.com/2019/08/05/hearing-change-in-the-chocolate-city-soundwalking-as-black-feminist-method/.

9. Jason Stanyek and Benjamin Piekut, "Deadness Technologies of the Intermundane," *TDR* 54 (Spring 2010): 20.

10. Stanyek and Piekut, "Deadness Technologies of the Intermundane," 19.

11. See, for example, David Novak, *Japanoise: Music at the Edge of Circulation* (Durham, NC: Duke University Press, 2013), 28–63.

12. This video was actually produced during my time at the house but not introduced into the tours until somewhat later. If you look closely, the author even makes a brief appearance in the background of a shot.

13. "Interpretive Program for the Louis Armstrong House," 5–6.

14. By my recollection, neighborhood residents were generally welcoming of the museum, rather than seeing it as an outsider institution or sign of encroaching gentrification. Cogswell made it a priority to work with neighborhood

organizations and plan events for the benefit of local residents. Area school kids would also often hang out in the museum's gift shop during open hours and sometimes helped out with small tasks like cleaning the sidewalk. Gentrification was certainly a concern for local residents, as many complained of encroaching developers tearing down single-family houses to construct multiunit apartments. But to my memory, most seemed to see Armstrong's house as a tie to the neighborhood's older life, rather than that of encroaching capital. Of course (and this is a significant caveat), as I was an outsider and a museum employee, it's possible that they did not express their full feelings on the subject, so more research would need to be done to confirm or contradict these impressions.

15. Abigail Fine, "Objects of Veneration: Music and Materiality in the Composer-Cults of Germany and Austria, 1870–1930," PhD dissertation, Music Department, University of Chicago, 2017, 6.

16. Fine, "Objects of Veneration," 17.

17. Fine, "Objects of Veneration," 18.

18. For an account of the tale of the Sosso Bala and its significance within Mande musical culture, see Eric S. Charry, *Mande Music: Traditional and Modern Music of the Maninka and Mandinka of Western Africa* (Chicago: University of Chicago Press, 2000), 142–45.

19. "Cultural Space of Sosso-Bala, Guinea," UNESCO, https://ich.unesco.org/en/RL/cultural-space-of-sosso-bala-00009 (accessed May 14, 2020).

20. In addition to such physical preservation, there is wide literature on the role of oral history and musical memorialization throughout West African cultures. As a product of African diasporic practices, jazz also makes extensive use of this manner of honoring a lineage of major figures. For more, see Patricia Tang, "The Rapper as Modern Griot: Reclaiming Ancient Traditions," in *Hip Hop Africa: New African Music in a Globalizing World* (Bloomington: Indiana University Press, 2012), 79–91; Nubia Kai, *Kuma Malinke Historiography: Sundiata Keita to Almamy Samori Toure* (Lanham, MD: Lexington Books, 2014); Barbara G. Hoffman, *Griots at War: Conflict, Conciliation, and Caste in Mande* (Bloomington: Indiana University Press, 2000); Thomas A. Hale, *Griots and Griottes: Masters of Words and Music* (Bloomington: Indiana University Press, 1998).

21. Victor Turner, *The Ritual Process: Structure and Anti-Structure* (Chicago: Aldine, 1969).

22. Brian Kane, *Sound Unseen: Acousmatic Sound in Theory and Practice* (New York: Oxford University Press, 2014), 147–59.

23. R. Murray Schafer, *The New Soundscape: A Handbook for the Modern Music Teacher* (Don Mills, Ontario: BMI Canada, 1969), 43.

24. Kane, *Sound Unseen*, 225, 245n7.

25. Peter Graff suggested in response to an earlier version of this chapter, that antischizophonic reattachment might also be a useful framework for thinking about the power of lip-synching.

26. Author interview with Michael Cogswell and Deslyn Dyer, Louis Armstrong House, Corona, NY, August 24, 2012.

27. "About Us," STQRY/Antenna International, www.antennainternational.com/about/ (accessed May 15, 2020).

28. Cogswell and Dyer interview.

29. Armstrong quoted in Jorge Daniel Veneciano, "Louis Armstrong, Bricolage, and the Aesthetics of Swing," in *Uptown Conversation*, ed. Robert G. O'Meally, Brent Hayes Edwards, and Farah Jasmine Griffin (Columbia University Press, 2004), 256–77, 258. For numerous reproduced examples of Armstrong's collage work, see Steven Brower, *Satchmo: The Wonderful World and Art of Louis Armstrong* (New York: Abrams, 2009).

30. Veneciano, "Louis Armstrong, Bricolage, and the Aesthetics of Swing," 274.

31. Veneciano, "Louis Armstrong, Bricolage, and the Aesthetics of Swing," 273.

32. Veneciano, "Louis Armstrong, Bricolage, and the Aesthetics of Swing," 274.

33. Kristin Gilger, "Otherwise Lost or Forgotten: Collecting Black History in L. S. Alexander Gumby's 'Negroana' Scrapbooks," *African American Review* 48, no. 1/2 (2015): 111–26, 113. See also Brent Hayes Edwards, "The Politics of Scraps (Black Radicalism and the Archive, Part 1)," W. E. B. Du Bois Lecture Series, Harvard University, March 24, 2015.

34. Gilger, "Otherwise Lost or Forgotten." 111.

35. Cogswell and Dyer interview.

36. Some years later, this clip would be subbed out for a different one of Armstrong saying grace.

37. Cogswell, "Interpretive Program for the Louis Armstrong House," 19.

38. Cogswell and Dyer interview.

39. Cogswell, "Interpretive Program for the Louis Armstrong House," 15.

40. Robin D. G. Kelley, "The Jazz Wife: Muse and Manager," *New York Times*, July 21, 2002.

41. Louis Armstrong, "Why I Like Dark Women," *Ebony Magazine*, August 1954, 61–68.

42. The tape in question deserves longer consideration, as uncomfortable a document as it is. It includes, at the conclusion of an evening of visiting and drinking with friends, a somewhat nasty fight between the couple. At one point Louis revisits the idea presented in the interview, telling Lucille: "You know that horn comes first. Then you and Joe Glaser." Lucille immediately responds: "Bullshit. I come first and then the horn. You can tell me what you want." Reel-to-reel tape recorded by Louis Armstrong, Louis Armstrong House Museum (LAHM) Tape 5/Louis Tape 4—Track 2, Louis Armstrong Archives, Flushing, NY.

43. Tammy L. Kernodle, "Black Women Working Together: Jazz, Gender, and the Politics of Validation," *Black Music Research Journal* 34, no. 1 (2014): 27–55, 35–36.

44. Sherrie Tucker, "Big Ears: Listening for Gender in Jazz Studies," *Current Musicology*, no. 71–73 (2002): 375–408, 378.

45. "About the Louis Armstrong Educational Foundation," https://louisarmstrongfoundation.org/about/ (accessed May 15, 2020).

46. "Interpretive Program for the Louis Armstrong House," 7.

47. "Louis Armstrong House Museum Historic House Tour: Interpretive Manual," updated July 9, 2019, internal document provided by Ricky Riccardi.

48. The most recent update (2019) to the home's interpretive manual makes this note explicit: "Inform visitors that they have just seen the public part of the house, and are about to visit the more private spaces—the Armstrongs' bedroom and Louis' Den." "Louis Armstrong House Museum Historic House Tour: Interpretive Manual."

49. Fine, *Objects of* Veneration, 177–244.

50. Fine, *Objects of* Veneration, 50–66.

51. "Interpretive Program for the Louis Armstrong House," 25.

52. Zora Neale Hurston, "The Characteristics of Negro Expression," in *Negro: An Anthology*, ed. Nancy Cunard (New York: Continuum, 1994), 24–31, 25–26.

53. Richard J. Powell, "Art History and Black Memory: Toward a 'Blues Aesthetic,'" in *History and Memory in African-American Culture*, ed. Geneviève Fabre and Robert G. O'Meally, 228–43 (New York: Oxford University Press, 1994).

54. Some work along these lines has taken place under the auspices of "hauntology," a term derived from Jacques Derrida. See, for instance, Derrida, *Specters of Marx* (New York: Routledge, 1994); Avery Gordon, *Ghostly Matters: Haunting and the Sociological Imagination* (Minneapolis: University of Minnesota Press, 1997); Kashif Jerome Powell, "Making #BlackLivesMatter: Michael Brown, Eric Garner, and the Specters of Black Life—Toward a Hauntology of Blackness," *Cultural Studies ↔ Critical Methodologies* 16, no. 3 (June 1, 2016): 253–60.

55. As of this writing, a movement is also under way to preserve Nina Simone's childhood home in Tryon, North Carolina.

CHAPTER 7

1. David Segal, "Elvis Fans All Shook Up Over Plan to Sell Bits of Reel," *Washington Post*, January 27, 2004, www.washingtonpost.com/archive/lifestyle/2004/01/27/elvis-fans-all-shook-up-over-plan-to-sell-bits-of-reel/926488fd-d38d-4190-b014-e5f3b1fe16e8/. My thanks to Ben Tausig for first pointing me toward this episode.

2. Segal, "Elvis Fans All Shook Up."

3. Jay Lustig, "The 'Reel' Elvis," January 26, 2004, www.talentondisplay.com/TakeNote/067.html.

4. Though the report was not released publicly, a copy was eventually posted in online discussion forums of tape aficionados. As of this writing, a copy remains online that was posted by a user at the Steve Hoffman Music Forums, "Elvis Presley Master Tapes to be cut and sold," forums.stevehoffman.tv

/threads/elvis-presley-master-tapes-to-be-cut-and-sold.27674/page-2 (accessed July 8, 2019).

5. Segal, "Elvis Fans All Shook Up"; Robin Pogrebin, "All Shook Up Over Cutting and Selling of Elvis Tape," *New York Times,* January 28, 2004.

6. This decision is in itself curious, as DAT is hardly a stable archival medium. However, many archival organizations had yet to establish agreed-upon standards for digital audio transfers in 2004. Several would do so in the years that followed. See, for example, Mike Casey and Bruce Gordon, *Sound Directions: Best Practices for Audio Preservation* (Bloomington: Indiana University Press; Cambridge, MA: Harvard University Press, 2007).

7. Pogrebin, "All Shook Up."

8. For discussion of sacred objects in relation to musical figures, see chapter 6.

9. See chapter 6.

10. This text (including all capitalization and punctuation errors) is copied from an image online at "Totally Cool: The Magazine," www.totallycool.net/ElvisTapeCut.html (accessed July 8, 2019).

11. Quoted in Pogrebin, "All Shook Up."

12. Segal, "Elvis Fans All Shook Up."

13. Marsh as quoted in Pogrebin, "All Shook Up."

14. Data from Internet Artchive, web.archive.org/web/20050302235451/http://www.mastertapecollection.com/ (accessed July 11, 2019).

15. An interesting parallel to the Presley story unfolding at the time of this writing, involved the planned sale of a digitized NFT (nonfungible token) of a painting by Jean-Michel Basquiat, for which the sellers initially indicated plans to destroy the original artwork after the sale ("Basquiat NFT Pulled from Auction after Sparking Controversy," *Artforum*, April 28, 2021, www.artforum.com/news/basquiat-nft-pulled-from-auction-after-sparking-controversy-85640).

16. Perusing message board responses to the Presley incident, it's remarkably easy to find comments corresponding to the classic (though today contested) "stages of grief" put forth by Elisabeth Kübler-Ross: denial ("It's hard to believe that they'd destroy the ORIGINAL master tape"; "Surely this is some sort of safety copy"; "It's a con job"); anger ("Reading something like this really makes me angry"; "If it is THE absolute master, this is SICK! It's greed taken to a whole new level"); bargaining ("Here's an idea: Let's all buy the entire mastertape, piece by piece, by ourselves, and then re-assemble the damn thing"); depression ("I felt like vomiting. I just can't imagine destroying a historic tape for any reason"); and acceptance ("I guess if you are the owner, you can do just about anything.") These quotes are taken from users at Steve Hoffman Music Forums, "Elvis Presley Master Tapes to be cut and sold," forums.stevehoffman.tv/threads/elvis-presley-master-tapes-to-be-cut-and-sold.27674/ (accessed July 8, 2019).

17. Andrea Bohlman and Peter McMurray, "Tape: Or, Rewinding the Phonographic Regime," *Twentieth-Century Music* (Cambridge) 14, no. 1 (2017): 9.

18. Bohlman and McMurray, "Tape," 10.

19. Bohlman and McMurray, "Tape," 10; and Peter McMurray, "Once Upon Time: A Superficial History of Early Tape," *Twentieth-Century Music* 14, no. 1 (2017): 25–48.

20. McMurray, "Once Upon Time."

21. For the notion of recombinatoriality of tape, particularly of dead artists, see Jason Stanyek and Benjamin Piekut, "Deadness Technologies of the Intermundane," *TDR* 54 (Spring 2010): 14–38.

22. For a general overview of sticky shed, see Sarah Norris, "Tape Baking," manuscript written in contribution to Stanford University's *Audio Preservation Manual*, 2007, www.sarahnorris.net/Papers%20&%20Research/Tape%20Baking.pdf.

23. Desmond A. Medeiros et al., "Restored magnetic recording media and method of producing same," US5236790 A, filed March 31, 1989, and issued August 17, 1993, www.google.com/patents/US5236790.

24. Philip De Lancie, "Sticky Shed Syndrome: Tips on Saving Your Damaged Master Tapes," *Mix: The Recording Industry Magazine*, May 1990, 149.

25. Michael Starling and John Emmett, "Audio Recording," in *National Association of Broadcasters Engineering Handbook*, 10th ed. (Waltham, MA: Focal Press, 2013); Mike Rivers and Graham Newton, "'Baking' Magnetic Tape to Overcome the 'Sticky-Shed' Problem," *Audio-Restoration by Graham Newton*, http://audio-restoration.com/baking.php (accessed June 16, 2016).

26. Eddie Ciletti, "If I Knew You Were Coming I'd Have Baked a Tape: A Recipe for Tape Restoration," 1998, www.tangible-technology.com/tape/baking1.html (accessed June 16, 2016).

27. This technique—which involves a brand of car polish called Nu Finish—remains a frequent subject of discussion on online forums like Tapeheads.net. See "Tape Trail: A Permanent Solution to Sticky Shed Syndrome (forum thread started by Jeff Koon)," *Audio Asylum*, May 2, 2007, www.audioasylum.com/messages/tape/8002/a-permane.nt-solution-to-sticky-shed-syndrome.

28. See, for example, Richard L. Hess, "Tape Degradation Factors and Challenges in Predicting Tape Life," *ARSC Journal* 39, no. 2 (Fall 2008): 240–74; Sarah Norris, "Effects of Desiccation on Degraded Binder Extraction in Magnetic Audio Tape," *ARSC Journal* 41, no. 2 (Fall 2010): 183–99; Charles A. Richardson, "The New 'Non-Baking' Cure for Sticky Shed Tapes: How Forensic Chemistry Saved the Annapolis Sounds Masters," *ARSC Journal* 44, no. 2 (Fall 2013): 217–48; Dietrich Schüller, "Magnetic Tape Stability: Talking to Experts of Former Tape Manufacturers," *IASA Journal* 42 (January 2014): 32–37.

29. Jim Lindner, "Magnetic Tape Deterioration: Tidal Wave at Our Shores," *Video Magazine*, February 1996, http://cool.conservation-us.org/byauth/lindner/tidal.html.

30. Bill Holland, "Industry's Catalog at Risk: Archived Tapes Could Be Lost to Binder Problem," *Billboard* 111, no. 23 (1999): 1.

31. Marissa Fessenden, "History and Culture of the 1960s to 1980s Is Disintegrating with the Tapes That Recorded It," *Smithsonian—Smart News*,

November 16, 2015, www.smithsonianmag.com/smart-news/culture-and-history-1960s-80s-disintegrating-chemistry-can-save-it-180957267.

32. Richardson, "New 'Non-Baking' Cure for Sticky Shed Tapes," 218.

33. Ann Armstrong, "The Master's Voice: Digitizing and Preserving Oral Histories of Architects," *Art Documentation: Journal of the Art Libraries Society of North America* 27, no. 2 (2008): 15.

34. Quoted in Bill Holland, "Analog: A Race against Time: Tapes Used for Masters Not Built to Last," *Billboard*, August 28, 2004, 78.

35. Michael C. Heller, *Loft Jazz: Improvising New York in the 1970s* (Oakland: University of California Press, 2017).

36. Lindner, "Magnetic Tape Deterioration."

37. For an extended history of archival appraisal, see Terry Cook, "What Is Past Is Prologue: A History of Archival Ideas since 1898 and the Future Paradigm Shift," *Archivaria* 43 (1997): 17–63.

38. McMurray, "Once Upon Time."

39. McMurray, "Once Upon Time."

40. My use of the Orpheus myth here differs from Mack Hagood's insightful theory of "orphic media," which refers to technologies that create a sense of sonic comfort by allowing users to users "remain unaffected in changeable, stressful, and distracting environments, sonically fabricating microspaces of freedom for the pursuit of happiness." Mack Hagood, *Hush: Media and Sonic Self-Control* (Durham, NC: Duke University Press, 2019), 3.

41. Ovid, *Metamorphoses*, trans. A.D. Melville (Oxford, UK: Oxford University Press, 1987), 226.

42. Ovid, *Metamorphoses*, 226.

43. Jan N. Bremmer, *Greek Religion and Culture, the Bible, and the Ancient Near East* (Boston: Brill, 2008), 117–32; Yasumaro Ō, *The Kojiki: An Account of Ancient Matters*, trans. Gustav Heldt (New York: Columbia University Press, 2014), 14–15.

44. Jody Rosen, "The Day the Music Burned," *New York Times Magazine*, June 11, 2019, www.nytimes.com/2019/06/11/magazine/universal-fire-master-recordings.html.

45. Rosen, "Day the Music Burned."

46. Jody Rosen, "Here Are Hundreds More Artists Whose Tapes Were Destroyed in the UMG Fire," *New York Times Magazine*, June 25, 2019, www.nytimes.com/2019/06/25/magazine/universal-music-fire-bands-list-umg.html.

47. Alexander G. Weheliye, *Phonographies: Grooves in Sonic Afro-Modernity* (Durham, NC: Duke University Press, 2005), 8.

48. Weheliye, *Phonographies*, 7.

49. Weheliye, *Phonographies*, 37.

50. Quoted in Rosen, "Day the Music Burned." Prince's phrasing explicitly references the problematic overtones embedded in the term "master" itself. While a reconsideration of similar terminology has begun taking place in other technical fields, such as computer science, no such conversation seems to be

active in sound recording. Elizabeth Landau, "Tech Confronts Its Use of the Labels 'Master' and 'Slave,'" *Wired,* July 6, 2020, www.wired.com/story/tech-confronts-use-labels-master-slave/.

51. Maxine Gordon, *Sophisticated Giant: The Life and Legacy of Dexter Gordon* (Oakland: University of California Press, 2018), 62–76.

52. See, for instance, Gerald Horne, *Jazz and Justice: Racism and the Political Economy of the Music* (New York: Monthly Review Press, 2019); Tim Brooks, *Lost Sounds: Blacks and the Birth of the Recording Industry, 1890–1919* (Urbana: University of Illinois Press, 2004); Fredric Dannen, *Hit Men: Power Brokers and Fast Money inside the Music Business* (New York: Vintage Books, 1991); Karl Hagstrom Miller, *Segregating Sound: Inventing Folk and Pop Music in the Age of Jim Crow* (Durham, NC: Duke University Press, 2010); Matt Stahl, *Unfree Masters: Recording Artists and the Politics of Work* (Durham, NC: Duke University Press, 2013), 183–225.

53. Matthew Morrison's work on Blacksound provides particular insight into the ways that copyright law since the nineteenth century failed to protect the "intellectual performance property" of Black artists and was often structured explicitly to allow its co-option by white performers, publishers, and other industry figures. This was often done through conceiving of Black performance material as existing within the public domain and therefore deeming it ineligible for protection. See Matthew D. Morrison, "Race, Blacksound, and the (Re)Making of Musicological Discourse," *Journal of the American Musicological Society* 72, no. 3 (2019): 781–823; Matthew D. Morrison, *Blacksound: Making Race and Popular Music in America* (Oakland: University of California Press, 2023).

54. See Stahl, *Unfree Masters.*

55. My thanks to reissue producer Carlos Kase for alerting me to this industry nomenclature.

56. Rosen, "Day the Music Burned."

57. Sven Spieker, *The Big Archive: Art from Bureaucracy* (Cambridge, MA: MIT Press, 2008), 21.

58. This is a common theme in archival studies literature. One recent shift has been a move toward an approach known as "more product, less process," in which archivists emphasize a streamlined approach to processing to make available a larger amount of material as quickly as possible. Mark Greene and Dennis Meissner, "More Product, Less Process: Revamping Traditional Archival Processing," *American Archivist* 68, no. 2 (September 1, 2005): 208–63.

59. Jonathan Sterne, *MP3:The Meaning of a Format* (Durham, NC: Duke University Press, 2012), 208–18.

60. Achille Mbembe, "Necropolitics," *Public Culture* 15, no. 1 (2003): 11.

61. Mbembe, "Necropolitics," 21.

62. Rosen, "Day the Music Burned."

63. Elaine Samantha Marston Penn, "Exploring Archival Value: An Axiological Approach," PhD dissertation, UCL University College London, 2014.

64. T. R. Schellenberg, *Modern Archives: Principles and Techniques* (Chicago: Society of American Archivists, 1996), 133.

65. Artists do tend to be featured much more prominently in coverage of legal disputes. See, for example, Stahl, *Unfree Masters,* 105–82.

66. Bill Holland, "Labels Strive to Rectify Past Archival Problems," *Billboard,* July 12, 1997, 3, 88–89; and Bill Holland, "Upgrading Labels' Vaults No Easy Archival Task," *Billboard,* July 19, 1997, 1, 98–99.

67. Holland, "Labels Strive to Rectify Past Archival Problems."

68. A fruitful area for future research would be to explore who has access to and authority over such materials in light of larger structural inequalities within the archival field. See, for example, Anthony W. Dunbar, "Introducing Critical Race Theory to Archival Discourse: Getting the Conversation Started," *Archival Science* 6, no. 1 (2006): 109–29; Mario H. Ramirez, "Being Assumed Not to Be: A Critique of Whiteness as an Archival Imperative," *American Archivist* 78, no. 2 (2015): 339–56.

69. Iron Mountain is an archival and information management company used by numerous recording companies to store various types of records (audio and otherwise).

70. Carlos Kase, post on Facebook.com, June 11, 2019, quoted with permission.

71. Rosen, "Day the Music Burned."

72. Rosen, "Day the Music Burned."

Bibliography

Abbate, Carolyn. "Music: Drastic or Gnostic?" *Critical Inquiry* 30, no. 3 (2004): 505–36.
Abbate, Carolyn, and Roger Parker. *A History of Opera*. New York: W.W. Norton & Company, 2012.
Anderson, Ben. "Becoming and Being Hopeful: Towards a Theory of Affect." *Environment and Planning D: Society and Space* 24, no. 5 (October 2006): 733–52.
Armstrong, Ann. "The Master's Voice: Digitizing and Preserving Oral Histories of Architects." *Art Documentation: Journal of the Art Libraries Society of North America* 27, no. 2 (2008): 15–21.
Attali, Jacques. *Noise: The Political Economy of Music*. Translated by Brian Massumi. Minneapolis: University of Minnesota Press, 1985.
Auslander, Philip. *Liveness: Performance in a Mediatized Culture*. London: Routledge, 1999.
Babbitt, Milton. "Brave New Worlds." *The Musical Times* 135, no. 1816 (1994): 330, 332–33.
Bailey, Moya. "On Misogynoir: Citation, Erasure, and Plagiarism." *Feminist Media Studies: Online Misogyny* 18, no. 4 (2018): 762–68.
Beattie, Heather. "Where Narratives Meet: Archival Description, Provenance, and Women's Diaries." *Libraries & the Cultural Record* 44, no. 1 (2009): 82–100.
Benjamin, Walter. *Selected Writings, Vol. 1, 1913–1926*. Edited by Marcus Bullock and Michael W. Jennings. Cambridge, MA: Belknap Press, 1996.
Beranek, Leo. *Riding the Waves: A Life in Sound, Science, and Industry*. Cambridge, MA: MIT Press, 2008.
Beranek, Leo, and Harvey P. Sleeper Jr. "The Design and Construction of Anechoic Sound Chambers." *Journal of the Acoustical Society of America* 18, no. 1 (1946): 140–50.
Bertram, H.N., and E.F. Cuddihy. "Kinetics of the Humid Aging of Magnetic Recording Tape." *IEEE Transactions on Magnetics* 18, no. 5 (September 1982): 993–99.

Biddle, Ian. "Love Thy Neighbour? The Political Economy of Musical Neighbours." *Radical Musicology* 2 (2007). www.radical-musicology.org.uk/2007/Biddle.htm.

Bijsterveld, Karin. *Mechanical Sound: Technology, Culture, and Public Problems of Noise in the Twentieth Century.* Cambridge, MA: MIT Press, 2008.

Bohlman, Andrea, and Peter McMurray. "Tape: Or, Rewinding the Phonographic Regime." *Twentieth-Century Music* 14, no. 1 (2017): 3–24.

Born, Georgina, and David Hesmondhalgh. *Western Music and Its Others: Difference, Representation, and Appropriation in Music.* Berkeley: University of California Press, 2000.

Braxton, Anthony. *Tri-Axium Writings.* Revised edition. 3 volumes. Lebanon, NH: Frog Peak Music, Forthcoming.

Bremmer, Jan N. *Greek Religion and Culture, the Bible, and the Ancient Near East.* Boston: Brill, 2008.

Brooks, Daphne. *Liner Notes for the Revolution: The Intellectual Life of Black Feminist Sound.* Cambridge, MA: Belknap Press, 2021.

Brooks, Tim. *Lost Sounds: Blacks and the Birth of the Recording Industry, 1890–1919.* Urbana: University of Illinois Press, 2004.

Brower, Steven. *Satchmo: The Wonderful World and Art of Louis Armstrong.* New York: Abrams, 2009.

Brown, Edward Fischer, E. B. Dennis, Jean Henry, and G. Edward Pendray, eds. "City Noise: The Report of the Commission Appointed by Dr. Shirley W. Wynne, Commissioner of Health, to Study Noise in New York City and to Develop Means of Abating It." New York Noise Abatement Commission, Department of Health, New York:,1930.

Burton, Antoinette M. *Archive Stories: Facts, Fictions, and the Writing of History.* Durham, NC: Duke University Press, 2005.

———. *Dwelling in the Archive: Women Writing House, Home, and History in Late Colonial India.* New York: Oxford University Press, 2003.

Cage, John. *Silence: Lectures and Writings.* Middletown, CT: Wesleyan University Press, 1961.

———. "Tokyo Lecture and Three Mesostics." *Perspectives of New Music* 26, no. 1 (1988): 6–25.

———. *A Year from Monday: New Lectures and Writings.* Middletown, CT: Wesleyan University Press, 1967.

Campt, Tina. *Image Matters: Archive, Photography, and the African Diaspora in Europe.* E-Duke Books Scholarly Collection. Durham, NC: Duke University Press, 2012.

Casey, Mike, and Bruce Gordon. *Sound Directions: Best Practices for Audio Preservation.* Bloomington: Indiana University Press; Cambridge, MA: Harvard University Press, 2007.

Caswell, Michelle L. "'The Archive' Is Not an Archives: On Acknowledging the Intellectual Contributions of Archival Studies." *Reconstruction: Studies in Contemporary Culture* 16, no. 1 (2016), reconstruction.digitalodu.com/Issues/161/Caswell.shtml.

———. "Owning Critical Archival Studies: A Plea." Lecture at Kent State University, 2016, https://escholarship.org/uc/item/75x090df.
Chandrasekaran, B., John R. Josephson, and V. Richard Benjamins. "What Are Ontologies, and Why Do We Need Them?" *Intelligent Systems and Their Applications, IEEE* 14, no. 1 (1999): 20–26.
Charry, Eric S. *Mande Music: Traditional and Modern Music of the Maninka and Mandinka of Western Africa*. Chicago: University of Chicago Press, 2000.
Cifor, Marika. "Affecting Relations: Introducing Affect Theory to Archival Discourse." *Archival Science* 16, no. 1 (March 2016): 7–31.
Cogswell, Michael. *Louis Armstrong: The Offstage Story of Satchmo*. Portland, OR: Collectors Press, 2003.
Connor, Steven. "Edison's Teeth: Touching Hearing." In *Hearing Cultures: Essays on Sound, Listening, and Modernity*. Edited by Veit Erlmann, 153–72. Oxford: Berg, 2004.
Cook, Terry. "What Is Past Is Prologue: A History of Archival Ideas since 1898 and the Future Paradigm Shift." *Archivaria* 43 (1997): 17–63.
Corbett, John. "Experimental Oriental: New Music and Other Others." In *Western Music and Its Others: Difference, Representation, and Appropriation in Music*. Edited by Georgina Born and David Hesmondhalgh, 163–86. Berkeley: University of California Press, 2000.
Crofton, Ian, and Donald Fraser, eds. *A Dictionary of Musical Quotations*. New York: Schirmer Books, 1985.
Culley, Margo. *A Day at a Time: The Diary Literature of American Women from 1764 to the Present*. New York: Feminist Press at the City University of New York, 1985.
Cusick, Suzanne G. "'You Are in a Place That Is Out of the World . . . ': Music in the Detention Camps of the 'Global War on Terror.'" *Journal of the Society for American Music* 2, no. 1 (2008): 1–26.
Cvetkovich, Ann. *An Archive of Feelings: Trauma, Sexuality, and Lesbian Public Cultures*. Durham, NC: Duke University Press, 2003.
Dannen, Fredric. *Hit Men: Power Brokers and Fast Money inside the Music Business*. New York: Vintage Books, 1991.
Daughtry, J. Martin. *Listening to War: Sound, Music, Trauma and Survival in Wartime Iraq*. New York: Oxford University Press, 2015.
———. "Thanatosonics: Ontologies of Acoustic Violence." *Social Text* 32, no. 2 (2014): 25–51.
Deleuze, Gilles, and Félix Guattari. *What Is Philosophy?* New York: Columbia University Press, 1994, 185.
Derrida, Jacques. *Archive Fever: A Freudian Impression*. Chicago: University of Chicago Press, 1996.
———. *Specters of Marx*. New York: Routledge, 1994.
Dickinson, Peter. *CageTalk: Dialogues with and about John Cage*. Rochester, NY: University of Rochester Press, 2006.
Dolar, Mladen. *A Voice and Nothing More*. Cambridge, MA: MIT Press, 2006.

Douglass, Frederick. "Narrative of the Life of Frederick Douglass, An American Slave." In *The Classic Slave Narratives*, edited by Henry Louis Gates, 243–331. New York: Mentor, 1987.
Drake, Jarrett M. "#ArchivesForBlackLives: Building a Community Archives of Police Violence in Cleveland." *Medium*. April 22, 2016. https://medium.com/on-archivy/archivesforblacklives-building-a-community-archives-of-police-violence-in-cleveland-93615d777289.
Dunbar, Anthony W. "Introducing Critical Race Theory to Archival Discourse: Getting the Conversation Started." *Archival Science* 6, no. 1 (2006): 109–29.
Echard, William. *Neil Young and the Poetics of Energy*. Bloomington: Indiana University Press, 2005.
Edwards, Brent Hayes. "The Politics of Scraps (Black Radicalism and the Archive, Part 1)." Lecture presented at the W.E.B. Du Bois Lecture Series, Harvard University, March 24, 2015.
———. "The Taste of the Archive." *Callaloo* 35, no. 4 (2012): 944–72.
Egoyan, Atom, and Ian Balfour, eds. *Subtitles: On the Foreignness of Film*. Cambridge, MA: MIT Press, 2004.
Eichhorn, Kate. *The Archival Turn in Feminism: Outrage in Order*. Philadelphia, PA: Temple University Press, 2013.
Eidsheim, Nina Sun. *The Race of Sound: Listening, Timbre, and Vocality in African American Music*. Durham, NC: Duke University Press, 2018.
———. *Sensing Sound: Singing and Listening as Vibrational Practice*. Durham, NC: Duke University Press, 2015.
Esse, Melina. "Don't Look Now: Opera, Liveness, and the Televisual." *Opera Quarterly* 26, no. 1 (2010): 81–95.
———. "A Note from the Guest Editor." *Opera Quarterly* 26, no. 1 (January 1, 2010): 1–3.
Farge, Arlette. *The Allure of the Archives*. Translated by Thomas Scott-Railton. New Haven, CT: Yale University Press, 2013.
Fine, Abigail. "Objects of Veneration: Music and Materiality in the Composer-Cults of Germany and Austria, 1870–1930." PhD dissertation, Music Department, University of Chicago, 2017.
Fleming, Richard, and William Duckworth, eds. *John Cage at Seventy-Five*. Lewisburg, PA: Bucknell University Press, 1989.
Fletcher, Harvey, and W.A. Munson. "Loudness, Its Definition, Measurement, and Calculation." *Bell System Technical Journal* 12, no. 4 (1933): 377–430.
Florentine, Mary, Arthur N. Popper, and Richard R. Fay, eds. *Loudness*. New York: Springer, 2010.
Fontaine, Dick, director. *Sound??* Documentary film. New Tempo, 1967.
Foucault, Michel. *The Archaeology of Knowledge and the Discourse on Language*. New York: Pantheon Books, 1972.
Frankenberg, Ruth. *White Women, Race Matters: The Social Construction of Whiteness*. Minneapolis: University of Minnesota Press, 1993.

Frith, Simon. Afterword. In *The Relentless Pursuit of Tone: Timbre in Popular Music*, edited by Robert Fink, Melinda Latour, and Zachary Wallmark, 367–76. New York: Oxford University Press, 2018.

Galambos, Robert. "Flight in the Dark: A Study of Bats." *Scientific Monthly* 56, no. 2 (1943): 155–62.

Galambos, Robert, and Donald R. Griffin. "Obstacle Avoidance by Flying Bats: The Cries of Bats." *Journal of Experimental Zoology* 89, no. 3 (April 1, 1942): 475–90.

Gann, Kyle. *No Such Thing as Silence: John Cage's 4'33"*. New Haven, CT: Yale University Press, 2010.

Gannon, Robert. *Hellions of the Deep: The Development of American Torpedoes in World War II*. University Park, PA: Penn State Press, 1996.

Gilger, Kristin. "Otherwise Lost or Forgotten: Collecting Black History in L. S. Alexander Gumby's 'Negroana' Scrapbooks." *African American Review* 48, no. 1/2 (2015): 111–26.

Gilliland, A. J., and M. Caswell. "Records and Their Imaginaries: Imagining the Impossible, Making Possible the Imagined." *Archival Science* 16, no. 1 (November 7, 2015): 53–75.

Goh, Annie. "Sounding Situated Knowledges: Echo in Archaeoacoustics." *Parallax* 23, no. 3 (2017): 283–304.

Goodman, Steve. *Sonic Warfare: Sound, Affect, and the Ecology of Fear*. Cambridge, MA: MIT Press, 2010.

Gordon, Avery. *Ghostly Matters: Haunting and the Sociological Imagination*. Minneapolis: University of Minnesota Press, 1997.

Gordon, Maxine. *Sophisticated Giant: The Life and Legacy of Dexter Gordon*. Oakland: University of California Press, 2018.

Gracyk, Theodore. *Rhythm and Noise: An Aesthetics of Rock*. Durham, NC: Duke University Press, 1996.

Greene, Mark, and Dennis Meissner. "More Product, Less Process: Revamping Traditional Archival Processing." *American Archivist* 68, no. 2 (September 1, 2005): 208–63.

Gregg, Melissa, and Gregory J. Seigworth. *The Affect Theory Reader*. Durham, NC: Duke University Press, 2010.

Griffiths, Ezer. "George William Clarkson Kaye. 1880–1941." *Obituary Notices of Fellows of the Royal Society* 3 (December 1941): 881–95.

Gumbrecht, Hans Ulrich. *Production of Presence: What Meaning Cannot Convey*. Stanford, CA: Stanford University Press, 2004.

Hagood, Mack. *Hush: Media and Sonic Self-Control*. Durham, NC: Duke University Press, 2019.

Hale, Thomas A. *Griots and Griottes: Masters of Words and Music*. Bloomington: Indiana University Press, 1998.

Harris, Verne. "The Archival Sliver: Power, Memory, and Archives in South Africa." *Archives & Museum Informatics* 2, no. 1–2 (2002): 63–86.

Hartman, Saidiya. "Venus in Two Acts." *Small Axe* 12, no. 2 (July 17, 2008): 1–14.

Hegarty, Paul. *Noise/Music: A History.* New York: Continuum, 2007.
Heller, Michael C. *Loft Jazz: Improvising New York in the 1970s.* Oakland: University of California Press, 2017.
Helmholtz, Hermann von. *On the Sensations of Tone as a Physiological Basis for the Theory of Music.* Translated by Alexander John Ellis. London: Longmans Green, 1875.
Helmreich, Stefan. "An Anthropologist Underwater: Immersive Soundscapes, Submarine Cyborgs, and Transductive Ethnography." *American Ethnologist* 34, no. 4 (November 1, 2007): 622.
Hess, Richard L. "Tape Degradation Factors and Challenges in Predicting Tape Life." *ARSC Journal* 39, no. 2 (Fall 2008): 240–74.
Hisama, Ellie M. *Gendering Musical Modernism: The Music of Ruth Crawford, Marion Bauer, and Miriam Gideon.* New York: Cambridge University Press, 2001.
———. "Getting to Count." *Music Theory Spectrum* 43, no. 2 (October 1, 2021): 349–63.
Hoffman, Barbara G. *Griots at War: Conflict, Conciliation, and Caste in Mande.* Bloomington: Indiana University Press, 2000.
Horne, Gerald. *Jazz and Justice: Racism and the Political Economy of the Music.* New York: Monthly Review Press, 2019.
Hurston, Zora Neale. "Characteristics of Negro Expression." In *Negro: An Anthology,* edited by Nancy Cunard, 24–31. New York: Continuum, 1994.
Jacquin, Maud, and Elsa Polverel. "'Dissolving Your Ear Plugs': The Unheard in Pauline Oliveros' Deep Listening Practice." *Auditive Perspektiven* (January 2020). https://edoc.hu-berlin.de/handle/18452/21842.
Kahn, Douglas. "John Cage: Silence and Silencing." *Musical Quarterly* 81, no. 4 (1997): 556–98.
Kai, Nubia. *Kuma Malinke Historiography: Sundiata Keita to Almamy Samori Toure.* Lanham, MD: Lexington Books, 2014.
Kane, Brian. "Sound Studies without Auditory Culture: A Critique of the Ontological Turn." *Sound Studies* 1, no. 1 (2015): 2–21.
———. *Sound Unseen: Acousmatic Sound in Theory and Practice.* New York: Oxford University Press, 2014.
Kapchan, Deborah. *Theorizing Sound Writing.* Middletown, CT: Wesleyan University Press, 2017.
Karpf, Anne. *The Human Voice: How This Extraordinary Instrument Reveals Essential Clues about Who We Are.* New York: Bloomsbury, 2006.
Kassabian, Anahid. *Ubiquitous Listening: Affect, Attention, and Distributed Subjectivity.* Berkeley: University of California Press, 2013.
Kaye, George William Clarkson. "The Measurement of Noise." *Reports on Progress in Physics* 3 (1936): 130–42.
Kernodle, Tammy L. "Black Women Working Together: Jazz, Gender, and the Politics of Validation." *Black Music Research Journal* 34, no. 1 (2014): 27–55.
Kim, Rebecca Y. "John Cage in Separate Togetherness with Jazz." *Contemporary Music Review* 31, no. 1 (February 1, 2012): 63–89.

Kittler, Friedrich A. *Gramophone, Film, Typewriter.* Stanford, CA: Stanford University Press, 1999.
Kneece, Jack. *Ghost Army of World War II.* Gretna, LA: Pelican, 2001.
Kostelanetz, Richard. *Conversing with Cage.* 2nd edition. New York: Routledge, 2003.
Kreuzer, Gundula Katharina. *Curtain, Gong, Steam: Wagnerian Technologies of Nineteenth-Century Opera.* Oakland: University of California Press, 2019.
Lange, Barbara Rose. "The Politics of Collaborative Performance in the Music of Pauline Oliveros." *Perspectives of New Music* 46, no. 1 (2008): 39–60.
Levin, David J. *Unsettling Opera: Staging Mozart, Verdi, Wagner, and Zemlinsky.* Chicago: University of Chicago Press, 2007.
Lewis, Eric. *Intents and Purposes: Philosophy and the Aesthetics of Improvisation.* Ann Arbor: University of Michigan Press, 2019.
Lewis, George E. "Afterword to 'Improvised Music after 1950': The Changing Same." In *The Other Side of Nowhere: Jazz, Improvisation, and Communities in Dialogue,* edited by Daniel Fischlin and Ajay Heble, 163–72. Middletown, CT: Wesleyan University Press, 2004.
———. "Improvised Music after 1950: Afrological and Eurological Perspectives." *Black Music Research Journal* 16, no. 1 (1996): 91–122.
———. *A Power Stronger Than Itself: The AACM and American Experimental Music.* Chicago: University of Chicago Press, 2008.
Lipsitz, George. *The Possessive Investment in Whiteness: How White People Profit from Identity Politics.* Philadelphia, PA: Temple University Press, 2018.
Lloyd, Llewelyn S. "What Are Phons?" *The Musical Times* 93, no. 1308 (1952): 62–63.
Lucas, Olivia. "MAXIMUM VOLUME YIELDS MAXIMUM RESULTS." *Journal of Sonic Studies* 7 (2014). http://sonicstudies.org/jss7.
Mansell, James G. "Hearing With: Researching the Histories of Sonic Encounter." In *The Bloomsbury Handbook of Sonic Methodologies,* edited by Michael Bull and Marcel Cobussen, 93–114. New York: Bloomsbury, 2020.
Mansouri, Lotfi, and Donald Arthur. *Lotfi Mansouri: An Operatic Journey.* Boston: Northeastern University Press, 2010.
Marks, Lawrence E., and Mary Florentine. "Measurement of Loudness, Part I: Methods, Problems and Pitfalls." In *Loudness,* edited by Mary Florentine, Arthur N. Popper, and Richard R. Fay. New York: Springer, 2010.
Marshall, Wayne. "Treble Culture." In *The Oxford Handbook of Mobile Music Studies, Volume 2,* edited by Sumanth Gopinath and Jason Stanyek. Oxford Handbooks in Music. New York: Oxford University Press, 2014.
Martin, Alison. "Hearing Change in the Chocolate City: Soundwalking as Black Feminist Method." *Sounding Out!* (blog), August 5, 2019. https://soundstudiesblog.com/2019/08/05/hearing-change-in-the-chocolate-city-soundwalking-as-black-feminist-method/.

Massumi, Brian. *Parables for the Virtual: Movement, Affect, Sensation.* Durham, NC: Duke University Press, 2002.

———. *What Animals Teach Us about Politics.* Durham, NC: Duke University Press, 2014.

Mathes, Carter. *Imagine the Sound: Experimental African American Literature after Civil Rights.* Minneapolis: University of Minnesota Press, 2015.

Mbembe, Achille. "Necropolitics." *Public Culture* 15, no. 1 (2003): 11–40.

———. "The Power of the Archive and Its Limits." In *Refiguring the Archive*, edited by Carolyn Hamilton, Verne Harris, Jane Taylor, Michele Pickover, Graeme Reid, and Razia Saleh. Dordrecht, Germany: Springer Netherlands, 2002.

McCartney, Andra. "Soundwalking." In *The Oxford Handbook of Mobile Music Studies*, edited by Sumanth Gopinath and Jason Stanyek, 212–37. New York: Oxford University Press, 2014.

McMullen, Tracy. "Jazz Education after 2017: The Berklee Institute of Jazz and Gender Justice and the Pedagogical Lineage." *Jazz & Culture* 4, no. 2 (2021): 27–55.

———. "Subject, Object, Improv: John Cage, Pauline Oliveros, and Eastern (Western) Philosophy in Music." *Critical Studies in Improvisation / Études Critiques En Improvisation* 6, no. 2 (December 1, 2010). https://doi.org/10.21083/csieci.v6i2.851.

McMurray, Peter. "Once Upon Time: A Superficial History of Early Tape." *Twentieth-Century Music* 14, no. 1 (2017): 25–48.

Menzel, Daniel, Hugo Fastl, Ralf Graf, and Jürgen Hellbrück. "Influence of Vehicle Color on Loudness Judgments." *Journal of the Acoustical Society of America* 123, no. 5 (2008): 2477–79.

Miller, Karl Hagstrom. *Segregating Sound: Inventing Folk and Pop Music in the Age of Jim Crow.* Durham, NC: Duke University Press, 2010.

Morrison, Matthew D. *Blacksound: Making Race and Popular Music in America.* Oakland: University of California Press, 2023.

———. "Race, Blacksound, and the (Re)Making of Musicological Discourse." *Journal of the American Musicological Society* 72, no. 3 (2019): 781–823.

Moten, Fred. *In the Break: The Aesthetics of the Black Radical Tradition.* Minneapolis: University of Minnesota Press, 2003.

Mowitt, John. *Sounds: The Ambient Humanities.* Oakland: University of California Press, 2015.

Nancy, Jean-Luc. *Listening.* Translated by Charlotte Mandell. New York: Fordham University Press, 2007.

Nornes, Abé Mark. "For an Abusive Subtitling." *Film Quarterly* 52, no. 3 (1999): 17–34.

Norris, Sarah. "Effects of Desiccation on Degraded Binder Extraction in Magnetic Audio Tape." *ARSC Journal* 41, no. 2 (Fall 2010): 183–99.

Novak, David. *Japanoise: Music at the Edge of Circulation.* Durham, NC: Duke University Press, 2013.

Nyong'o, Tavia. "Afro-Philo-Sonic Fictions: Black Sound Studies after the Millennium." *Small Axe* 18, no. 2 (2014): 173–79.

Ō Yasumaro. *The Kojiki: An Account of Ancient Matters*. Translated by Gustav Heldt. New York: Columbia University Press, 2014.

Ochoa Gautier, Ana María. *Aurality: Listening and Knowledge in Nineteenth-Century Colombia*. Durham, NC: Duke University Press, 2014.

———. "Silence." In *Keywords in Sound*, edited by Matt Sakakeeny and David Novak, 183–92. Durham, NC: Duke University Press, 2015.

Okiji, Fumi. *Jazz As Critique: Adorno and Black Expression Revisited*. Redwood City, CA: Stanford University Press, 2018.

Oliveros, Pauline. *Deep Listening: A Composer's Sound Practice*. New York: iUniverse, Inc, 2005.

———. *Software for People: Collected Writings, 1963–80*. Baltimore, MD: Smith Publications, 1984.

———. *Sonic Meditations*. Baltimore, MD: Smith Publications, 1974.

Ouzounian, Gascia. *Stereophonica: Sound and Space in Science, Technology, and the Arts*. Cambridge, MA: MIT Press, 2021.

Ovid. *Metamorphoses*. Translated by A.D. Melville. Oxford, UK: Oxford University Press, 1987.

Pais, Ana. "Almost Imperceptible Rhythms and Stuff Like That: The Power of Affect in Live Performance." In *Theorizing Sound Writing*, edited by Deborah Kapchan, 233–49. Hanover, NH: Wesleyan University Press, 2017.

Pattuelli, M. Cristina, Alexandra Provo, and Hilary Thorsen. "Ontology Building for Linked Open Data: A Pragmatic Perspective." *Journal of Library Metadata* 15, no. 3–4 (2015): 265–94.

Penn, Elaine Samantha Marston. "Exploring Archival Value: An Axiological Approach." PhD dissertation, University College London, 2014.

Pestorius, Frederick M., and David T. Blackstock. "Contributions to the Development of Underwater Acoustics at the Harvard Underwater Sound Laboratory (HUSL)." *Proceedings of Meetings on Acoustics* 23, no. 1 (May 18, 2015).

Pinch, Trevor, and Karin Bijsterveld. *The Oxford Handbook of Sound Studies*. New York: Oxford University Press, 2012.

Poizat, Michel. *The Angel's Cry: Beyond the Pleasure Principle in Opera*. Ithaca, NY: Cornell University Press, 1992.

Powell, Kashif Jerome. "Making #BlackLivesMatter: Michael Brown, Eric Garner, and the Specters of Black Life—Toward a Hauntology of Blackness." *Cultural Studies ↔ Critical Methodologies* 16, no. 3 (June 1, 2016): 253–60.

Powell, Richard J. "Art History and Black Memory: Toward a 'Blues Aesthetic.'" In *History and Memory in African-American Culture*, edited by Geneviève Fabre and Robert G. O'Meally, 228–43. New York: Oxford University Press, 1994.

Preston, Katherine K. "Between the Cracks: The Performance of English-Language Opera in Late Nineteenth-Century America." *American Music* 21, no. 3 (2003): 349–74.

Quashie, Kevin Everod. *The Sovereignty of Quiet: Beyond Resistance in Black Culture*. New Brunswick, NJ: Rutgers University Press, 2012.
Rainer, Yvonne. "Looking Myself in the Mouth." *October* 17 (1981): 65–76.
Ramirez, Mario H. "Being Assumed Not to Be: A Critique of Whiteness as an Archival Imperative." *American Archivist* 78, no. 2 (2015): 339–56.
Revill, David. *The Roaring Silence: John Cage: A Life*. New York: Arcade Publishing, 2012.
Rice, Tom. "Listening." In *Keywords in Sound*, edited by Matt Sakakeeny and David Novak, 99–111. Durham, NC: Duke University Press, 2015.
Rich, B. Ruby. "To Read or Not to Read: Subtitles, Trailers, and Monolingualism." In *Subtitles: On the Foreignness of Film*, edited by Atom Egoyan and Ian Balfour, 153–69. Cambridge, MA: MIT Press, 2004.
Richardson, Charles A. "The New 'Non-Baking' Cure for Sticky Shed Tapes: How Forensic Chemistry Saved the Annapolis Sounds Masters." *ARSC Journal* 44, no. 2 (Fall 2013): 217–48.
Riesz, R. R. "The Relationship between Loudness and the Minimum Perceptible Increment of Intensity." *Journal of the Acoustical Society of America* 4, no. 3 (1933): 211–16.
Roads, Curtis. *Microsound*. Cambridge, MA: MIT Press, 2001.
Robinson, Dylan. *Hungry Listening: Resonant Theory for Indigenous Sound Studies*. Minneapolis: University of Minnesota Press, 2020.
Robinson, Paul A. *Opera, Sex, and Other Vital Matters*. Chicago: University of Chicago Press, 2002.
Rodgers, Tara. "Toward a Feminist Epistemology of Sound: Refiguring Waves in Audio-Technical Discourse." In *Engaging the World: Thinking after Irigaray*, edited by Mary C. Rawlinson, 195–213. Albany: State University of New York Press, 2016.
Rose, Tricia. *Black Noise: Rap Music and Black Culture in Contemporary America*. African American Music Reference. Hanover, NH: Wesleyan University Press, 1994.
Rosen, Jody. "The Day the Music Burned." *New York Times Magazine*, June 11, 2019. www.nytimes.com/2019/06/11/magazine/universal-fire-master-recordings.html.
———. "Here Are Hundreds More Artists Whose Tapes Were Destroyed in the UMG Fire." *New York Times Magazine*, June 25, 2019. www.nytimes.com/2019/06/25/magazine/universal-music-fire-bands-list-umg.html.
Sakakeeny, Matt, and David Novak, eds. *Keywords in Sound*. Durham, NC: Duke University Press, 2015.
Scarry, Elaine. *The Body in Pain: The Making and Unmaking of the World*. New York: Oxford University Press, 1985.
Scarth, Richard N., and Hythe Civic Society. *Echoes from the Sky: A Story of Acoustic Defence*. Kent, UK: Hythe Civic Society, 1999.
Schafer, R. Murray. *The New Soundscape: A Handbook for the Modern Music Teacher*. Don Mills, Ontario: BMI Canada, 1969.

———. *The Soundscape: Our Sonic Environment and the Tuning of the World.* Rochester, VT: Destiny Books, 1993.

Schellenberg, T.R. *Modern Archives: Principles and Techniques.* Chicago: Society of American Archivists, 1996.

Schüller, Dietrich. "Magnetic Tape Stability: Talking to Experts of Former Tape Manufacturers." *IASA Journal* 42 (January 2014): 32–37.

Schwartz, Joan M., and Terry Cook. "Archives, Records, and Power: The Making of Modern Memory." *Archival Science* 2 (2002): 1–19.

Scott, David. "Introduction: On the Archaeologies of Black Memory." *Small Axe* 12, no. 2 (2008): v–xvi.

Shackelford, Brandon Gary. "When the Noise Signals Change: The Electro-Acoustic and Psycho-Acoustic Laboratories from 1940 to 1945." AB thesis, Harvard University, 1997.

Sheppard, W. Anthony. "Review of the Metropolitan Opera's New HD Movie Theater Broadcasts." *American Music* 25, no. 3 (2007): 383–87.

Sinha, Amresh. "The Use and Abuse of Subtitles." In *Subtitles: On the Foreignness of Film*, edited by Atom Egoyan and Ian Balfour, 171–90. Cambridge, MA: MIT Press, 2004.

Smeds, Karolina, and Arne Leijon. "Loudness and Hearing Loss." In *Loudness*, edited by Mary Florentine, Arthur N. Popper, and Richard R. Fay, 223–59. Springer Handbook of Auditory Research 37. New York: Springer, 2010.

Smith, Sidonie, and Julia Watson. "Introduction: Situating Subjectivity in Women's Autobiographical Practices." In *Women, Autobiography, Theory: A Reader*, 3–52. Madison: University of Wisconsin Press, 1998.

Smith, Wadada Leo. *Notes (8 Pieces).* Reprint edition. Chicago: Renaissance Society at the University of Chicago, 2015.

Sontag, Susan. "Notes on Camp." In *Against Interpretation, and Other Essays*, 275–92. New York: Picador, 2001.

Spieker, Sven. *The Big Archive: Art from Bureaucracy.* Cambridge, MA: MIT Press, 2008.

Stahl, Matt. *Unfree Masters: Recording Artists and the Politics of Work.* Durham, NC: Duke University Press, 2013.

Stanyek, Jason, and Benjamin Piekut. "Deadness Technologies of the Intermundane." *TDR* 54 (Spring 2010): 14–38.

Starling, Michael, and John Emmett. "Audio Recording." In *National Association of Broadcasters Engineering Handbook*, 10th edition. Waltham, MA: Focal Press, 2013.

Steedman, Carolyn. *Dust: The Archive and Cultural History.* New Brunswick, NJ: Rutgers University Press, 2002.

Steichen, James. "HD Opera: A Love/Hate Story." *Opera Quarterly* 27, no. 4 (2011): 443–59.

Steingo, Gavin, and Jim Sykes, eds. *Remapping Sound Studies.* Durham, NC: Duke University Press, 2019.

Sterne, Jonathan. "Hearing." In *Keywords in Sound*, edited by Matt Sakakeeny and David Novak, 65–77. Durham, NC: Duke University Press, 2015.

———. *MP3: The Meaning of a Format*. Durham, NC: Duke University Press, 2012.

Stoever, Jennifer Lynn. *The Sonic Color Line: Race and the Cultural Politics of Listening*. New York: New York University Press, 2016.

Stoler, Ann Laura. *Along the Archival Grain: Epistemic Anxieties and Colonial Common Sense*. Princeton, NJ: Princeton University Press, 2009.

Sun Ra and John Cage. *John Cage Meets Sun Ra*. LP. Meltdown Records MPA-1, 1987.

———. *John Cage Meets Sun Ra: The Complete Concert*. Compact Disc. Modern Harmonic MHCD-020, 2016.

Sutherland, Tonia. "Archival Amnesty: In Search of Black American Transitional and Restorative Justice." *Journal of Critical Library and Information Studies* 1, no. 2 (2017). journals.litwinbooks.com/index.php/jclis/article/view/42.

Szwed, John F. *So What: The Life of Miles Davis*. New York: Simon & Schuster, 2002.

———. *Space Is the Place: The Lives and Times of Sun Ra*. New York: Pantheon Books, 1997.

Tang, Patricia. "The Rapper as Modern Griot: Reclaiming Ancient Traditions." In *Hip Hop Africa: New African Music in a Globalizing World*, 79–91. Bloomington: Indiana University Press, 2012.

Tausig, Benjamin. *Bangkok Is Ringing: Sound, Protest, and Constraint*. New York: Oxford University Press, 2019.

Taylor, Diana. *The Archive and the Repertoire: Performing Cultural Memory in the Americas*. Durham, NC: Duke University Press, 2003.

———. *Villa Grimaldi (From History to Memory: Walking through Villa Grimaldi)*. Hemi Press, n.d. http://villagrimaldi.typefold.com/.

Thompson, Emily Ann. *The Soundscape of Modernity: Architectural Acoustics and the Culture of Listening in America, 1900–1933*. Cambridge, MA: MIT Press, 2002.

Thompson, Marie. "Whiteness and the Ontological Turn in Sound Studies." *Parallax* 23, no. 3 (2017): 266–82.

Trippett, David. "Facing Digital Realities: Where Media Do Not Mix." *Cambridge Opera Journal* 26, no. 1 (2014): 41–64.

Trouillot, Michel-Rolph. *Silencing the Past: Power and the Production of History*. Boston: Beacon Press, 1995.

Tucker, Sherrie. "Big Ears: Listening for Gender in Jazz Studies." *Current Musicology*, no. 71–73 (2002): 375–408.

Turner, Victor. *The Ritual Process: Structure and Anti-Structure*. Chicago: Aldine, 1969.

Veneciano, Jorge Daniel. "Louis Armstrong, Bricolage, and the Aesthetics of Swing." In *Uptown Conversation*, edited by Robert G. O'Meally, Brent Hayes Edwards, and Farah Jasmine Griffin, 256–77. New York: Columbia University Press, 2004.

Waleson, Heidi. *Mad Scenes and Exit Arias: The Death of the New York City Opera and the Future of Opera in America.* New York: Metropolitan Books, Henry Holt and Company, 2018.
Wallach, Jeremy, Harris M. Berger, and Paul D. Greene. "Affective Overdrive, Scene Dynamics, and Identity in the Global Metal Scene." In *Metal Rules the Globe: Heavy Metal Music Around the World*, 3–33. Durham, NC: Duke University Press, 2011.
Walser, Robert. *Running with the Devil: Power, Gender, and Madness in Heavy Metal Music.* Middletown, CT: Wesleyan University Press, 1993.
Wegel, R. L. "The Physical Characteristics of Audition and Dynamical Analysis of the External Ear." *Bell System Technical Journal* 1, no. 2 (1922): 56–68.
———. "The Physical Examination of Hearing and Binaural Aids for the Deaf." *Proceedings of the National Academy of Sciences of the United States of America* 8, no. 7 (1922): 155–60.
Weheliye, Alexander G. *Phonographies: Grooves in Sonic Afro-Modernity.* E-Duke Books Scholarly Collection. Durham, NC: Duke University Press, 2005.
Westerkamp, Hildegard. "Soundwalking." *Sound Heritage* 3, no. 4 (1974): 18–27.
Wittgenstein, Ludwig. *Philosophical Investigations.* Translated by G. E. M. Anscombe. Malden, MA: Blackwell, 1997.
Zwerin, Michael. "A Lethal Measurement." In *John Cage: An Anthology*, edited by Richard Kostelanetz, 161–67. New York: Da Capo Press, 1991.

Index

♀ Ensemble, 78, 82
4′33″ (Cage, 1952), 5, 57, 65, 67, 71, 73–74; affective analysis, 54–56; Cage's ("two sounds") analysis, 48–50, 52; as theatrical, 55, 222n67

A&M Records, 196, 205
AACM (Association for the Advancement of Creative Musicians), 59–61, 66, 74, 81; silence/quietude and, 67
Abbate, Carolyn, 103
ABC Records, 196
absence, 14, 172, 182; silence as, 25–27, 37–39, 49–50, 53–55, 73, 75, 79, 82
absurdism, 116–18, 120–25
acousmatic sound, 6, 158–59, 175, 179
acoustic locator, 32, 45, 218n1
acoustics (field), 12, 35–38, 43–45, 54
adhesion, 185, 187, 190–92
Adorno, Theodor, 184
aesthetics, 44, 67, 70, 90, 124, 136; aesthetic thickening, 72; archiving and, 165; Black aesthetics, 28, 72–74, 81–82, 165, 175–77; bricolage aesthetic, 165; loudness and, 16–20; of AACM, 74; of the operatic voice, 25–28, 88; polylogical aesthetics, 100, 102–103; silence as, 49, 72–73; space and, 44–57; war and, 40–43
affect, 3–5, 25–31, 90, 94, 103–105, 133, 136–38, 145–46, 155–57, 179–
80; archives and, 107–109, 112, 115; distinct from emotion, 46; as forces of encounter/transfer of intensities, 14; hearing/listening and, 46; intermundane affect, 178; investment in (absent) sound as, 187; loudness and, 18–19, 22; relationships between sound, space, and, 44, 146; silence and, 52, 75–78; translation and, 101
Afrofuturism, 62
AGFA, 188
Aiken, Conrad, 126
Alden, David, 100
aleatoricism, 58, 73, 111, 121
alternate takes, 200, 207
American Federation of Musicians, 196
Ampex Corporation, 188
Anderson, Ben, 47
anechoic chamber, 5, 43–45, 55, 57, 62, 67, 75, 77–8, 81, 146, 151, 219n21; bat echolocation research in, 48; early chambers, 43; experience of entering, 45, 51–52, 55; Harvard chambers, 36–9, 48; origin of word "anechoic," 44; visit by John Cage, 48–53
Annie (musical, 1977), 117
anonymity, 109–110, 114–15
Antenna International, 162
antinoise movement, 11
antiquing, 182

257

Index

antischizophonia, 6, 158–59, 179, 234n25
Apple Music, 199
Appleton, Edward, 91, 97
appraisal theory, 202
archives, 6–7, 106–117, 120–26, 130, 132–38, 160–61, 165, 170, 184, 190–92; access concerns, 197–201; activist-archives, 114, 137; appraisal, 112–14, 202; #ArchivesForBlackLives, 114; archival amnesty, 115; archival empathy, 106–107, 111–15, 132, 136; archival impulse, 165; archival intimacy, 106, 109, 111–12; archival privilege, 113; #ArchivesForBlackLives, 114; community-based archives, 113; conceptions of value, 198, 202; digital archives, 114, 190; distinction from vaults, 187, 194, 197–201; Louis Armstrong Archive, 161; nonpositivist archiving, 166; relation to social power structures, 229n9, 241n68
Argento, Dominick, 104
Argo Records, 205
Armstrong, Louis, 6, 141–44, 147–52, 154–67, 170–77, 179–80, 194, 204, 235n42; as collage artist, 164–66, 175–77; as curator of his own legacy, 163–66; private tapes, 155–57, 161–66, 168, 173–75, 180
Armstrong, Lucille, 142–43, 149, 154–55, 158, 162–3, 168–72, 174–75, 177, 179–80, 235n42; as curator, 168–71
Aronson, Randy, 193–94, 198, 200, 204
artifacts, 146–48, 170, 181–82, 184; audio, 68–70, 75, 200; archives preserving, 107–115, 124, 133, 137
Atlantic Records, 203–204
Attali, Jacques, 23–4, 29
auditory hallucinations, 51
Augoyard, Jean Francois, 145
Aunt Hester's scream (Douglass), 15, 25, 28–31
aura/auratic, 182, 184–86, 202
aurality, 16, 23, 28, 46, 51
Auslander, Philip, 88, 105
authenticity, 92, 96, 99, 181–82

autoethnography, 4
Avery Fisher Hall, Lincoln Center, New York, NY, 44
Ayler, Albert, 29–30

"back catalog," 196, 202
Barad, Karen, 147
Barenboim, Daniel, 101
Basquiat, Jean-Michel, 237n15
bats, 48
Bayreuth, Germany, 85
BBC Orchestra, 55–56
"Beale Street Blues," 174
Beatles, The, 117
Beethoven, Ludwig van, 153, 173
Bell Telephone Laboratory, 43
Bennett, Don, 206
Bennett, Tony, 163
Benjamin, Walter, 93, 227n35
Beranek, Leo, 35–39, 48–51, 53; accounts of building the anechoic chamber, 43–45
Berlin, Germany, 43
Berliner, Emile, 184
Berry, Chuck, 194
Bijsterveld, Karin, 22
Billboard, 203
binder (audio tape), 187–91
biography, 137
biopolitics/biopower, 37, 200
Black aesthetic and expressive traditions, 72–74, 81–82, 175–77; audio technology and, 194–95; exploitation and, 186–87, 194–96, 205–206; Black radicalism and, 29–30
Blacksound, 240n53
Blige, Mary J., 194
BMG Records, 203
bodies/corporeality, 14, 17–18, 24–25, 27–30, 79–80; erasure of, 46–47, 80; fleshy bodies, 32, 45, 48, 108, 147, 154; in 4'33", 55; hearing the body in an anechoic chamber, 48–9, 51–2, 78; listening as touch, 16; recording as rupture of body and voice, 195; sound-becoming-body/body-becoming-sound, 52
Bohlman, Andrea, 184–85

Bolt, Beranek, and Newman, 44
Bonn, Austria, 153
Born, Georgina, 59, 63
Boston, MA, 40, 48
Bourgeois, Jacques, 91
Braxton, Anthony, 3–4, 67, 72
breath, 54, 69, 71, 79, 154, 192
bricolage/bricoleur, 165
Britten, Benjamin, 86
Brown, James, 29–30
Burns, Ken, 170

Cage, John, 5, 38, 69–70, 76–78, 80–82, 116, 120; *4'33"* and, 5, 48–50, 52, 54–57, 65, 67, 71, 73–74; critiques of jazz, 58–60, 65–66; encounter with the anechoic chamber, 48–49; interactions with jazz musicians, 58–66
camp, 117–20
Canadian Opera Company, 85
Canela, Patricio, 148, 157
capitalism, 24, 178, 184, 199–201
Capitol Records, 203
Carpenters, The, 205
cataloguing, 120, 125, 136, 173, 198–99
CBS Records, 204
Chéreau, Patrice, 85
Chess Records, 196, 205
Chicago, IL, 59, 101, 142
Cicero, 93
Cifor, Marika, 112–14, 136
clairaudience, 157
class, 3, 87, 90; 153, 177
Cline, Patsy, 194
Cogswell, Michael, 144, 148, 151, 154, 159–64, 166, 168, 174, 179
Cole, Nat "King," 147
Cole, Natalie, 147
collage, 164–66, 173, 175–77, 179; "collage sensibility," 177
colonialism, 4, 201; decolonizing strategies in archives, 113–14
Coltrane, John, 205
Columbia Records, 203–204
Columbus, Georgia, 180
compact disc (CD), 143, 161, 199, 205; boom of the 1980s-90s, 202–203
commodification, 28–30, 195, 199

"Composer, The" (pseudonym), 106–107, 109–125, 127–138; relationship with "the Virtuoso," 128–33
composer houses, 153–54
"Composition As Process" (Cage, 1958), 61–62
Coney Island, NY, 63–64
Coomaraswamy, Ananda, 49
co-presence, 162, 179, 195
copyability/duplication (of audio), 185–86, 188, 199, 206–207, 237n16; and schizophonia, 158–59
copyright, 195–96, 240n53
Corbett, John, 59
Corona, Queens, NY, 141, 148, 155, 157; Armstrong's neighborhood in, 142–44, 146, 149, 178
"corpaurality," 147
Cosey, Pete, 205
Cotton Club, 168
counterculture, 66, 110, 118–20
Crawford, Bruce, 94
Crutchfield, Will, 92, 94, 96–98, 104
cry (in opera), 15, 25–29, 31, 99, 227n28
curation, 115, 145–46, 160–66, 168–71, 175, 177–79; *curare* and, 166, 206; curatorial agency, 178; curatorial choices, 137, 171, 175; curatorial impulse, 165; relation to social power structures, 229n9
curing, 188
cyborg, 48

DAT (digital audio tape), 182, 237n6
data, 3, 16, 34–35, 40; noisy data, 38; storage within media, 185, 187 190–91; transformation of sound into, 45–7
Davis, Miles, 21, 224n32; and Harmon mute, 21
De Lancie, Philip, 188–89
De Re, Catarina, 78
deadness, 6, 139, 141, 147–48, 155–59, 178–80, 200
death chambers, 171–73
"death-in-life," 201
death masks, 173

Index

Decca Records, 196, 205
decibel, 11, 18, 215n4
Declaration of Independence (U.S.), 183–84
decoration/decor, 170–74, 177, 180; as gendered, 170–71; "decorating a decoration," 176
Deep Listening, 5, 75–80, 82, Center for Deep Listening, 76, 82
Deep Listening: A Composer's Sound Practice (Oliveros, 2005), 75
democratization, 89–90, 93
detached listening, 16–17
devotionalia, 153
diaries, 125–35, 137; as sources in historical scholarship, 125, 232n39
digital rights management (DRM), 199
"direct address" clips (category of audio clip), 162
disability, 49
distortion (sound effect), 20–21
"distraction argument" (supertitles), 92, 102–104
Dolar, Mladen, 98–99
domesticity, 145, 151, 153, 155, 162, 165, 170, 178, 180
Don Giovanni (Mozart, 1788), 97
Dornemann, Joan, 94–95
Douglass, Frederick, 28–29
Drake, Jarrett, 114
dramaturgy, 100–102
drastic (mode of listening), 47, 90, 103–104
Dyer, Deslyn Downes, 144, 161–62, 168
dynamic equivalence (translation), 93

Echard, William, 23–4
echo, 34 36, 39, 44, 54, 62, 70, 151
echolocation, 48
ecological sound practices, 145–46, 215n4
Edison, NJ, 205
Edison, Thomas, 184
Edwards, Brent Hayes, 107
"effort argument" (supertitles), 92–95, 99
ego, 58, 65, 73–75, 80–81

Eidsheim, Nina Sun, 3–4, 109
elitism, 89, 95
Empty Words (Cage, 1974), 63–64
energy music, 67
enslavement, 28–29, 195, 201
environmental sound, 58, 72–73, 76–78, 80, 145–46; environmental noise, 11; museum sound environments, 162
ephemera, 165, 182
ephemerality, 191–92, 194. 206
erasure, 17, 19, 47, 126, 177, 206
Esposito, Michael, 181–83
Esse, Melina, 87
ethnicity, 87, 90
Europe/European culture, 24, 61, 87, 91, 96, 107, 153–54; Euro-American classical music, 22, 27, 72, 118; Eurocentrism, 4, 74, 111–12; as exoticized other, 97
Eurydice, 186–87, 191–92
exoticization, 97
experimentalism, 59, 61, 65, 72, 81, 112, 116
expressivity, 133, 135–36

Facebook, 204–206
Farge, Arlette, 107–108, 136
Fechner, Gustav, 15–6
Feldman, Morton, 116
fidelity (audio), 35, 185–86, 206
film, 88–89
Fine, Abigail, 153–54, 173
Fontaine, Dick, 61–63
foreignness, 88–89, 91, 93, 95–97, 99
forensic reports, 181–82, 184, 236–37n4
formal equivalence (translation), 93
Foucault, Michel, 200
Frankenberg, Ruth, 74
frequency (of sound waves), 15, 21, 81, 187
futurity, 59, 72, 126, 131, 147, 157, 167, 183, 187, 195, 198–201, 205–206

Gann, Kyle, 52
gatekeeping, 6, 65, 90, 95

Geffen Records, 196
gender, 3, 22, 40, 110–112, 125, 133, 138, 146, 231n26; in jazz, 168–71, 180
genre, 24
gentrification, 233–34n14
ghosts/haunting, 6, 28–29, 144, 155, 157, 171, 175, 177–78, 200
ghost army (WWII military unit), 35–36
Gilger, Kristin, 166
Gillespie, Lorraine, 168
"Glow" (pseudonym), 106–107, 119, 123, 134–36
gnostic (mode of listening), 90, 103–104, 228–29n67
Gordon, Dexter, 195–96
Gordon, Maxine, 195–96
Gracyk, Theodore, 17, 19, 23
Gregg, Melissa, 4, 14
Grossberg, Morris, 168
Guinness Book of World Records, 53
Gumbrecht, Hans Ulrich, 89–90
Gumby, Alexander, 165–66
gun wave, 45

hagiography, 179–80
Hahn, Tomie, 76
haptic experience, 14, 17, 20, 148
Hardin, Lil, 169–70
Harlem, New York, 165
Harvard University military acoustics laboratories, 35; Electro-Acoustic Laboratory, 35–37, 44, 48; Psycho-Acoustic Laboratory, 35; Underwater Sound Laboratory, 35, 39–42
haunting/ghosts, 6, 28–29, 157, 171, 177–78; hauntology, 200, 236n54
headphones, 17, 35, 45, 161
hearing, 45–49, 56; as affective register, 46–7
heavy metal, 17, 19–20
Hegarty, Paul, 22
hegemony, 22–24
Helmreich, Stefan, 47–48
Henahan, Donal, 86, 94
Hendrix, Jimi, 20–21
Heraldo, Selma, 149, 178

hermeneutics, 101, 103, 105
Hesmondhalgh, David, 59, 63
himpathy, 115, 231n21
historic house museums, 153–54
historiography, 153, 159, 170
Holiday, Billie, 194, 205, 224n32
Holland, Bill, 203–204
Horace, 93
Houston Grand Opera, 92
Hunt, Frederick, 39, 48
Hurston, Zora Neale, 175–77
hyperechoic chamber, 62

I Ching, 49, 116, 128; hexagrams in, 120; yarrow sticks used for, 120, 129, 232n33
imagined loudness, 5, 16, 19–22, 28, 30
imagined sound, 76, 79; of the past, 146–47
improvisation, 58–60, 63, 65, 72–75, 165
Impulse Records, 196, 205
in-between-ness, 14, 30
L'incoronazione di Poppea (Monteverdi, 1643), 85
indeterminacy, 58–59
Indian classical music, 49
individualism, 77
inscription, 190
intensity, 16, 29–31; affect and, 13–15, 46–47
intermundane, 147–48, 178–79
Internet Archive, 183
Interscope Records, 197
intersubjectivity, 81–82
Iron Mountain, 205, 241n69
Ivey, Bill, 189
Izanami and Izanagi, 192

Jacquin, Maud, 76
Jamal, Ahmad, 224n32
Janszen, Arthur A., 36
Jarman, Joseph, 59–61, 65, 74
jazz, 74, 81, 130, 144, 144, 146, 160, 177, 196, 200; gender and, 168–70, 180; John Cage's relationship with, 58–67; loft jazz, 111–12, 114; under-recognition of wives of male jazz artists, 168–70

Jenkins, Leroy, 67, 72
jouissance, 91, 96, 99
Journal of the Acoustical Society of America (JASA), 43
Juilliard School, 127–28

Kahn, Douglass, 49–50
Kane, Brian, 158
Karpf, Anne, 21
Kase, Carlos, 204–206
Kaye, George William Clarkson, 11–13
Keita, Sundiata, 154
Kelley, Robin D.G., 168
Kernodle, Tammy, 169
Kim, Rebecca K., 58–60
Kirk, Rahsaan Roland, 61–62, 65
Kittler, Friedrich, 184
Koussevitzky Music Shed, Stockbridge, MA, 44
Kouyate, Bala Faseke, 154
Kreuzer, Gundula, 87
Kübler-Ross, Elisabeth, 237n16
Kusama, Maika Yuri, 80

Lab Echo, 40–41
labor, 6–7, 87; stored/dead labor, 147, 157, 178, 195, 197–98, 200; musical labor, 202–203
Lacan, Jacques, 26–27, 98–99
Latour, Bruno, 147
Levin, David, 99–100, 103
Lewis, Eric, 71
Lewis, George, 59–60
librettos, 85, 92–97, 99–103; reading during performance, 93–95
liminality, 90, 148, 157, 165, 179, 190
limit of audibility, 76–77, 79
Lincoln, Abbey, 29–30
listener collapse, 5, 16–19, 27, 29–30
listening, 16, 68–69; Deep Listening, 75–80; distinct from sonic encounter, 2–3; listening again, 206; listening communities, 20, 23–24, 75; posthuman/nonhuman, 45–48; relation to hearing, 46–7, 56; situated, 233n8
liveness, 88, 105
logic of mutual inclusion, 5

long range acoustic device (LRAD), 25, 35
Lot's wife, 192
loudness, 5, 11–12, 26–31, 135; bodies and, 16–19; desired by certain listening communities, 23–4; distinction from volume, 215n9; imagined loudness, 19–22, 30; John Cage attribution of, 60–61; loudness effects, 5, 15–25; power of low loudness, 21–22; undertheorized in music studies, 13–4, 31; wave amplitude and, 15
Louis Armstrong Archive, 161
Louis Armstrong Educational Foundation, 170, 172
Louis Armstrong House Museum, 6, 141–146, 148–175, 178–80; audio clips used in, 155–59, 161–63, 166–68, 171, 173–74, 179; tour script, 144, 154, 163, 168–70, 173, 179
LP records, 65, 204–206
Lucas, Olivia, 17–19
Lyric Opera of Chicago, 101

magic square, 120
Mamas & the Papas, The, 116
Mande people, 154
Manne, Kate, 115
Mansell, James G., 3
Mansouri, Lotfi, 85
Mansouri, Marjorie, 85
Marriage of Figaro, The (Mozart, 1786), 101
marijuana, 117–19
Marsh, Dave, 183
Marton, Eva, 92
Marx, Karl, 24, 28–29
Massumi, Brian, 5, 46
"master" tapes, 181–86, 189–90, 195, 197, 200, 202–206; as uncopiable, 186; problematic naming, 239–40n50
Master Tape Collection, 182
materiality, 18, 72–74, 136–38, 153–54, 173, 184, 190, 194–95
Maus, Fred, 19

Mbembe, Achille, 113–14, 200–201
MCA Records, 196, 204
McCartney, Andra, 145–46
McMullen, Tracy, 80
McMurray, Peter, 44, 184–85, 190
mechanical ears, 45, 47
media/mediation, 23, 87–90, 147–48, 161, 165–66, 187, 191, 195; agency of, 147; cultural, 16; self-remediation, 165; unmediated communication, 94, 96, 98–99, 104
meditation, 64, 75, 78–80, 82
memory/remembering, 2–5, 20, 177–78, 190–92, 207; cultural memory, 145; memoria, 153; remembered sound, 76, 79
Methodism, 80
Metropolitan Opera, New York, NY, 94, 100; *Live in HD* series, 87; Met Titles, 86, 102, 225n5
MGM Records, 204
microphones, 21, 45
military research, 42, 81; and acoustics, 32–45, 57
Milnes, Rodney, 86
mise-en-scène, 98, 100
Mix Magazine, 188
Moby Dick, 183–84
modernism, 110, 120, 125
modernity, 11, 62, 194–95
Mona Lisa, 183–84
Monk, Nellie, 168
Monk, Thelonious, 224n32
"more product, less process," 240n58
Morrison, Matthew D., 240n53
Mostel, Zero, 97
Moten, Fred, 15, 25, 28–31, 72
mourning, 7, 184, 187, 201, 207; silence and 173
Mowitt, John, 53–54
Mozart, Wolfgang Amadeus, 97, 153
museum audio curation, 161–62
"musical" clips (category of audio clip), 163
music vs. text binary, 25–7, 91, 99–100, 103
musique concrete, 158
My Bloody Valentine, 17

mycology, 110, 116
Myrbeck, Edward R., 36, 42

Nancy, Jean-Luc, 16–17, 19
Napster, 199
narrative, 87, 136; accounts of the anechoic chamber, 43–4; interpretations of sound, 2; military acoustics research and, 40–42
National Endowment for the Humanities, 197
National Historic Landmark designation, 6, 146, 166, 170
necropolitics, 200–201; necro-technopolitics, 193, 201
"Neville" (pseudonym), 117–119, 121–123, 130, 134
New York, NY, 6, 67, 86, 119, 141, 149, 155; Department of Cultural Affairs, 170; subway, 141, 144
New York City Opera, 86, 101
New York Times, 52, 63, 85–86, 101, 168, 183, 193
Niagassola, Guinea, 154
Nirvana, 194
noise, 16, 20; abatement of, 50; definitions of, 22, 217n36; noise music, 16–7; noisy data, 38; relation to loudness, 22–3; relation to political power, 23–5; underwater, 34–35
noise occupation, 5, 16, 22–25, 29–30, 217n44
non-fungible token (NFT), 237n15
nonhuman bodies/listeners/subjects, 14, 34, 47–8
"nonmeaning argument" (supertitles), 92, 96–99
non-sonic/extra-sonic addenda, 2–4, 14, 55
"Norman" (pseudonym), 116–119, 134
Notes (8 Pieces) (Smith, 1973), 71–73
Notre Dame Cathedral, 1–3
Novak, David, 17–19

"object voice," 26–27, 98–99
Ochoa Gautier, Ana María, 37, 82
ocular-centrism, 145
Oliveros, Pauline, 5, 38, 58, 75–82

ontology, 19, 89–90, 98, 180, 186–87, 193–95; in information theory, 39–40; in sound studies, 3
opera, 25–27, 85–105; aesthetics, 88, 100, 102–103; dialogue opera, 91; *Singspiel*, 91; "unsettledness" of, 100, 103
Opera (journal), 86
Opera News, 86, 97, 104
Opera Quarterly, 87
Orfield Laboratory, Minneapolis, MN, 51–52
Orfield, Steven, 51
Orpheus, 186–87, 191–92, 239n40
"overcomprehension argument" (supertitles), 92, 95–96
Ovid, 191–92
oxide (magnetic), 70, 156, 187–88, 190–92

pain, 14, 18–19, 27
"paper music," 121, 125, 135
Pappano, Antonio, 101
Paris, France, 1–3
pastness, 146–47, 149, 162, 167, 178, 187, 200, 202
patriarchy, 114, 131–32, 169, 180, 192
perception, 46, 87
perisonic (intensity), 14
Petry, Laura, 170
Phillips, Sam, 181
phon (measurement of loudness), 11–13
phonograph, 184–86, 199
Piekut, Benjamin, 147, 156–57, 178, 195
ping (SONAR), 34–35, 47
Piper, Adrian, 30
"place referential" clips (category of audio clip), 162–3
Plato, 127
playback, 21, 147, 159, 186–88, 191, 201
"Poetics of Environmental Sound, The" (Oliveros, 1968), 76–77
Poizat, Michel, 15, 25–31, 49, 91, 98–99
Polverel, Elsa, 76
polylogical framework (of opera), 90, 99–100, 102–103

popular music, 59–61, 63, 110–11, 183, 196, 200
Porter, Andrew, 97
Portland, Maine, 42
postcards, 109, 115–21, 124–25, 135, 137
posthumanism, 47–48
postproduction (of sound recordings), 185
Powell, Richard J., 177
power evasiveness, 74
pre-listening preparation, 3, 115
presence, 14, 23, 30, 88, 180, 185; co-presence, 162, 179; ghostly, 70, 144, 155–57, 171, 173; in archives, 108, 113, 116, 133; of language, 98–99; presence-based vs. meaning-based framework, 89–90; silence as, 49–50, 74; sonic, 18, 27–8, 39, 52, 54–55, 66, 165; supertitles as, 94, 99–105
presentness, 146–47, 156–57, 178, 192, 195, 198, 200
preservation, 111, 113–14, 153–54, 156–57, 159–61, 170, 174, 177, 184–86, 189–90, 197–99, 201, 234n20; anxieties surrounding, 190; of the dead, 185; phonograph as "eternal preservation," 185
Presley, Elvis, 181–86
prima le parole/prima la musica, 91
Prince, 195, 197, 239n50
print-through, 68, 70, 75
privilege, 3, 6, 60, 106, 109–116, 120, 124, 132, 134, 138, 231n21
process-based composition, 120–23, 125
protest music, 24
prune whip yogurt, 123, 125
psychedelic drugs, 110–11
psychical distance, 17
psychoacoustics/psychophysics, 15–6, 216n31
"Purple Haze" (Hendrix, 1967), 20–21
Pythagoras, 158

Quashie, Kevin, 66
quietness, 13–14, 21–22, 38, 50–51, 58–60, 66–67, 71, 79, 151; Black quiet, 66; quietest place on earth, 53

Ra, Sun, 62–65, 74
race, 3–4, 90, 138, 223n7; and timbre, 217n33; racism, 117, 231n26
The Race of Sound (Eidsheim, 2018), 3
radar, 32
Rainer, Yvonne, 73
Rainey, Gertrude "Ma," 180
Rauschenberg, Robert, 49
RCA Records, 181, 204
reanimation, 144, 177–78, 200
recombinatoriality, 147, 157, 178, 185–86, 238n21
record contracts, 195–96, 199
record pops, 70
recordings (sound), 20, 70, 94, 171, 178, 181–206; anti/schizophonia and, 158–59; deadness and, 147–48; as dis/embodiment, 184, 195, 197; emotional investment in, 184; as "freezing of time," 155, 185; perceptions of value, 178, 183, 187, 194, 201–206; private recordings, 6, 155–57, 161–66, 168, 173–75, 180
reduced listening, 158, 213n6
reissues (of recordings), 64, 200, 202–205
relics/reliquary, 151, 153, 155, 182, 185
remix, 186, 194
reproduction, 19–20, 165, 174, 177–78; lossy, 186; of systems of privilege, 110, 112–15, 138
resistance (political), 22–23, 29–30, 66, 195, 204
reverb/reverberation, 36, 44, 70, 75, 186
revertability, 147, 157, 178
Rice, Tom, 47
Rich, B. Ruby, 88–89
Riding the Waves (Beranek, 2008), 43–4
"Rip, Rig, and Panic" (Kirk, 1965), 62
ritual, 19, 55, 151, 154, 157, 179
Rizzo, Francis, 100–101
Roach, Max, 29–30
Roads, Curtis, 14
Robinson, Paul, 95–98
Rock and Roll Hall of Fame, 181
rock music, 16–17, 118, 181–82

room sound, 157–58
Rosen, Jody, 193–95, 198, 201–204, 206
Rucker, Bronwyn, 63
Rumsfeld, Donald, 189
Russo, Rick, 63

sacredness, 101, 151, 154, 156–57, 178–79, 182, 206
saints/saintliness, 153–54, 157, 173, 180
Salzburg, Austria, 153
Savoy Records, 196
Scarry, Elaine, 18
Schaeffer, Pierre, 158
Schafer, R. Murray, 145, 158–59, 215n4
Schellenberg, Theodore, 202
schizophonia, 6, 158–59, 179
scientism, 5, 38, 43–45, 52–54, 78, 81
score (musical) 94, 103, 109, 120, 122–24, 133; overemphasis in opera scholarship, 99–100; text-based scores, 79
scrapbooks, 166
Seigworth, Gregory, 4, 14
Sellars, Peter, 101
semantics, 46–47
semiotics, 26–27, 46–47, 52, 98–99, 103–104
sensation, 46, 87
senses, 18, 47, 89–90, 157, 171; encroachment of, 86–87; multisensory experience, 2–3, 103, 148, 178–79; in museums, 161–62; networks of, 105; sensoria of deadness, 179; "thick events and," 4
Sensing Sound (Eidsheim, 2015), 3
serialism, 110–11, 118, 120–21, 135
sexual harassment, 128–31
sexism, 131–33
Shangri-Las, 116
shell wave (ballistics), 45
shrines, 148, 151, 155, 179
Sideshows By The Seashore, 63
signification, linguistic, 25–30, 89–90, 97–99, 104; musical, 104

silence, 5, 12–13, 37–45, 48–57, 64–65, 66–82; as absence, 25–27, 37–39, 49–50, 53–55, 73, 75, 79, 82; boundary with sound, 70–71; as intention, 50, 53; pain and, 13–14, 31; as presence, 55; as resistance, 30, 72–73; silence that speaks/silence that screams, 26–28, 49, 71, 75; silencing, 5, 22, 37, 54, 58–59, 62, 65, 74, 82; as space, 73–74, 224n32
Silence (Cage, 1961), 49, 63
Silence (Smith, 1969), 5, 67–69
silent cudgel, 5, 58–59, 81
Sills, Beverley, 86
Simone, Nina, 236n55
Sinha, Amresh, 88
Smith, Alpha, 170
Smith, Wadada Leo, 5, 38, 66–75
Smithsonian Institution, 181, 189
social death, 201
social experience of sound, 17, 19–20, 100
"Somewhere Over the Rainbow," 174
SONAR, 34–35, 47–48
sonic encounter, 2–6, 14, 19, 31, 37–8, 45–46, 51–54, 57, 75–76, 78, 81–82, 86–87, 89–90, 97, 101–105, 109, 115, 120, 124, 134, 136–38, 144–45, 148–49, 151, 155, 157–58, 161–62, 179, 181, 184, 186–87, 201, 207
Sonic Meditations (Oliveros, 1974), 5, 78–79
sonic reduction, 4
sonic weapons, 18, 24–25
Sontag, Susan, 120
Sony, 203
Sophocles, 85
Sosso Bala, 154
sound-rhythm, 73
sound studies, 3–4, 13, 22–3, 145, 158
sound waves, 15, 32, 34
soundscape, 44, 67, 141, 143, 145–46, 149, 151, 158, 179
soundwalking, 6, 141, 145–46, 179
Southern, Hugh, 102

space, 16–7, 34–35, 39, 144–46, 151, 177–78; designing acoustic spaces, 44; domestic, 151, 165, 180; "dry," 151; embalmed, 178; re/suturing of sound and, 145, sacred spaces, 151, 156–57, 178–79; silence as, 73, 82; 158–59, 179; smells and, 161; and soundwalking, 146
Spieker, Sven, 198
spirituality, 51, 125
Spotify, 199
stages of grief, 237n16
Stanyek, Jason, 147, 156–57, 178, 195
Steely Dan, 205
sticky-shed syndrome, 7, 186–92, 238n22
Strauss, Richard, 85
street noise, 11, 143, 149, 151, 178
sublimity, 19
submarines, 34, 39–40, 42, 48
subsonic (intensity), 14
subtitles, 85, 88–89
Sultan, Juma, 114, 190
Sumanguru, 154
Sun Ra, 62–65, 74
superfice, 190
supertitles, 6, 85–105
sung translation (opera), 93, 96
Sun Records, 181–82
Sunn O))), 17–18
Sutherland, Tonia, 115
swing, 66, 165
sympathetic listening, 47
Szwed, John, 21, 64

Tannhäuser (Wagner, 1845), 101
tape (adhesive), 165, 178
tape (audio), 70, 75, 180; affordances of, 185–86; cassette tapes, 185, 199; DAT tape, 182, 237n6; reel-to-reel, 181, 187–88, 191–92
tape death, 7, 181, 183–87, 194, 197, 200–204, 206–207; tape life and, 201
tape hiss, 70
tarot, 110, 116
Taylor, Diana, 233n7

technophilia/technophobia, 87, 164
techno-sonic culture, 195
"Ted" (pseudonym), 116–119
televisuality, 88, 105
temporality, 146–47
"termination of transfers," 196
text, 3, 6; as gnostic/drastic, 103, 228–29n67; opera reception and, 93–96; textual anticipation/textual arousal, 97, 104
text-based scores, 79
textual interference, 6, 83, 94–96, 102, 115
Thompson, Marie, 3
threshold of pain/threshold of hearing, 12–13, 18, 79
timbre, 15, 20–21, 135, 217n33
time capsules, 160, 170, 178
tinnitus, 49
Tokyo Opera City Concert Hall, 44
torpedoes, 40–41; listening torpedoes, 35, 39, 218n4
Tosca (Puccini, 1900), 92
translation, 6, 88–89, 92–93, 95–97, 101–102, 227n35
"translation argument" (supertitles), 92–93
triage, 190
Tri-Axium Writings (Braxton, 1985), 3
Trippett, David, 87
Troy, NY, 76
Tucker microphone, 45
Tucker, Sherrie, 170
Tucker, William Sansome, 45
Twentieth Century Music, 184

uncomfortable loudness level (UCL), 13
underwater sound, 34–35, 39–42, 219n12
"Unforgettable" (recording by Cole and Cole, 1991), 147–48
United States Department of Defense, 35
Universal Music Group fire, 7, 186–87, 193–99, 201, 203–206
urbanity, 177
USS *Galaxy* (Navy research vessel), 40

Vancouver, Canada, 145
Varèse, Edgard, 61
vaults, 7, 186–87, 193–94, 197–202, 204; logic of, 197–98, 202–203
veiling (hiding sound source), 158, 179
Veneciano, Jorge Daniel, 165
vibration, 13, 32, 37, 52–4, 75–78, 81–82, 201, 217n36; shared in act of listening, 16–19; "vibrational" approaches to sound studies, 3
Vienna, Austria, 173
"Virtuoso, The" (pseudonym), 107, 109, 114–16, 125–38; relationship with "the Composer," 128–33
voice, 21, 54, 58–60, 73, 75, 78, 91, 129, 185, 191; adjusting in quiet space, 151; autonomous, 81; Black voices, 195; in film, 88; hagiography and, 179; of Louis Armstrong, 6, 143, 155, 157–58, 160–61, 171, 173; of Lucille Armstrong, 171; mediated/unmediated, 98–99; non-linguistic utterance and, 25–30, 98; operatic, 25–27, 88, 95; unseen voices, 179
volume, 14, 17, 23, 25, 215n9
von Hofmannsthal, Hugo, 85
"voyeuristic" clips (category of audio clip), 162, 166, 174
vulnerability, 131, 134, 177

Wagner, Richard, 27, 87, 103
Waits, Tom, 205
Walküre, Die (Wagner, 1870), 85
wallpaper, 151, 167–168, 170, 174, 180
Walser, Robert, 19–20
Warner Brothers Records, 203
Washington Post, 181–82
Waters, Muddy, 205
Weaver, Caity, 52
Wegel, R. L., 13, 17
Weheliye, Alexander, 194–95, 197
Westerkamp, Hildegard, 145
Whitely, Sheila, 20

whiteness, 3–4, 60–61, 74, 110–12, 114, 117, 126, 132, 138, 146, 227n24
"will to adorn," 176
Williams, Tony, 205
Wittgenstein, Ludwig, 102
WKCR-FM, 172
World Soundscape Project, 145–46
World War I, 32

World War II, 35–37, 41–42, 169
Wozzeck (Berg, 1925), 100

Youtube, 51

Zen Buddhism, 49, 53, 58, 60, 75, 80–81, 221n44; koans, 52; zazen, 80

www.ingramcontent.com/pod-product-compliance
Lightning Source LLC
Chambersburg PA
CBHW021342230426
43666CB00006B/372